THE STRATEGIC APPLICATION OF INFORMATION TECHNOLOGY IN HEALTHCARE ORGANIZATIONS

THE STRATEGIC APPLICATION OF INFORMATION TECHNOLOGY IN HEALTHCARE ORGANIZATIONS

JOHN P. GLASER, Ph.D.
LESLIE D. HSU, MPH

McGraw-Hill

New York   San Francisco   Washington, D.C.   Auckland   Bogotá
Caracas   Lisbon   London   Madrid   Mexico City   Milan
Montreal   New Delhi   San Juan   Singapore
Sydney   Tokyo   Toronto

Library of Congress Cataloging-in-Publication Data
Glaser, John (John P.)
    The strategic application of information technology in healthcare organizations / John Glaser, Leslie Hsu.
        p.   cm.
    Includes bibliographical references and index.
    ISBN 0-07-134631-7
    1. Information technology—Management.   2. Strategic planning.
I. Hsu, Leslie.   II. Title.
T58.64.G55   1999
362.1′068′4—DC21   99-12323
                                                                                                              CIP

McGraw-Hill
A Division of The McGraw·Hill Companies

Copyright © 1999 by the McGraw-Hill Companies, Inc. All rights reserved. Printed in the United States of America. Except as permitted under the United States Copyright Act of 1976, no part of this publication may be reproduced or distributed in any form or by any means, or stored in a database or retrieval system, without the prior written permission of the publisher.

1 2 3 4 5 6 7 8 9 0 BKM / BKM 9 0 9 8 7

ISBN 0-07-134631-7

Printed and bound by Book-Mart Press, Inc.

Cover illustration by Steve Dininno.

This book was typeset using 11 point Times Roman.

This publication is designed to provide accurate and authoritative information in regard to the subject matter covered. It is sold with the understanding that neither the author nor the publisher is engaged in rendering legal, accounting, or other professional service. If legal advice or other expert assistance is required, the services of a competent professional person should be sought.

            —*From a declaration of Principles jointly adopted by a Committee of
            the American Bar Association and a Committee of Publishers.*

To
The Information Systems Staff of Partners HealthCare System, Inc.
and
H. Richard Nesson, M.D.

They have made a difference.

PREFACE

Information technology (IT) can be a critical contributor to the strategic plans of healthcare providers to reduce costs, respond to managed care, develop a continuum of care, manage the cost and quality of that care, and improve the quality of service to patients, payors, and physicians. However, on several fronts, the leadership of healthcare organizations struggles with its organization's use of and commitment to IT.

The aggregate capital projections for these systems often convey staggering numbers: tens or, at times, hundreds of millions of dollars. The percentage of the organization's overall capital and operating budgets devoted to information systems appears to be increasing and is on its way to being double current percentages. While organizational leadership understands from colleagues, consultants, and trade press that these numbers are becoming common, information system capital and operating budget requests carry sticker shock and are often growing much faster than any other segment of the budget. Moreover, the demands for information technology capital compete with other pressing capital demands: opportunities to expand the delivery system through acquisition, improve service quality through facilities improvements, or enhance the ability to delivery efficacious care through new medical technology.

Healthcare executives have a belief, often tenuous, that information systems will provide some form of competitive advantage and will be a major contributor to organizational strategies and plans. However, it is difficult for most executives to point to a large number of prior information system investments that have led to significant and unarguable returns to the fiscal and competitive performance of the organization. Even successful information investments may be difficult to empirically and convincingly defend. It may not be hard to point to examples of information systems' failures or significant overruns.

Healthcare leadership observes a gap between the perceived importance of IT and its organization's preparedness to address it. The 1998 *Hospitals and Health Networks* Leadership Survey (Solovy and Sunseri, 1998) of hospital, managed care, and physician group executives identified those issues that had the largest strategic gap. Strategic gap was defined as the difference between the importance of an issue and the organization's preparedness to address the issue. The survey found that IT was one of the top three gap issues for all three groups of executives. Healthcare leadership appears to be no different from leadership across all industries in its concern about IT. A survey presented in *The New York Times* (1995) found that 96% of business executives believe that "IT is immensely important for their business." However, 20% felt that "their organization knows how to exploit IT fully" and only 25% stated that "their IT department is providing value for the money."

This book is intended to improve the ability of the leadership of healthcare organizations to invest strategically and thoughtfully in information technology. The book will focus on strategies and strategic thinking in the planning and implementation of information technology for the provider organization.

This book will not focus on the "how to" aspects of several areas of IT[1] management (e.g., application system selection, project management, or development of IS service levels). This should not lead the reader to believe that such topics are unimportant.

Rather, the book is premised on the author's experiences and observations, from 10 years as a CIO in a provider organization and as a leader in healthcare IT industry organizations, that a consistent and deep problem facing the industry is insufficient healthcare IT strategy. Cash, McFarlan, and McKenney (1992) note that there are two major categories of risk that confront significant IT investments (where risk is defined as failure to achieve intended objectives): conceptualization failures and implementation failures.

Conceptualization failures are failures to adequately link the organization strategies and IT strategies and poor definition and focus of the IT initiative. An example of a conceptualization failure would be an intellectually anemic response to the question of "What real, measurable, and significant problems will the computerized medical record solve for us?" Conceptualization failures are almost always strategy failures.

Implementation failures occur when projects run significantly over budget, deliver a shadow of the expected capabilities, or just don't work. Implementation failures are often due to strategy failures because the

---

[1] Information technology (IT) will refer to the field and domain in general. As such it will encompass the technology, technical staff, data, application systems, and policies and procedures that govern the use of computers. Information systems (IS) will refer to that part of the organization responsible for managing IT.

organization has not thought strategically about the form and characteristics of the staff, technologies, and applications that should be brought to bear on an initiative.

This book has the perspective of the use of IT in a large provider organization, particularly the integrated delivery system. This should not preclude the utility of the book's content for those who are executives in other sectors of the healthcare industry. Those readers who are healthcare IT executives, industry vendors and consultants, and healthcare leadership with an interest and modest knowledge of IT management issues, should find the book informative and stimulating.

The book contains the following chapters.

Chapter 1 provides an overview of strategy. Strategy is defined. The three major areas of healthcare IT that require strategy are described: linkage of IT to organizational strategies, internal organizational factors that contribute to the effectiveness of IT use, and concepts that frame the organization's view of major initiatives and new technologies.

Chapter 2 discusses the linkage of IT to organizational strategy. The use of IT to further an organization's competitive position is discussed drawing on lessons learned from other industries. Strategic information systems planning is reviewed. Example planning frameworks are presented and lessons learned about the nature of IT planning are described.

Chapter 3 examines factors, internal to the organization, that have a large influence on how well the organization applies IT. One class of factors is the IT asset that is composed of applications, technical architecture, data, IS staff, and IT governance. The importance and nature of strategies directed to advancing the asset are explored. The second class of factors is IT-centric organizational attributes (e.g., the relationship between the IS group and the rest of the organization). Studies that have examined this class of factors are presented. The limitations of industry surveys, fads, and IT evaluation methodologies are also reviewed.

Chapter 4 focuses on examples of IT strategy. Three examples of IT strategy are discussed: clinical information systems, integration, and the World Wide Web. These examples, drawn from the experiences of Partners HealthCare System, illustrate the role of developing "strategic views" and bring together concepts and lessons discussed in the earlier sections of the book.

Chapter 5 presents some conclusions.

The reader should find that the book develops a well integrated blend of management concepts and theories with the practical realities of implementing complex information systems in complex healthcare organizations.

We hope you find the book useful.

REFERENCES

Cash, J., McFarlan, W., McKenney, J. (1992). *Corporate Information Systems Management: The Issues Facing Senior Executives.* Chicago, Ill.: Irwin.

Solovy, A., Sunseri, R. (1998). Leading the Way. *Hospitals and Health Networks.* August. *The New York Times,* November 22, 1995.

CONTENTS

PREFACE   vii

Chapter 1

An Overview of Strategy   1

Definition of Strategy   1
- *Formulation*   2
- *Implementation*   3
- *Observations on Strategy Definition*   4

Competitive Strategy   6
The Need for IT Strategy   7
- *Areas of IT Strategy*   7
- *Linkage to Organizational Goals and Initiatives*   8
- *Internal Capabilities and Characteristics*   10
- *Concepts That Frame the IT Challenge*   11

Characteristics of Strategic Thinking   12
Summary   14

Chapter 2

Linkage of IT Strategy to Organizational Strategy   17

Strategic IT Planning Methodologies and Frameworks   18
- *Derived IT Linkage*   19
- *Linkage Based on Fundamental Views*   23
- *Observations on IT Frameworks and Planning*   29
- *Summary*   33

Information Technology as a Competitive Weapon   33
- *Case Studies*   34
- *Lessons Learned*   40

Summary   57

Chapter 3

Internal Capabilities and Characteristics 61

Asset Composition and Overview 62
Asset Discussion 64
    Application Systems 64
    Technical Architecture 70
    Data 77
    IS Staff 81
    Governance 91
    The Chief Information Officer 93
Asset Lessons Learned and Observations 95
    Plans for the Asset 95
    Asset Investment 96
Factors That Influence Organizational IT Asset Decisions 98
    Evaluation of IT Investments 98
    Fads 106
    Surveys of Issues and IT Adoption 111
IT-Centric Organizational Attributes 118
    Financial Executives Research Foundation 118
    Ross, Beath, and Goodhue 119
    McKenney, Copeland, and Goodhue 121
    Weil and Broadbent (1998) 122
    Summary of Studies 123
Summary 126

Chapter 4

Examples of IT Strategy 131

Clinical Information Systems 133
    Underlying Core Business Concepts and Views 136
    IT Application Concepts 136
    Sources of Complexity 139
    Brigham and Women's Hospital Care Improvement Efforts 144
    Clinical Information Systems Across a Continuum of Care 152
    Summary of Clinical Information System Concepts and Views 159
Integration of Information Systems 160
    What Does Integration Mean? 162

Contents

xiii

> *Views That Guide the Improvement of Integration* 164
> *Integration IT Strategies* 166
> *Summary* 173

The World Wide Web 174
> *Core Characteristics of the WWW* 177
> *Examples of Use by Healthcare Organizations* 178
> *Roles of the WWW in Healthcare* 180
> *WWW Support of the Healthcare Organization's Strategies* 187
> *Impact of the WWW on IT Governance* 190
> *WWW Summary* 194

Summary 195

Chapter 5

Conclusion 199

Appendix A

Levels of Integration of Information Systems at Partners (1997) 203

Levels of Integration 203
PCHI Affiliates 204
Partners Wide 204
Constellations 205
Urban Core 206
> *Technical Infrastructure* 207
> *Clinical Information Systems* 207
> *Consolidated Operations* 207

Clinical Joint Ventures 208
External Linkages 209

Appendix B

The Impact of Clinical Information Systems in Brigham Women's Hospital 211

ABOUT THE AUTHORS 219

INDEX 221

CHAPTER 1

An Overview of Strategy

The art, science, and practice of strategy has been a centerpiece of management and information technology (IT) literature and discussion for many years and will remain a major management concern for the foreseeable future. Effective strategies are a key determinant of organizational performance. Developing effective strategies is difficult. A plethora of approaches to assist in strategy formation has been created over the years (Harvard Business School, 1998; Stern and Stalk, 1998).

In this chapter we discuss the nature of strategy and the different ways in which we should apply strategy to IT in healthcare. The chapter will present the following.

- A definition of strategy
- A review of competitive strategy
- A discussion of the need for IT strategy and the types of IT strategy
- Characteristics of strategic thinking

DEFINITION OF STRATEGY

The strategy of an organization has two major components (Henderson and Venkatraman, 1993): formulation and implementation.

Formulation

Formulation involves making decisions about the mission and goals of the organization and the activities and initiatives that it will undertake to achieve that mission and those goals. Formulation could involve, for example, determining that

- Our mission is to provide high quality medical care.
- We have a goal of reducing the cost of care while at least preserving the quality of that care.
- One of our greatest leverage points lies in reducing inappropriate and unnecessary care.
- To achieve this goal we will place emphasis on, for example, reducing the number of inappropriate radiology procedures.
- We will carry out initiatives that enable us to intervene at the time of procedure ordering if we need to suggest a more cost-effective modality.

We can imagine other goals directed to achieving this mission. For each goal, we can envision multiple leverage points and for each leverage point we may see multiple initiatives. An inverted tree that cascades from our mission to a series of initiatives would emerge.

Formulation involves developing a core set of ideas and concepts that form the foundation of our view, or definition, of our goals and the manner by which we will achieve them.

Formulation involves understanding competing ideas and choosing between them. In the example above, we could have arrived at a different set of ideas. We could have decided to improve quality with less emphasis on care costs. We could have decided to focus on reducing the cost per procedure. We could have decided to produce reports, by provider, of radiology utilization and used this feedback to lead to ordering behavior change rather than intervening at time of ordering.

In IT we also have a need for formulation. In keeping with our IT mission to use the technology to support the improvement of the quality of care, we may have a goal to integrate our clinical application systems. We can have different concepts that define our view of this goal. We may decide that our definition of the goal of integration is

- A common look and feel across all applications
- Process interoperability

- Application interfaces using an interface standard
- A shared database of common clinical data used by all applications and users
- The implementation of the same clinical application across all organizations in the delivery system
- Some combination of the above

Although different, in each of these cases we have a core set of concepts and ideas that define our goal of integration. The initiatives that we will undertake will depend on the view of the goal of integration that we choose. Each of the ideas above represents, to a degree, competing ideas and we are likely to have to choose which subset of ideas we will apply.

Implementation

Implementation involves decisions about how we structure ourselves, acquire skills, establish organizational capabilities, and/or alter organizational processes in order to achieve the goals and carry out the activities and approaches that we have defined during the formulation of our strategy. For example, if we have decided to reduce care costs by reducing inappropriate procedure utilization, we may need to implement

- An organizational unit of providers with health services research training to analyze care practices and identify deficiencies
- A steering committee of clinical leadership to guide these efforts and provide political support
- A provider order entry system to provide real time feedback on order appropriateness
- Data warehouse technologies to support the analyses of utilization

Using our integration example, we may determine that

- A Web-based front end to all applications will provide necessary integration.
- The adoption of the Health Level 7 (HL7) standard and the implementation of interface engine technology will provide the needed level of interoperability.
- All of our clinical applications will use Cache, Oracle, SQL 7, or some other database technology.

- All delivery system organizations will utilize the application suite provided by Eclipsys.
- We must create a department in Information Systems that is responsible for all integration projects.
- Some combination of the above will be used.

The implementation component of strategy development is not the development of project plans and budgets. Rather it is the identification of those capabilities, capacities, and competencies that the organization will need if it is to carry out the results of the formulation component of strategy.

Observations on Strategy Definition

In IT we "conduct strategy," whether we realize it or not, when we formulate our definition of a goal and how we will approach that goal, and when we define the staff, technologies, and decision making structures needed to implement that goal. If we do not realize that we are engaged in a set of strategic decisions, we may carry out one component but not the other.

At times it may not be clear whether a particular IT strategy discussion is engaged in the formulation or implementation component of strategy. At a practical level, it may be irrelevant whether a specific insightful observation is one strategic component or the other. What does matter is that both components occur and occur well.

One's perspective may influence whether one views a conversation as strategic or tactical. The Board, having blessed an overall organizational strategy, may regard an IT conversation on the related clinical information systems as a tactical conversation. From the perspective of the CIO, that same conversation may be quite strategic. The CIO may regard the conversation that the clinical information systems project team has about the approach to implementation as tactical while the project team, rightfully so from their perspective, views that conversation as strategic. Pragmatically it may not be particularly worth the exercise to develop an irrefutable, perspective-invariant litmus test of whether a particular conversation is strategic or not. For this book, we adopt the perspective of the CIO and the other members of the senior leadership of the organization.

We can have IT strategy failures in both formulation and implementation. Formulation failures are the most serious since they can mean that the implementation strategies, no matter how well conceived and executed, are heading down the wrong path.

Following are potential examples of formulation strategy failures.

- *We may decide to integrate the applications in our integrated delivery system (IDS).* But our integrated delivery system isn't all that integrated. Rather, it is a loose confederation of relatively independent entities. If our strategy is to put the same system in all entities and thereby achieve integration we may fail to match the IT view of tight integration with the IDS practice of loose integration. We may spend a lot of money and not have advanced the cause of integration.
- *We may decide to implement a computer-based referral system* that steers the referring physician to one of our specialists and guides the collection of patient history. This system would invoke medical management rules to determine if the referral was necessary and ensure that all of the tests, that need to be done prior to the consult, have been performed. We may not realize that, from the referring physician's perspective, the primary problem with the referral process is the failure of the specialist to follow up rapidly on evaluation results. Hence, from the referring physician's perspective we have solved the wrong problem.
- *We may decide to construct an organizational home page to attract the consumer to our organization to receive care.* We may fail to recognize that, in our market, the key decision maker for where a family receives care is a demographic stereotype of a middle-aged woman who makes care decisions for herself, her children, and often her spouse and parents. This person, on average, is not a user of the Web and hence our page will miss the most important consumer.

Following are potential examples of implementation strategy failures.

- *We may decide to quickly move to message-based architectures* but not realize that our current legacy systems are incapable of supporting that architecture. Message technologies are too immature to scale well, and message standards are embryonic.
- *We may decide to embrace a three-tiered architecture strategy for our new applications* without any real understanding if such

tiering will enable us to be more agile, reduce our support costs or improve the functioning of applications. The significant exercise of replacing an architecture, which may be described as "legacy," with one that may be described as "state of the art" may not result in the organization believing that it is better off.

- *We may decide to create an IDS-wide steering committee,* but not realize that the vast majority of capital decision-making power lies in the member hospitals and hence our committee is impotent.
- *We may decide to standardize on key data elements that measure IDS patient volume* but fail to realize that changing data definitions changes counts, which changes power, which causes political "issues."

COMPETITIVE STRATEGY

An important aspect of "competitive" strategy is identifying goals and ways to achieve those goals that are materially superior to the way our competitor has defined them (formulation). We must also develop capabilities that are materially superior to the capabilities of our competitor (implementation) (Lipton, 1996). For example, we and our competitors may both decide that we need to create a network of primary care providers. However, we might believe that we can move faster and utilize less capital than our competition if we contract with existing providers rather than buy their practices. We and our competition may both have a mission to deliver high quality care, but our competitor has decided to focus on selected carve-outs or "focused factories" (Herzlinger, 1997) while we attempt to create a full-spectrum care delivery capacity.

Competitive strategy should attempt to define superiority that can be sustained. For example, we may believe that if our organization moves quickly, it can capture a large network of primary care providers and limit the ability of the competition to create its own network. "First to market" can provide a sustainable advantage although no advantage is sustainable for long periods of time. Similarly, an integrated delivery system with access to large amounts of capital can have an advantage over a system that does not. Wealth can provide a sustainable advantage.

In IT, while our competitor is focusing on implementing the computer-based patient record, we will focus on improving the referral

An Overview of Strategy

process because we believe that focus will have greater relative leverage on improving care and enhancing service to the primary care provider. We may also assess whether we can develop means that will enable us to implement systems faster or deliver richer and more critical functionality than our competition. For example, if we could implement systems for half the cost, because of vendor partnerships, or three times faster, because of efficient implementation decision making, then clearly an advantage, perhaps sustainable, accrues to the organization.

THE NEED FOR IT STRATEGY

There are many times in IT activities (mindful of our perspective) in which the goal, or our core approaches to achieving the goal, are not particularly strategic; strategy formulation and implementation are not needed. Replacing an inpatient pharmacy system, correcting Year 2000 issues, and delivering word processing capabilities organization wide, while requiring well-executed projects, do not always require the organization to be particularly clever or original in its approach to the challenge. There may be a penalty to attempting to be innovative because the associated risk may not have a sufficient reward.

There are many times in which there is little likelihood that the way we achieve the goal will create a distinct or competitive advantage. For example, an organization may decide that it needs a common e-mail network across its hospitals, clinics, and physician offices but it does not expect that the delivered e-mail system, or its implementation, is so superior to a competitor's e-mail system that an advantage is accrued to the organization.

Much of what information systems (IS) do is not strategic nor does it require strategic thinking. Most IS projects do not require hard looks at organizational mission, thoughtful discussions of fundamental approaches to achieving those organizational goals, or significant changes in organizational capabilities. However, the fact that all activities are not strategic should not reduce the need for the IS organization to find the best technology and continuously improve its own performance. Nonstrategic activities remain important.

Areas of IT Strategy

There are three major areas where IT strategy is very important. The areas are listed below and discussed in subsequent chapters.

- Those activities that establish a well-conceived linkage between organizational goals and initiatives and IT plans
- Approaches and initiatives designed to improve internal organizational characteristics, which significantly enhance our ability to be effective in our application of IT (e.g., creating a robust IT infrastructure or improving the relationships between IS and the rest of the organization)
- Concepts that will govern the approach to a class of initiatives and applications (e.g., are Internet technologies viewed as an integration opportunity or as a zero cost distribution channel for information, or both?)

Developing sound strategy in these areas can be very important for one simple reason: If you define what you have to do incorrectly or partially correctly, you run the risk that significant organizational resources will be misdirected. This risk has nothing to do with how well you execute the direction you choose. Being on time, on budget, and on spec is of diminished utility if you are doing the wrong thing.

Linkage to Organizational Goals and Initiatives

Organizations develop missions, goals, and plans. At times, these may not be written, have elements that are vague, or be volatile.

IS initiatives and capabilities, as any organizational resource, should be directed to supporting and advancing the organization's goals and plans. IS achieves strategic alignment with the organization by ensuring that it formulates its goals, activities, and plans and effects the implementation of its capabilities in a way that leverages the organization's ability to carry out its strategies. This alignment occurs through two basic mechanisms.

IT Strategies Derived from Organizational Strategies

The first mechanism involves deriving the IS agenda directly from the organization's goals and plans. For example, an organization may decide that it intends to become the low cost provider of care. It may decide to achieve this goal through the implementation of disease management, the reengineering of inpatient care, and the reduction of the unit costs of certain tests and procedures that it believes are inordinately expensive.

The IT strategy development centers on answering questions such as the following: "How do we apply IT to support disease management?"

The answers can range from Web-based publication of disease management protocols, data warehouse technology to assess the conformance of care practice to the protocols, provider documentation systems based on protocols, and provider order entry systems that guide ordering decisions based on the protocols. An organization may choose all or some of these responses and arrive at different sequences of implementation. Nonetheless, it has developed an answer to the question "What is our basic approach (formulation) to using IT to support the goal of reducing costs through the implementation of disease management?" The IT plan may define the application systems and staff that are needed to support the goals (implementation).

IT Strategies "Creating" Organizational Strategies

The second mechanism involves IT capabilities enabling the organization to consider new, or significantly altering current, strategic formulations and implementations. For example, Telemedicine capabilities may enable the organization to consider a strategy that it had not considered, extending the reach of its specialists across the globe, or alter its approach to achieving an existing strategy (e.g., relying less on specialists visiting regional health centers and relying more on teleconsultation).

An "extreme" form of this mechanism occurs when a new technology or application suggests that the very fundamental strategies of the organization, or the organization's existence, may be called into question or need to undergo significant transformation. Although rare in healthcare,[1] this form has been observed in other industries. The Internet, for example, is challenging the existence, or at least transforming, a range of companies that distribute "content." Example types of companies include book stores, record/CD stores, publishers of specific books, travel agents, and consumer software sales.

Changing Core Organizational Capabilities

Most of the time the linkage between organizational strategy and IT strategy involves organizational efforts such as adding or changing services and products or growing market share. However, at times, an organization may decide that it needs to change or add basic, core capabilities.

---

[1] Technologies, other than IT, have significantly altered the strategies of healthcare organizations. Example technologies include minimally invasive surgeries, chemotherapy and a wide range of medications. Advances in genetics are likely to have a dramatic impact on organizational strategy.

The organization may decide that it needs its staff to be more care-quality or service-delivery or bottom-line oriented. It may decide that it needs to decentralize decision making or to recentralize decision making. The organization may decide to improve its ability to manage knowledge or it may not. These characteristics, and there are many others, can point to initiatives for IS.

In these cases, IS must develop strategies that answer, for example, the question "What is our basic approach to supporting a decentralized decision making structure?" We might answer the question by permitting decentralized choices of applications as long as those application meet certain standards (e.g., run on a common platform or support an interapplication messaging standard). We might answer the question of how we support an emphasis on knowledge management by developing an Intranet service that inventories knowledge.

Internal Capabilities and Characteristics

Organizational effectiveness in applying IT is heavily influenced by the following two classes of organizational capabilities and characteristics.

- The IT asset
- IT-centric organizational attributes

The IT asset is composed of those IT resources, which the organization has or can obtain, that are applied to further the goals, plans, and initiatives of the organization. Strategies regarding the IT asset are generally implementation strategies. The IT asset, discussed in more detail in Chapter 3, has the following five components.

1. *Applications* are the systems with which users interact (e.g., scheduling, billing, and computerized record systems).
2. *Technical architecture* is composed of the base technology (e.g., networks, operating systems, and workstations that form the foundation for applications, and the approaches adopted to ensuring that these technologies "fit together").
3. *Data* are composed of the organization's data and analysis and access technologies.
4. *IS staff* are the analysts, programmers, computer operators, and so on who daily manage and advance information systems in an organization. This portion of the asset also includes IS

organization structure, core competencies, and IS organization characteristics.
5. *IT governance* is the organizational mechanism by which activities such as IS priorities are set, IT policies and procedures are developed, and IT management responsibility is distributed.

In those cases where there is a very explicit effort to link IT strategies to organizational strategies, activities directed to altering the IT asset can result. The organization's strategy may call for new applications, development of more reliable infrastructure, or the creation of new departments (e.g., quality measurement). There are often, however, needs to develop strategies for the IT asset for reasons that cut across organizational plans and activities. For example, strategies may be developed as a response to the following possible questions.

- What is our approach to ensuring that our infrastructure is more agile?
- What is our approach to attracting and retaining superb IS talent?
- How do we improve our prioritization of IT initiatives?
- Is there a way we can significantly improve the impact of our clinical information systems on our care processes?

A variety of studies, discussed in Chapter 3, have identified IT-centric organizational attributes, which appear to have a significant influence on the effectiveness of the organization in applying IT. Some of these factors are those mentioned as being part of the IT asset. Other factors include the following.

- The relationship between the IS group and the rest of the organization
- The presence of top management support for IT
- Organizational comfort with "visionary" IT applications
- Organizational experience with IT

These factors can be created or changed. If creation or change is desired, strategies will need to be developed.

Concepts that Frame the IT Challenge

There are classes of technology, applications, or management techniques that can appear to have the potential for a significant impact on our industry, organizations, and the way we implement and apply information systems. Examples today include the Internet, component-based architectures, knowledge management, and computerized medical record systems.

It may not be initially clear how these "technologies" will further organizational strategies or the impact, if adopted, on the IT asset. As organizations adopt, or explore the adoption of, these kinds of technologies, they develop formulation and implementation concepts that guide how they think about the technology, which in turn has great influence over whether they will adopt the technology, how they approach the implementation, and how they will evaluate the technology's success. For example, there are several ways to think about the Internet and its technologies.

- As a universal presentation layer allowing access to a diverse array of legacy systems by a diverse array of workstations
- As a means to publish organizational knowledge
- As a means to find services and information offered by others
- As a means to extend an organization's services into the home
- As a replacement for EDI
- As an approach to the alteration of a distribution channel (e.g., ordering your personal computer directly from the manufacturer rather than the local distributor)

All of these views are correct in that all can be effective. However, once an organization chooses a concept or concepts, it tends to think about the technology that way, often to the exclusion of other ways to think about it. Moreover the organization's concept can be wrong or half potent. For example, if an organization viewed Internet technologies solely as the universal front end, it would miss an extraordinary set of other opportunities for the technology.

The discussion of concepts that frame the IT challenge will be discussed in more detail in Chapter 4.

CHARACTERISTICS OF STRATEGIC THINKING

Strategic thinking and discussion have several characteristics.

Strategic thinking centers on discussions of the formulation of core concepts and ideas that determine goals and initiatives, and the definition of organizational capabilities and competencies needed if we are to implement those goals and initiatives.

The consequences of being wrong are generally serious. A hardware manufacturer that had a strategy that did not include the client server revolution generally paid for that strategy. Many healthcare provider organizations that failed to identify the tension between providing care and ensuring care and then integrated both wound up in trouble with the two.

A strategic decision has clear and illuminating ramifications for many other decisions. For example, an organization can decide that the critical component of a clinical information system is the introduction of decision support that guides a provider's decisions on ordering and referring. Such a strategy tells the organization that a provider order entry application and medical logic processors are critical aspects of its clinical system infrastructure. The organization would know that it needs a group of physicians, and organizational processes, to develop and monitor decision rules. The organization would know that it needs to code data for medications, lab tests, procedures, and problems since these form the basis for many rules. These decisions and calls fall naturally from a strategy of centering on decision support.

Strategic decisions often imply relatively significant changes in how business is conducted. Strategic decisions usually involve changes in the core concepts which guide organizational activity. Any time the concepts that underlie an organization undergo fundamental change, the organization's activities, market position, processes, and structure can undergo significant change. Similarly, the IS organization can experience significant change as a result of strategic decisions such as moving to client server architectures or investing heavily in computerized medical records.

The implementation of strategic decisions will require significant resources and intense political activity. Extensive resource commitments and political activity are the natural consequence and antecedent of the introduction of major organizational change.

Strategies take time, multiple iterations, and lots of analyses to develop, and they must be monitored. Organizations rarely fully understand either the consequences of their strategies or the complete set of organizational activities and investments required to implement their strategies. Strategies can be wrong or "off by 15 degrees." The organization learns as it adjusts itself and assesses the effectiveness of its changes.

In IS we often confuse tactical decisions with strategic decisions. "Should we use Java?" is not a strategic question. The question needs a formulation or implementation strategic context before it can be answered. One might be able to arrive at the Java question through a line of reasoning as follows.

- A major goal in our development of our technical architecture is the creation of the attribute of architectural agility (formulation).

- We would define agility as the ability to change a major component of our architecture without having to change other components of our architecture (formulation).
- If we could run complex applications in a way that essentially ignores, or need not be aware of, the client operating system, then we would have established some reasonably high level of agility since we could change clients and client operating systems without having to change the applications (formulation).
- To the degree that Java and virtual client machines provide such agility, we should pursue them (implementation).
- If we pursue this technology we will need, among other things, Java development expertise and means to manage the distribution of the Java software (implementation).

Unless we have started from some level of strategic thinking, it is hard to give a good answer to the Java question.

Nor can we directly answer the question of "Should we computerize the patient record?" We have to ask and answer the question "What is our basic approach to applying the technology to improve care?" If the answer is "We must improve the accessibility of patient data and improve the comprehensiveness of patient documentation," then we are in a position to assess whether the computerized patient record is a solid approach to improving care.

SUMMARY

It is critical that healthcare organizations apply strategic thinking, questioning, and analyses to their investments in information technology. Strategic thinking requires that we pursue fundamental questions regarding the formulation of goals and activities needed to achieve those goals. Strategic thinking requires that we pursue fundamental implementation questions such as the need to add or change core organizational capabilities.

Strategic thinking should be applied during conversations that link IT investments to organizational initiatives, development of plans to improve internal IT capabilities, and the examination of major classes of technology, applications, or management techniques.

Strategic thinking has several characteristics, and organizations can confuse a strategic question with a tactical question.

Not all conversations are strategic conversations. Not all IT investments are strategic investments. Classifying a tactical conversation, regardless of its importance, as strategic does not enhance the quality of the conversation.

REFERENCES

Harvard Business School. (1998). *Competitive Strategy—Articles from the Harvard Business Review and Case Studies from the Harvard Business School.* Cambridge, MA: Harvard Business School Publishing.

Henderson, J., Venkatraman, N. (1993). Strategic Alignment: Leveraging Information Technology for Transforming Organizations. *IBM Systems Journal* 32(1):4–16.

Herzlinger, R. (1997). *Market Driven Health Care* Reading, MA: Addison-Wesley.

Lipton, M. (1996). Opinion: Demystifying the Development of an Organizational Vision. *Sloan Management Review* 37(4):83–92, Summer.

Porter, M. (1996). What is Strategy? *Harvard Business Review* 74(6):61–78, November–December.

Stern, C., Stalk, G. (Eds.). (1998). *Perspectives on Strategy.* New York: John Wiley and Sons.

CHAPTER 2

Linkage of IT Strategy to Organizational Strategy

Information technology can support and, at times, be a critical contributor to affecting organizational strategies. Efforts to improve care quality can require clinical information systems and databases to analyze patterns of care. The integration of the integrated delivery system can be advanced through the development of a common e-mail platform, telephone directory, and an enterprise master person index.

Information technology can enable the organization to consider new elements and aspects of its strategy. The organization could use the World Wide Web as a way of reaching consumers with health information and providing access to the organization's health services. Provider order entry systems can be used to proactively guide medication decisions as a way of managing within a medication sub-capitation and reduce medication errors.

In this chapter we explore this linkage between organizational strategies and IT strategies. We will cover the following two major topics.
1. IT strategic planning frameworks and methodologies
2. Lessons learned from efforts to apply IT as a "competitive weapon"

STRATEGIC IT PLANNING METHODOLOGIES AND FRAMEWORKS

The IT strategic planning process has several objectives.

- Ensure that information technology plans and activities "align" with the plans and activities of the organization (i.e., the IT needs of each aspect of organizational strategy is clear and the portfolio of IT plans and activities can be mapped to organizational strategies and operational needs)
- Ensure that the alignment is comprehensive, that is,
- Each aspect of strategy has been addressed from an IT perspective recognizing that not all aspects have an IT component and not all components will be funded
- The non-IT organizational initiatives needed to ensure maximum leverage of the IT initiative (e.g., process reengineering), are understood
- The organization has not missed a strategic IT opportunity (e.g., those that might result from new technologies)
- Develop the tactical plan that details approved project descriptions, timetables, budgets, staffing plans, and plan risk factors
- Create a communication tool that can inform the organization of the IT initiatives that will be undertaken and those that will not
- Establish a political process that helps to ensure the plan results have sufficient organizational support

The above seems simple. Simple in the same way that the statement "Figure out what you want to do and then do it," seems like a one-sentence description of the entire set of responsibilities of an organization's CEO. However, alignment of IT with the organization has been notoriously difficult for many years and there appears to be no reason that such an alignment will become significantly easier over time.

Over the years, several methodologies have been developed in an effort to assist the organization in its effort to develop well-aligned IT plans. There are two major types of methodologies.

1. Those that utilize assessments of a specific organization's environment, strategies, missions, and goals and from that derive the related IT plans

2. Those that arrive at IT plans based on very fundamental views of the nature of organizations and their processes and the nature of forces, such as competition

In both types, the methodologies assist in developing organizational support, serve to communicate the plan, and lead to the eventual tactical plans of projects, timetables, and budgets.

Derived IT Linkage

Most IT planning methodologies used in healthcare today derive the IT plan from a thorough review of the organization's external environment, mission, goals, strategies, capabilities, and immediate competitive position. Three such methodologies are presented below.

Generic Methodology

A generic methodology is depicted in Figure 2–1.

In this methodology, interviews are conducted, often by consultants, to review organizational plans and strategies with organizational leadership and define operational needs with middle management. A portfolio of application and technical infrastructure needs is developed. Current IS resources are surveyed and the gap between those resources and the needed resources determined. Priorities are defined and budgets, timetables, and projects are eventually developed. These methodologies also include provisions and support for the formation of committees, to ensure broad input and garner political support for the plan's conclusions, and the delivery of sets of data that can limit the need of the organization to engage in original data gathering (e.g., the average costs of implementing a particular type of application system).

Minard Methodology

The annual planning cycle presented by Minard (1990) offers a strategy of reevaluation, modification, and evolution of ideas or issues. The cycle is presented in Figure 2–2.

There are six steps to the annual planning cycle. Arrows pointing into the rectangle represent plans and issues that are reviewed and analyzed, while arrows pointing out of the rectangle represent plans that are being updated. The shaded circles indicate planning items that correspond to the step.

FIGURE 2-1

Generic IT Strategic Planning Methodology

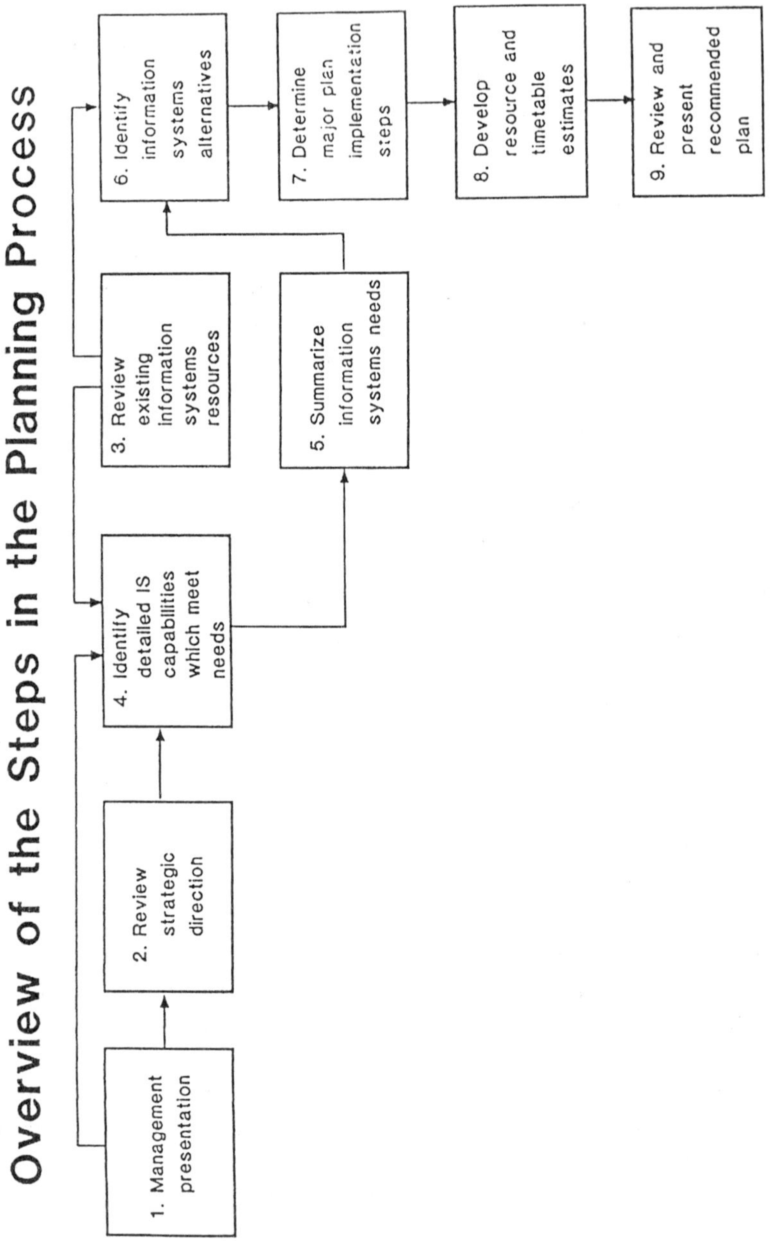

FIGURE 2-2
Minard Model

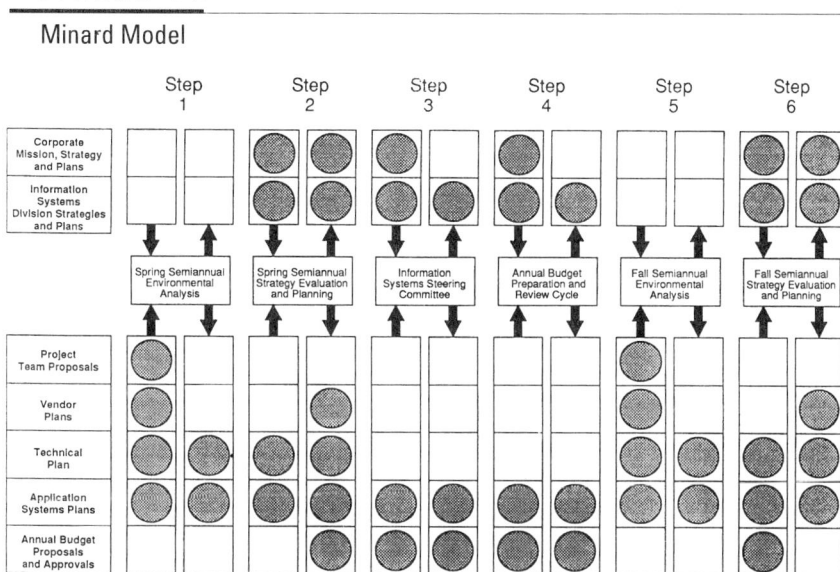

Source: Used with permission from *Health Care Computer Systems for the 1990s: Critical Executive Decisions*, by Bernie Minard (Chicago: Health Administration Press, 1991).

The first step in the annual planning cycle is the "Spring Semiannual Environmental Analysis," which involves reevaluation of new IT opportunities. The analysis can take place through conferences or presentations by vendors, consultants, hospital managers, and technical experts. Data analysis, data gathering, and learning experiences occur at this level, and proposed alterations to application system's plans are recorded.

The second step is the "Spring Semiannual Strategy Evaluation and Planning," which requires participants to review proposed changes in corporate plans, information system plans, technical plans, and application system plans. Consensus is vital at this stage.

Step three involves the meeting of the "Information Systems Steering Committee," the highest level executive group. They meet to review and approve proposed IT plans.

Step four is the "Annual Budget Preparation and Review Cycle," where budget items are approved and planned projects become planned objectives for the following year.

FIGURE 2-3

Component Alignment Model

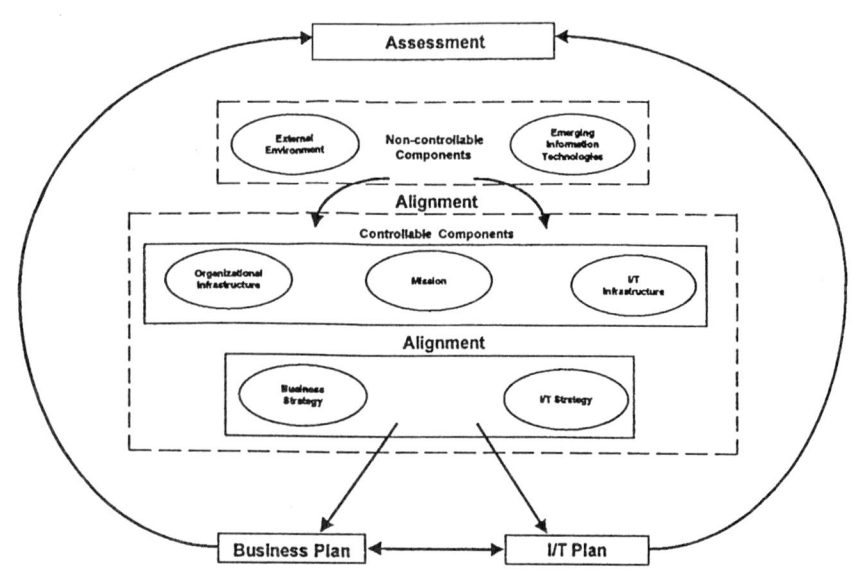

Source: Martin, J., Wilins, A., Stawski, S. (1998). The Component Alignment Model: A New Approach to Health Care Information Technology Strategic Planning. *Topics in Health Information Management* 19(1):1–10.

Step five is the "Fall Semiannual Environmental Analysis," which repeats the procedures of step one.

Step six is the "Fall Semiannual Strategy Evaluation and Planning," which repeats procedures of step two. Goals and objectives for next year are finalized and divided among project teams or individuals.

Component Alignment Model

The Component Alignment Model (CAM) (Martin, Wilkins, and Stawski, 1998) is based on the premise that strategic IT planning requires that the organization adopt a systems mentality where it sees itself as part of a whole entity, rather than as a confederation of individual business units. CAM consists of seven components, which are grouped into two major components: uncontrollable components and controllable components. CAM is presented in Figure 2–3.

Uncontrollable components (external environment and emerging information technologies) can not be affected by an organization's strategic plans, while controllable components (organization infrastructure and processes, mission, IT infrastructure and processes, business strategy, and IT strategy) can be directly affected by an organization's strategic plan.

The external environment component describes everything that occurs outside of the organization's corporate environment (e.g., mergers and affiliations, public perception of the healthcare environment, and federal regulation and reimbursement). The emerging information technology component describes any new technologies currently being developed (e.g., applications based on the client–server architecture). The organizational infrastructure and processes component describes an organization's services and management structures and philosophies (e.g., whether the organization emphasizes patient-focused or department-focused care). The mission component describes the main goals or objectives of the organization. The IT infrastructure and processes component describes the software, hardware, and personnel being used currently as a resource for delivering IT services. Business strategy describes an organization's business strategy (e.g., downsizing or developing centers of excellence in specialty areas). IT strategy describes an organization's IT goals, objectives, and strategic plans.

All of the components are interdependent and must be coordinated in response to changes in the healthcare industry and organizational direction. Each component outlined above needs to undergo continuous reassessment and modification known as alignment. There are two types of alignment: unidirectional and multidimensional. Unidirectional is the alignment of controllable components in response to changes in the uncontrollable components. Multidimensional is alignment among the five controllable components.

The CAM process defines each component and seeks to establish alignment through three phases: assessment, visioning, and plan development.

Linkage Based on Fundamental Views

Several IT strategic planning methodologies are based on fundamental views of the nature of organizations and organizational processes and the nature of competition. Often these views are originally presented in literature, which examines organizations and management and strategy issues in general, and then is adapted for use in IT strategic planning. For example, Porter's work on competitive forces (1980) was subsequently adapted by McFarlan (1984) for use in IT planning. Three examples of IT linkage based on fundamental views are discussed below.

The Value Chain

A useful framework for analyzing the strategic significance of information technology is the "value chain" described by Porter and Millar (1985). The "value chain" is a system of interdependent activities connected by linkages. The value chain divides company activities into technologically and economically distinct activities it performs to do business called "value activities." The value chain is depicted in Figure 2–4.

Value activities must be performed at a lower cost or lead to differentiation and a premium price in order for a company to gain competitive advantage. In other words, the value, the amount that buyers are willing to pay for a product or service, must exceed the cost of performing the value activity. These activities fall into nine categories, which are summarized into two overall activities. Primary activities are those that are involved in the physical creation of the product such as inbound logistics, operations, outbound logistics, marketing and sales, and service, while support activities are those that provide inputs and infrastructure that allow primary activities to take place such as firm infrastructure, human resource management, technology development, and procurement.

Linkages occur when the way in which one activity is performed affects the cost or effectiveness of other activities. Because they can create

FIGURE 2–4

The Value Chain

EXHIBIT I
The value chain

Support activities	Firm infrastructure					
	Human resource management					
	Technology development					
	Procurement					
		Inbound logistics	Operations	Outbound logistics	Marketing and sales	Service
		Primary activities				Margin

Source: Porter, M., Millar, V. (1985). How Information Gives You a Competitive Advantage. *Harvard Business Review* 63(4):149–160, July–August.

trade-offs, be optimized, and require good coordination of activities (e.g., just-in-time deliveries of supplies), it is important to carefully manage linkages as they can be a powerful source of competitive advantage.

Companies can also differ in competitive scope, or the breadth of their activities, with scope being a potential source of competitive advantage. Competitive scope ranges from broad to narrow scope. An organization can potentially serve more industries or geographic areas by performing more activities internally (i.e., an organization does not need to establish across several regions relationships with others in order to perform the activities). An organization can narrow scope by tailoring the value chain to a specific product, buyer, or geographic region.

Porter and Millar note that information technology has gained strategic significance because it is constantly transforming linkages, the way value activities are performed, and the competitive scope. For every value activity, there is an information-processing unit, which stores, manipulates, and transmits any data needed to perform the value activity, and a physical-processing unit, which includes all physical tasks required to perform the value activity. Information technology is transforming both of these units making information processes cost less and physical processes faster, more accurate, and more flexible. Information systems also can alter competitive scope by allowing companies to coordinate value activities in distant geographic locations.

In healthcare we might define such activities broadly (e.g., patient access), and narrowly (e.g., dispense medication). Linkages can include procedure orders, referrals, and eligibility determination.

The value chain approach to IT strategic planning represents a very different approach than one that begins by reading the organization's strategic plan. One identifies the IT strategy by defining value activities and linkages that can be improved or altered, rather than through a direct examination of the organization's strategy.

Competitive Forces

The competitive forces model (Porter, 1980) examines forces that shape the competitive environment and hence an industry's, and its member organization's, profitability. Porter identifies five competitive forces that determine an industry's profitability: the bargaining power of buyers, the bargaining power of suppliers, the threat of new entrants, the threat of substitute products, and the rivalry among existing competitors. In order to gain a competitive advantage, companies must devise methods to counter each of these forces. Figure 2–5 present Porter's competitive forces model.

The model can be used to evaluate how information technology can alter each of these competitive forces (McFarlan, 1984). For example, the bargaining power of buyers may be increased by electronic catalogs and consumer report web sites. Barriers to entry in some industries have increased due to the large investments that need to be spent to remain on the cutting edge of technology (e.g., organizations often join integrated delivery systems because of the capital costs of the information technology, which is viewed as necessary in order to compete, and some banks have sold themselves to larger banks to avoid the prohibitive costs of correcting the Year 2000 problem).

Information technology can also create competitive advantage by lowering cost, enhancing differentiation, and changing competitive scope. IT is enabling the creation of new industries and new businesses (e.g., direct ordering of merchandise through the Internet).

FIGURE 2–5

Competitive Forces

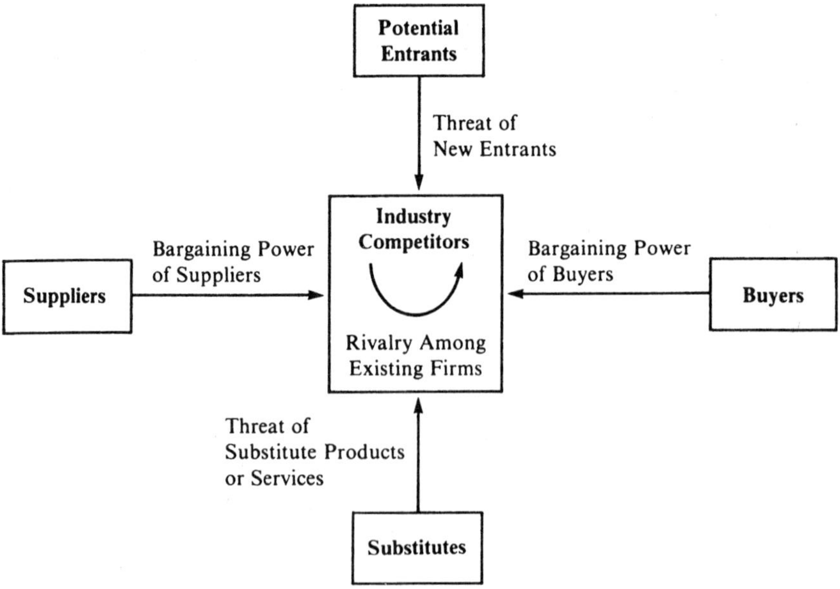

```
                        ┌──────────────┐
                        │  Potential   │
                        │   Entrants   │
                        └──────┬───────┘
                               │
                           Threat of
                          New Entrants
                               │
                               ▼
                        ┌──────────────┐
                        │   Industry   │
   Bargaining Power     │ Competitors  │    Bargaining Power
    of Suppliers        │      ↷       │     of Buyers
┌──────────┐            │              │            ┌──────────┐
│Suppliers │───────────▶│              │◀───────────│  Buyers  │
└──────────┘            │ Rivalry Among│            └──────────┘
                        │Existing Firms│
                        └──────┬───────┘
                               ▲
                           Threat of
                       Substitute Products
                           or Services
                               │
                        ┌──────┴───────┐
                        │  Substitutes │
                        └──────────────┘
```

Source: Porter, M. (1980). *Competitive Strategy.* New York: The Free Press.

Porter and Millar (1985) offer IS managers five steps in taking advantage of IT.

1. Assess information intensity (i.e., how essential and pervasive information processing generically is in the industry).
2. Determine the role of information technology in industry structure (i.e., to what degree IT has lead to the current industry structure, with international banking being an example of an industry whose current form is significantly shaped by IT).
3. Identify and rank the ways in which information technology might create a competitive advantage (e.g., providing referring physicians with access to the specialist's schedule).
4. Investigate how information technology might spawn new businesses (e.g., the examination of disease management, as a business, by pharmaceutical companies).
5. Develop a plan for taking advantage of information technology.

We can see examples in healthcare where IT can alter competitive forces although it is not clear that such examples were developed using the framework. IT enables providers to assume full delegation under capitation. Management of delegation would be effectively impossible without IT. Delegation alters the power between the supplier (the managed care company) and the buyer (the provider). Telemedicine can act as a means to provide a substitute product wherein one provider "invades" the market of another provider with a different approach to obtaining access to specialists. Many healthcare provider organizations are attempting to strengthen their relationships with their buyers (referring physicians) by providing real-time access to information about the hospital care of the referring physician's patient.

As with the value change analysis, the process of arriving at an IT strategic plan using the competitive forces framework has a very different conversation than the conversation that centers on the published organizational strategic plan.

Customer Resource Life Cycle

While the value chain and competitive forces models present frameworks that evaluate whether strategic opportunities exist and categorize existing applications, Ives and Learmouth (1984) offer the "customer resource life cycle" (CRLC), which not only identifies and categorizes strategic applications on the basis of differentiating a company's product from its competitors, but also identifies what specific strategic applications to develop. It focuses on the relationship between customer and the provider of goods or services. There are thirteen steps to the CRLC model (Figure 2–6).

A product or resource generally has four stages in its life cycle that are supported by a supplier's application of IT: requirements, acquisition or implementation, stewardship, and retirement or disposition. Within the four stages, thirteen steps define in more detail exactly where suppliers can develop more strategic IT systems.

FIGURE 2–6

Customer Resource Life Cycle

IBM Stage	Extended Model	Description
Requirements	Establish requirements	To determine how much of a resource is required.
	Specify	To determine a resource's attributes.
Acquisition	Select source	To determine where customers will buy a resource.
	Order	To order a quantity of a resource from the supplier.
	Authorize and pay for	To transfer funds or extend credit.
	Aquire	To take possession of a resource.
	Test and except	To ensure that a resource meets specifications.
Stewardship	Integrate	To add to an existing inventory.
	Monitor	To control access and use of a resource.
	Upgrade	To upgrade a resource if conditions change.
	Maintain	To repair a resource, if necessary.
Retirement	Transfer or dispose	To move, return, or dispose of inventory as necessary.
	Account for	To monitor where and how much is spent on a resource.

Source: Ives, B., Learmonth, G. (1984). The Information as a Competitive Weapon. *Communications of the ACM* 27(12):1193–1201, December.

1. Establish requirements and estimate future needs of a particular resource.
2. Specify attributes of a particular resource.
3. Select a source and match a client's needs with an appropriate supplier.
4. Order systems that offer around-the-clock or just-in-time services.
5. Authorize and arrange payments through debit or credit card systems.
6. Acquire products or services in the quickest and most convenient ways.
7. Customers should be allowed to test the acceptability of the new resource.
8. Integrate into and manage inventory—the resource must be included in existing inventory of resources and be managed.
9. Monitor use and behavior—resources should remain acceptable.
10. Upgrade resources if requirements change.
11. Maintain—suppliers need to make repairs to keep resources in good condition.
12. Customers will transfer or dispose of a resource.
13. Account for—customer can receive reports on how much money is spent for resources.

While the product orientation of the CRLC might make it seem inappropriate in a service industry such as healthcare, the thirteen steps can be helpful. One can find that most of the thirteen steps might be germane in a discussion of the creation of a women's health service or a set of service improvements directed to the referring physician.

Observations on IT Frameworks and Planning

Processes and methodologies that help organizations develop IT plans, whether based on derived linkage or the examination of more fundamental characteristics of organizations, can be very helpful. If well executed they can accomplish the following.

- Enhance and ensure necessary leadership participation and support

- Contribute to a more thorough analysis of the major aspects of the plan
- Help the organization to be more decisive
- Ensure that the allocation of resources among the competing alternative is more rational and politically defensible
- Identify alternatives and approaches that might not have occurred without the process
- Enhance communication of the developed plan

Persistence of the Alignment Problem

Despite the useful attributes, the IT alignment issue has been a top concern of senior leadership for many years. The annual Computer Science Corporation surveys of top IT issues (which will be discussed in Chapter 3) note that the issue of aligning IT with the rest of the organization has been a top IT issue for several years in a row. There are several reasons for the persistent difficulty in alignment (Bensaou and Earl, 1998).

- Business strategies are often not clear or are volatile.
- IT opportunities are poorly understood.
- The different parts of the organization have different priorities.
- The resulting IT strategies can be incoherent.

Weill and Broadbent (1998) note that effective IT alignment requires that organizational leadership understand, with clarity, and integrate well, strategically and tactically, (a) the organization's strategic context (i.e., its strategies and market position), (b) the organization's environment, (c) the IT strategy and (d) the IT portfolio (e.g., the current applications, technology, and staff skills). Understanding and integrating these four continuously evolving and complex areas is exceptionally difficult.

The following reasons could be added to these lists of factors that make alignment difficult.

- The organization finds that it has not achieved the gains, apparently achieved by others, that it has heard or read about, nor have the promises of the vendors of the technologies materialized. Organizations can view these gaps, perhaps incorrectly, as an alignment problem.
- Often the value of IT, particularly infrastructure, is difficult to quantify. IT can also be expensive. Alignment can refer to the

challenge of determining how expensive infrastructure and applications actually contribute to organizational goals (e .g., what's the business value of staff having the newest personal computer technology?).

The Limitations of Alignment

As we shall see in Chapter 3, while alignment is important, there are several other factors that influence organizational IT excellence (e.g., the relationship between IS and the rest of the organization and the presence of a sound IT technology infrastructure). Planning methodologies cannot by themselves overcome these other factors if they are weak, although they can improve an organization and help them to be better IT planners and develop better IT plans. Planning methodologies also cannot overcome unclear strategies or organizational inability (which would affect IT and non-IT decisions) to resolve competing priorities other than by trying to appease all.

In an analogous fashion, if one has mediocre painting skills, a class on painting technique will make one a better painter but will not turn one into Picasso. Perhaps, this reason, more than any other, is why the alignment issue remains persistently as a top-ranked IT issue. Organizations are searching for excellence in the wrong place, it cannot be purely delivered by methodologies.

Alignment at Maturity

Organizations that have a history of IT excellence would appear to evolve to a state where there alignment process is "methodology-less." A study by Earl (1993) of organizations in the UK that had a history of IT excellence found that their IT planning processes had several characteristics.

- *IT planning was not a separate process.* IT planning, and the strategic discussion of IT, occurred as an integral part of organizational strategic planning processes and management discussions. In these organizations, management did not think of separating out an IT discussion, during the course of strategy development, any more than they would run a separate Finance planning process or Human Resources planning processes. IT planning was an unseverable, intertwined component of the normal management conversation. This would suggest that there is no separate IS Steering Committee.

- *IT planning had neither a beginning nor an end.* Often IT planning processes start in one month every year and are done, for example, three months later. In the studied organizations, the IT planning and strategy conversation went on all of the time. This does not mean that an organization doesn't have to have a temporally de-marked process designed to form a budget every year. Rather it means that IT planning is a continuous process reflecting the continuous change in the environment and organizational plans and strategies.
- *IT planning involved shared decision making and shared learning between IS and the organization.* IS leadership informed organizational leadership of the potential contribution of new technologies and constraints of current technologies. Organizational leadership ensured that IS leadership understood the business plans and strategies and constraints. The IT budget and annual tactical plan resulted from a shared analysis and set of conclusions.
- *The IT plan emphasized themes.*[1] For example, a provider organization may have themes of improving care quality, reducing costs and integrating the IDS. During the course of any given year, it will have initiatives that are intended to advance the organization along these themes. The mixture of initiatives will change from year to year but the themes endure over the course of many years. Themes serve as a foundation for criteria for choosing between alternative activities. Themes help organizations understand infrastructure creation (e.g., the establishment of a group to measure care quality or the standardization on common vocabularies for clinical data become important if care improvement is a primary organizational theme). Themes provide a basis for crafting architecture (e.g., infrastructure reliability and performance become exceptionally important if significant, multi-year investments will be made in systems to be used directly by care providers).

---

[1] Weill and Broadbent (1998) would refer to a theme as a "maxim." Examples of maxims would be "develop partnerships with customers on a world-wide basis" and "relentless cost reduction."

Summarizing Earl's work would suggest that mature IT alignment, as it occurs in the course of normal management conversation

- Is iterative and ongoing,
- Focuses on core, strategic themes,
- Has short time horizons for initiatives, and
- Is conducted by the same senior management in the same conversations that decide and develop strategies overall.

Summary

IT strategic planning methodologies and frameworks can be very helpful. They can provide a needed discipline and process. They can help organizational leadership "see" new IT opportunities. However, these methodologies and frameworks are not a panacea; they will not overcome other organizational limitations. It appears that organizations that have become quite mature in their IT use and have evolved these alignment processes to the point where they are no longer distinguishable as separate processes. This observation should not be construed as advice to cease using such methodologies or disband effective steering committees. Such an evolution, to the degree that it is normative (e.g., kids will grow up [at least most of them will]), may occur naturally.

INFORMATION TECHNOLOGY AS A COMPETITIVE WEAPON

A large segment of the provider sector of the healthcare industry still seems to struggle with the fact that it competes and that identifying and implementing competitive strategies and "weapons" is important. Competition should not be characterized as involving clubbing an opponent into submission and running rough shod over well-meaning nurses and physicians. Competition does mean ensuring that one's organization fares well and meets the goals it has established. Since the world, at times, has attributes of a zero sum game, this success may come at the expense of someone else.

As organizations examine strategies and capabilities, an entirely reasonable question is "Can the application of information technology provide a competitive advantage to an organization?"

Over the last two decades, across a wide range of industries, answers to this question have been explored. Answers continue to be explored[2] and developed and perhaps, as a result of continued evolution of the technology and continued transformation of industries and economies, will always be explored.

In this section of the chapter, we will review several cases of non-healthcare organizations where information technology has appeared to provide a competitive advantage. We will also discuss lessons learned and answers developed to the question posed at the beginning of this section.

Case Studies

Several superb examples of the use of IT to achieve a competitive advantage have been developed, documented, and studied (McKenney, Copeland, and Mason, 1995). In this section we will summarize three examples: the American Airlines SABRE system, the American Hospital Supply Co. ASAP system, and a set of systems implemented by Federal Express. Summary lessons from each of these cases will also be presented.

SABRE

The American Airlines' reservation system, SABRE, is regarded as one of the legendary examples of the competitive use of IT. The development of SABRE can be traced back to the late 1940s. American Airlines was seeking to address operational issues and inefficiencies associated with the manual keeping of records of passenger names. By the mid 1970s, SABRE was providing to travel agents the ability to book airline flights interactively. SABRE, the name of a reservation system, eventually became the name of a business.

Since its genesis, SABRE, the business, centered on a massive IT infrastructure. Today, with over 450 clients in 73 countries, American Airlines is a world leader in electronic distribution and information technology solutions for travel and travel-related services. SABRE provides their clients with travel reservation automation, advanced decision-support systems, customized software development and software products, transaction processing, systems integration, consulting, and IT

---

[2] *Business Week*, in its cover story on June 22, 1998, examined the implications of the Internet for a diverse set of industries.

outsourcing. Their clients include travel agencies, airlines, railroads, lodging companies, transportation services, oil and gas companies, and the financial services industry.

Located underground in Tulsa, Oklahoma, SABRE consists of 17 mainframes with more than 15.3 terabytes of electronic storage, over 4,000 MIPS of processing power, and 180 communications processors. Not only does this protect the system from natural disasters, but it also handles over 45 million fares in the database, 40 million changes each month, 2,000 messages per second, and creates more than 500,000 passenger name records every day (Hopper, 1990). There are over 130,000 terminals located in travel agencies that link to SABRE. SABRE also manages 200,000 personal computers, 45,370 telephone numbers, and 10,200 voice mailboxes. It is the world's largest privately owned, real-time computer system.

American Airlines had five strategic objectives in 1982 with SABRE (McKenney, Copeland, and Mason, 1995).

1. Display American's products preferentially at the retail level (e.g., if an agent wanted to book a flight from Boston to Los Angeles, SABRE would list the American Airlines offerings first).
2. Maintain SABRE's superiority among automated reservations systems.
3. Receive revenue from every booking made by subscribers to SABRE, regardless of the carrier chosen for the flight.
4. Increase the amount paid by third parties (e.g., other carriers who utilized the SABRE system such as Continental Airlines).
5. Receive a satisfactory return on investment without consideration of incremental passenger revenues.

It is difficult to question the success of SABRE. By 1983 American Airlines had captured 27% of automated travel agent locations and accounted for 43% of the travel revenues booked through airline-sponsored computerized reservation systems. American Airlines reports a return on investment of 500%. From 1977 to 1986, SABRE contributed $1.5 billion to the bottom line of American Airlines.

American Airlines has demonstrated a series of competitive insights and capitalized on them over the course of the years. They did the following.

- *Understood and implemented new technologies,* which enabled SABRE to continue to expand its contribution to American Airlines. Example technologies include time-sharing, which dramatically improved the level of capabilities that could be offered to travel agents, and access, through the Internet, to enable direct consumer ordering of tickets.
- *Recognized how to leverage a process.* Some argue that SABRE gave travel agents a bias toward booking American Airlines, either by offering incentives to the agents or having a "screen bias" (i.e., showing the American flight first) (Hopper, 1990).
- *Recognized the value of the data* contained in SABRE. This data enabled American to offer frequent flyer programs and successfully manage fare wars and plane yield (i.e., ensuring that barely full flights occurred infrequently).
- *Understood the customer.* SABRE has launched "Travelocity"sm, an Internet and online service that allows travelers to coordinate their own travel plans, from reserving and purchasing airline tickets to accessing travel and entertainment information to purchasing customized travel guides. Customers can also share travel experiences through chat groups, postings, and conferences (http://www.amrcorp.com).
- *Understood, and leveraged, opportunities created when a competitive advantage had ceased to be an advantage.* American eventually sold their software and expertise to competitors and others in the travel business. They recognized that their expertise and investment could generate more revenue by selling them than by continuing to hold them within the company. For example, in 1997 American made $21.9 million by having Dollar Rent A Car System, Inc., and Thrifty Rent A Car System Inc., outsource their data center and system engineering functions to SABRE.

ASAP

Another legendary example of the use of IT to improve competitive position, the American Hospital Supply Corporation's (AHSC) Analytic Systems Automatic Purchasing (ASAP) is an efficient ordering, tracking, computerized system for managing hospital supplies.

ASAP evolved from efforts in the 1950s, by AHSC, to improve hospital supply inventory control, order processing, and billing through the utilization of punch cards. In the 1970s ASAP was created when these core capabilities were extended to allow direct access to the ordering system using time-sharing technology by hospital materials managers.

ASAP evolved from a focus on supply order-entry and reporting to a focus on quality of service, cost management, and value-added materials management (Short and Venkatraman, 1992). A key to ASAP's success is its ability to reconceptualize business relationships. As the market shifts from product/price-based exchange to value-added services approach, AHSC went beyond just ordering and tracking hospital supplies and focused on customizing their system to each hospital. ASAP and its successors (ASAP 2, 3, 4, and 5) gave customers more power. For example, ASAP 2 allowed messages to be transmitted electronically from AHSC to sales representatives to customers. Also, for items that were not in stock, ASAP 2 automatically suggested substitutions. ASAP 3 allowed customers to build their own electronic files, using the hospital's own internal stock numbers. ASAP 5 allowed customers to place orders on their own personal computer, which eliminated telephone expenses (Konsynski and Vitale, 1991). They responded to the personal needs of their customers, adding more value to their services by setting up teams of sales, marketing, distribution, and IS staff to analyze a hospital's ordering and receiving patterns. Like SABRE, ASAP provides market power and competitive advantage because it provides is creators access to information that their competitors cannot obtain.

AHSC also gained a competitive edge by achieving status of "prime vendor of choice" among hospitals. As prime vendor of choice AHSC negotiates volume purchase agreements with the customer on a fixed-price basis, thus shifting purchasing decisions from price to service (Short and Venkatraman, 1992). In other words, hospitals would contract a major portion of their supplies from AHSC in return, for example, for lower inventory, reduced paper handling, guaranteed service, and fewer purchase orders. This status of prime vendor was achieved not only with ASAP, but also with AHSC's broad product line. With an extensive range of products, hospitals have the advantage of "one-stop shopping" with AHSC as their supplier. "Prime vendor of choice" also helps hospitals lower administrative charges and inventory carrying costs.

Another way AHSC maintains competitive advantage is by shifting its strategic emphasis over time. In the 1960s, ASAP was a dedicated system providing efficient, nationwide distribution of hospital supplies. Now, ASAP Express, designed to be the first all-vendor, all-transaction clearing house, is an electronic data exchange platform, similar to SABRE, where data regarding price and product availability of their competitors can be made available. Customers can conduct business with all vendors using one system, anytime of the day (Konsynski and Vitale, 1991). Along with this strategic shift to a multivendor platform, Baxter's[3] ValueLink program is changing AHSC's traditional role as a distributor by assuming the role of materials manager for the hospital. This strategic partnership requires hospitals to sign a long-term contract while Baxter provides 100% fill rate, customized procedures, and lower inventory levels. This demonstrates the importance of shifting strategic emphasis to accommodate the evolution of traditional customer-supplier relationships.

It is difficult to argue the contribution of ASAP to AHSC. ASAP can be accessed in 80% of US hospitals. AHSC's earnings from continued operations grew from $42 million (1974) to $237 million (1984) (McKenney, Copeland, and Mason, 1995).

AHSC, like American Airlines, was able to leverage its core IT application competitively because they did several things very well.

- *Took advantage, over several years, of new technologies* (e.g., the touch tone phone, timesharing, personal computers, and now the Internet) and technology concepts (e.g., EDI)
- *Evolved the role of the system as their customers' needs and sophistication evolved.* What began as a means to improve the efficiency of the ordering processing for the supplies of one vendor has now evolved to e-mail capabilities, hospitals maintaining their own profiles, and just-in-time supply delivery.
- *Leveraged other, perhaps more core strengths* of AHSC, specifically the ability of AHSC to offer a broad array of competitively priced and high quality products and supplies.
- *Was able to correctly visualize and act on significant changes in the industry* (e.g., healthcare cost pressures enabled Baxter to develop approaches to shared risk in hospital materials management) and changes in the basis of IT-centric competition (e.g., abandoning the narrow role of ASAP, which channeled orders only to AHSC to a role of the system as an industry utility acting as an all-vendor materials electronic clearing house).

---

[3] Baxter Travenol acquired American Hospital Supply in 1985.

Federal Express

The world's largest express transportation company, Federal Express (FedEx) provides fast, reliable services for documents, packages, and freight. They transport time-sensitive, high-value cargo to more than 211 countries, which represent over 99% of the world's GDP.

A critical element of their success is their use of IT. Customers prefer FedEx as their express package delivery company because of IT's leverage in providing reliable, speedy service, and accurate information on the status of their shipments.

FedEx's systems are used to improve the efficiency and effectiveness of internal operations by, for example, performing customer-by-customer assessment of pricing, developing earlier in the day delivery options, consolidating FedEx trucking contracts, and generating Courier Route Planner Information System that streamlines pickup and delivery routes.

FedEx has also used IT to extend and enhance the customer's capabilities. FedEx's POWERSHIP system brings a variety of services from automated tracking, self-invoicing, stored shipping database, and report compilation and generation to the customer's desktop. Nearly one-third of all FedEx's volume was processed through POWERSHIP. COSMOS is the multipurpose, multifaceted tracking system built in 1979 that connects POWERSHIP to Digitally Assisted Dispatch System (DADS), a computer link in the courier's van. SuperTracker, which is a handheld barcode scanner, is used by the courier to scan the package information.

Another IT enhancement of business activities is the FedEx Web site with over 1.4 million hits per month, and over 360,000 tracking requests so far (http://WWW.fedex.com). The Web site offers "InterNetShip," which means customers do not need to call FedEx or write international airbills. They can print barcodes for themselves with a laser printer, arrange for a courier pick-up, and then track their FedEx item. The Web offers customers career opportunities, provides financial and corporate information for stockholders, notes locations of dropoff sites, identifies easy delivery options, and provides software that customers can download like "FedExShip" and "FedEx Tracking." FedEx continues to provide their customers with new services like their new time-of-day deliveries, new Asian routes, and instructions in different languages.

With FedEx, as in the other two cases, we see a deep understanding of the customer, an ability to capitalize on new technologies, a leverage of other strengths (in FedEx's case it owns a package delivery system of 500 aircraft and 35,000 vehicles), and a continuous extension of system capabilities. We also see, and saw to varying degrees in the other cases, the following.

- *A radical reengineering of the business processes that surround package delivery.* This successful reengineering of this organization, and as a result that of its industry, was done in conjunction with conversations about the ability of IT to support various process options. This is an example, in addition to IT support of significant reengineering, of the IT strategy being developed in parallel and intertwined with the business strategy, rather than the IT strategy "falling out" or being derived from the business strategy.
- *A progressive transfer of control, power, and information to the customer.* This transfer (e.g., generating your own shipping documents or directly determining the status of your packages) reduced FedEx's costs and improved customer satisfaction without jeopardizing the core capabilities and value of FedEx. On the contrary, by giving customers greater power FedEx's value has increased.

Lessons Learned

The experiences cited above, and those of other organizations, have led to a series of observations and conclusions, some mentioned above, about the ability of IT to provide a competitive advantage.

Core Sources of Advantage

In most cases, organizations utilize IT to provide a competitive advantage in four general ways.

1. Leverage organizational processes
2. Enable rapid and accurate provision of critical data
3. Enable product and service differentiation and, occasionally, creation
4. Support the alteration of overall organizational form or characteristics

Leverage Organizational Processes IT can be applied in effort to improve organizational processes by making them faster, less error prone, less expensive, more convenient, and more available (e.g., can be conducted from home at 2 AM). In effect, the "transaction cost" of the process, from the "customer's" perspective, has been reduced. Examples abound, including the following.

- Automated Teller Machines have made the process of obtaining cash more convenient.
- Accounts receivable applications have made that process less expensive, faster, and less error prone.
- Outpatient scheduling systems can improve the management and utilization of expensive staff, room, and equipment resources.
- Results reporting systems enable the process of obtaining test results to be faster, less error prone, and more convenient.
- Computerized record systems can enable the process of accessing information about a patient's prior encounters more efficient and more accessible.

These examples and countless others have highlighted several lessons.

IT leverage of processes is most effective when the processes being leveraged are critical, core processes that

- Customers use to judge the performance of the organization and
- Define the core business of the organization.[4]

Patients are more likely to judge a provider organization on the basis of its ambulatory scheduling processes and billing processes than they are on its accounts payable and human resources processes. Moreover, there are attributes of these processes, and their end products, that matter more than other attributes. For example, patients may judge appointment availability as more important than the organization's ability to process no-shows.

Making diagnostic and therapeutic decisions is a core provider organization process; a process that is essential to its core business. It is

---

[4] Keen (1997) defines the importance of processes along two dimensions. Worth is a measure to the difference between the cost of a process and the revenue it generates. Salience is a measure of the degree to which a process is critical to the identity of an organization or is critical to its effectiveness. The referral process may have high worth. The ambulatory scheduling process may be a critical contributor to the organization's efforts to be identified as "patient friendly." Order entry and communication may be critical to a hospital's effectiveness.

unlikely that there are a large number of organizational processes that have no bearing on and make no contribution to organizational performance. However, there are processes that are more essential to the mission of the organization and its goals than others. Customers may have limited ability to judge or evaluate these processes. For example, most patients cannot judge how well a provider organization makes diagnostic and therapeutic decisions despite the growing use and sophistication of quality measures.

While provider organizations have lots of customers (e.g., patients, providers, referring physicians, employees, and trustees), some customers matter more than others. Those who design and select information systems are not always the most important customer and/or have limited understanding of how the customer judges the process.

IT can enable an organization to materially alter the nature of its processes. For example, the technology can enable processes or business activities to be extended over a wider geographic area than the immediate service area. Telemedicine enables consultation to occur with patients across the globe. The Internet can enable patients in many countries to enroll in clinical trials. IT can support an organization's efforts to franchise care operations in other states by providing access to "home" expertise.

Process can be altered or created in a manner that enables the organization to craft or significantly enhance strategic partnerships with other organizations. A process can be moved from one organization to another; a form of outsourcing. For example, a hospital and a managed care organization, rather than both conducting utilization review and case management, could share that responsibility. Providers and materials suppliers have established just-in-time inventory replenishment processes. Both examples, and others that one can imagine, are predicated upon a strong IT core.

Process reexamination should accompany any effort to apply IT to process improvement. If underlying problems with processes are not remedied, the IT investment can be wasted or diluted. IT applications can result in existing processes continuing to perform poorly only faster. Moreover, it can be harder to fix flawed processes after the application of IT because the "new" IT-supported process has an additional source of complexity, cost, and ossification to address: the "new computer system." Process reexamination, addressed extensively and well in several books, can range from incremental, although valuable change, to more radical reengineering.

Linkage of IT Strategy to Organizational Strategy

In addition to the examination and improvement of the mechanics of the process that is the target of the information system, the reexamination should question whether the process is defined correctly. Process definitions often incorporate the mechanics of the process into the core definition of the process leading reexamination to inappropriately narrow its efforts. For example

- A statement of the process as "obtaining cash from the bank" might lead reengineering efforts to locate ATMs only at the bank. Such ATMs might ease the burden of standing in line on a Saturday morning and hence be viewed as an improvement. However, a statement of the process as "obtaining cash" might lead one to consider all of the places where one needs cash: malls, theaters, and airports. This might result in placement of ATMs everywhere leading to a far more powerful improvement in the process. A statement of the process as "buying something" might lead one to create debit cards as cash surrogates.
- A statement of the process as "obtaining a referral number" might lead one to construct an EDI link between the managed care application and the systems in the physician's office.
  A statement of the process as "managing referrals" might lead one to abandon entirely the process of obtaining the referral number.

Recently there has been great interest in using IT to alter the "intermediation" structures of various processes. These processes generally link a customer to a supplier.

Dis-intermediation would involve removing a process "middleman" (e.g., selling airline tickets through the World Wide Web, bypassing the travel agent, ordering a personal computer from the manufacturer, rather than a local distributor, or specialists offering medical information on the Web allowing patients to bypass the primary care provider).

Cementing a current intermediation role might, for example, lead a stock brokerage to offer the ability to purchase stocks through the Internet in addition to the use of their brokers, a book distributor might support the ordering of books over the Web as a supplement to their chain of book stores or a mortgage firm might enable the initiation of the mortgage application in addition to providing access to their brokers.

Re-intermediation involves creating a middle man where effectively, for you, there was none. The Web is being used to enable customers to find, for example, rare music recordings, specialized material for hobbies, or uncommon services. Before these offerings were available a customer may not have had any middleman to work with.

Alteration of an intermediation structure can be effective if the following occurs.

- One reduces transaction costs (e.g., improves convenience and availability)
- One understands the process well enough to know when IT use is inappropriate. For example, efforts to use the Web to enable a customer to perform all of the activities behind purchasing a house have had limited success since the customer *wants* a real person to help with the complexities of the legal work, and wants to hear from a *person* about the neighborhood schools.

Overall the most important class of processes is coordination (Malone and Rockart, 1991; Keen, 1997). Sociologists who have studied organizational form and its effect on performance note that, for the hospital, the coordination of tasks is the most critical organizational process. Coordination takes many forms.

- Communication between the referring and consulting physician
- Discussion among nurses at shift change
- Propagation of managed care rules to staff in ambulatory registration and accounts receivable
- Communication between pharmacy and nursing
- Management of the operating room's schedule
- Interchange among nursing, central transport, and the ancillary departments

Coordination involves ensuring that task performers receive the information they need in order to perform their jobs. This information describes the nature of the "input" (e.g., the patient's problems), the desired approach to "transforming the input" (e.g., the treatment plan), the desired output (e.g., a consult report), and, if the "input" has to be transferred to another task performer, the information garnered by the transferring task performer (e.g., the care provided).

Rapid Accurate Provision of Critical Data Organizations define critical elements of their plans, operations and environment. These elements must be monitored to ensure that the plan is working, service and care quality is high, and the environment is behaving as anticipated. Clearly data are required to perform such monitoring.

IT can improve a competitive position by providing such data. Examples include the following.

- Gathering data during registration about the patient's referring physician can help a hospital understand whether its outreach activities and market share growth strategies are working.
- Bar code scanners at supermarkets and department stores inform product suppliers regarding which products are being purchased. This knowledge can ensure that valuable shelf space is filled with the optimal mix of product. This knowledge can also improve inventory management and manufacturing capacity utilization. This data, when combined with data about the customer (which can be obtained when the customer presents a store card to obtain discounts) enable the store and the product manufacturer to understand the demographics of their customers, leading to more focused advertising.
- Provider order entry systems that request the reason or clinical indication for a procedure being ordered not only assist the receiving department in understanding what they are supposed to do, but also assist quality assurance and utilization review efforts in understanding the dynamics of procedure utilization.

These examples and several others have generated several lessons.

The terms *rapid* and *accurate* are relative. Data about product movement should be gathered and analyzed in as close to real time as possible because one can change shelf space composition almost instantly. Analysis of physician referral patterns need not be real time because the organization is unlikely to be able to effect a change in patterns instantly. Complete accuracy of the cost of performing laboratory tests may not be necessary because it can be clear from allocations whether a cost structure is too high or reasonable. Accuracy of the linkage between a provider and medications being ordered may be critical in order to get acceptance of any utilization analysis.

The rapid and accurate gathering of data may be the most significant and important source of a competitive advantage. Having good data about utilization may be more important than efficient ordering processes. Having good data about referring physicians may be more important than an error-free registration process. Knowing the demographics of the customer who consumes your snack food, what else they buy when they buy your product, and where and when they buy may be far more important than well-run inventory management. Knowing who your passengers are, their fare tolerance, what time of year they fly, and their destination may be more important than managing full utilization of the aircraft.

The role of data should not imply that well-run processes are irrelevant. People would prefer to obtain services from organizations with well-run processes than from organizations that appear to out do the Three Stooges. Often a well-run, efficient, and convenient process may be necessary to get high quality data. But in some cases the process is subordinate to the need for the data. We see in many examples of the competitive use of IT where the organization accepts that its rivals will mimic their process gains and focuses on the utilization of the data. For example, systems to support the making of an airline reservation evolved into the use of the reservation data to develop frequent flyer programs, establish mileage programs linked to credit cards, and engage in fare wars. Those organizations who developed the reservation systems "sold them" to their competitors recognizing that such a system did not provide a sustainable process advantage.

Product and Service Differentiation   IT can be used to differentiate and customize products and services. Following are some examples.

- Financial planners will offer prospective customers free software that helps the customer assess the savings needed to achieve financial goals such as funding college for children or having a certain income at retirement. Customers discover, after running the software, that they will be insolvent within a week after retirement. Fortunately, the financial planner is there to work with the customer to ensure that such a gloomy outcome does not occur.
- Providers will establish Web sites that include information about health news, classes to reduce health risk, information on new research, and basic triage algorithms. Such information is an effort to differentiate their care from that of others.
- Supermarkets will send information to customers about upcoming sales. This information is often based on knowledge of prior customer purchases. Hence, a family that has purchased

diapers and baby food will be seen as a household with young children. Information on sales on infant products and products directed to young parents will be sent to that household and not to households in which the purchase patterns (e.g., a steady pattern of purchasing hot dogs, snack food, and beer, indicate a single male). The supermarket is attempting to differentiate its service by helping the household plan its purchases around "specials."

Customization and differentiation often rely on data. Effective customization presumes that we know something about the customer. Differentiation assumes that we know something about the customer's criteria for evaluating our organization so that we can differentiate our processes, products, and services in a way that is deemed to have value.

Customization and differentiation often center on organizational processes. These processes can be made unique. New processes can be created as a means of differentiation. For example, financial services firms that enable one to move one's money among money market, stock, and bond accounts create new processes that enable asset movement across diverse financial instruments.

IT has enabled new products and services to be developed and new companies and industries to be formed. New Internet-based services and companies seem to be spawning daily. Companies that provide comparative analysis of claims and utilization data owe their existence to IT. Capitation as a scheme for financing and managing risk would be extraordinarily difficult without information technology. Several academic medical centers provide international Telemedicine consultations (although it's arguable whether that's an extension of existing service or a new business).

Change in Organizational Form or Characteristics IT can be utilized to improve or change certain organizational attributes or characteristics. Example characteristics might include service quality orientation, communication, decision making, or collaboration.

Several examples exist.

- Some business and medical schools require students to own a personal computer and perform their assignments using the PC and the school's network. This emphasis is intended to

accomplish several objectives, one of which is to enhance the student's comfort and skill with the technology.
- Organizations will implement groupware (e.g., IBM's Lotus Notes), in an effort to foster collaboration.
- Senior management may implement an Executive Information System in an effort to encourage organizational management to be more data driven and focused on key organizational parameters.

The value of these efforts or their impact is often unclear since the organization is often different in the end. Moreover, these characteristics tend to be quite difficult to measure at anything other than a very crude level.

Often the change in organizational characteristics is inadvertent or an unintended consequence of an IT implementation. Electronic mail can be implemented to improve communication. E-mail also has the affect of speeding up decision making and altering power structures: staff will seek information from other staff, using e-mail, whom they would feel uncomfortable approaching face to face (e.g., scheduling a meeting with the Chief of Medicine).

Sustainability of an Advantage

It is difficult to sustain an IT-enabled or IT-centric advantage. Competitors, noting the advantage, are quick to attempt to copy the application, lure away the original developers, or obtain a version of the application from a vendor who has seen a market opportunity as a result of the success of the original developers. And a sufficient number of them will be successful. Often their success may be less expensive and faster to achieve than the first organization to achieve the advantage because they learn from the mistakes of those who are first. A provider organization that offers computer-based access to patient results to its referring physicians finds that its competitors will also provide such capabilities. A managed care organization that provides consumer health information to its subscribers finds that its competitors are quite capable of doing the same.

The effect can be a form of an IT arms race. A race that provides no advantage for long. A race you often have to run since these systems become accepted by customers as an aspect of basic service. No one would bank at a bank that did not offer ATM service.

In the cases discussed above, the organization recognized, and perhaps knew up front, that an advantage attained at any point in time was not sustainable. Knowing that today's IT-advantage is tomorrow's core capability possessed by all industry participants, the organization has several strategies that it can adopt.

- *Attempt to out-hustle the competition* by aggressive and focused introduction of a series of enhancements to the then core system that enables that system to evolve faster than the competition can and "hold a lead."
- *Transform the nature of an advantage* (e.g., SABRE's transforming the SABRE system advantage into a SABRE business advantage of generating revenues from the selling of the system, and the expertise that created it), to others including competitors
- *"Freezing the system"* (i.e., ceasing major investments in its continued progress and relegating the system to the role of a core production system where efficiency and reliability of operation, rather than the possession of superior capabilities, become the objectives). In this case, the organization may turn its sights to new systems that attempt to create an advantage in other ways.

There are ways that an advantage can be sustained over a prolonged period of time. In no case does a single application, by itself, result in a prolonged sustained advantage. However, an advantage can be sustained for longer than a brief period of time by doing the following.

- Leveraging some other, significant organizational strength
- Leveraging a well developed, strong IT asset

Leveraging Other Strengths Organizations can have strengths that are quite difficult for their competitors to also garner (Cecil and Goldstein, 1990). Such strengths can include market share, access to capital, brand name recognition, and proprietary know-how. IT can be used to reinforce or extend the strengths. Some examples follow.

- A large integrated delivery system and a large retail pharmacy chain, both with significant market shares in a region, may decide to link the provider's medication ambulatory order entry system to the pharmacy's dispensing and medication management systems. The delivery system receives, from the pharmacy system, information as to whether the entered medication was filled, which improves its medical management programs. The delivery system is also able to provide a service to its patients since it can route the prescription to a pharmacy near to the patient's home. The pharmacy is able to channel customers to its stores where it believes that, as the patient picks up the medications, they will also make other purchases.

The delivery system and the retail pharmacy chain find each other attractive because of their respective shares of the market. The delivery system is able to ensure significant geographic coverage for its patients filling their prescriptions. The pharmacy chain is able to ensure a large volume of customers visiting its stores. Neither party might find another party, with less market share, as attractive of a partner. In both cases, the partnership was able to leverage an existing strength of market share.

- An academic medical center having developed, over the years, significant applied Medical Informatics expertise may find that such knowledge and experience enable it to develop and implement clinical information systems more efficiently and effectively than its competitors. These systems would enable the medical center to effect IT-based improvements in the care process more rapidly than its competitors. The medical center is leveraging proprietary or scarce know-how.

- A well-known academic medical center may be able to leverage its brand name and base of foreign-born physicians, who trained at the medical center, to establish a Telemedicine-based international consultation service. It may also be able to leverage its brand name to improve the attractiveness of its consumer-oriented health information Web site. Consumers, confused and worried about the quality of information on the World Wide Web, may take comfort in knowing that information is being generated by a respected source.

These advantages do not result purely from an application system nor inherently from process improvement, data gathering, or service differentiation or customization. The advantages result from utilizing some core, difficult to replicate, strength of the organization through IT.

Leveraging the IT Asset For most of the healthcare industry, the technology and applications being implemented are available to all industry participants including competitors. Any provider organization can acquire and implement systems from Eclipsys, Cerner, HBOC, or SMS. If this is true, why would a provider organization believe that it will garner an advantage from the implementation of a clinical data repository from one of these vendors if their competitor can implement the same (or similar) repository? Particularly if the organization has no other advantage (e.g., market share), that it is able to leverage with the system.

An advantage can be obtained if one or both of two things happen. First, one organization does a more thoughtful and effective job at understanding and then effecting the changes in processes or data gathering, associated with the system to be implemented, than its competitors. The application does not provide the advantage but the way that it is implemented does. We see the difference that execution makes every day in all facets of our lives. It is the difference between a great restaurant and a mediocre one. Or a terrific movie and a terrible one. In neither case is the idea (e.g., let's make meals and sell them), nor the fact that one executes on the idea (e.g., we've hired a cook and purchased silverware), the "advantage." It is the manner of execution that distinguishes.

Second, if one organization is consistently able to out run the other, it may be able to sustain an advantage. If an organization is able to develop means to implement faster or cheaper, it may be able to out run its competition even if its implementations, one for one, are of no higher quality than its competitor's. In a period of time, one organization implements four applications while the other implements three. For the same amount of capital, one organization implements five applications while the other implements three.

Such speed and efficiency can be garnered through a variety of mechanisms, none of them sufficient in and of themselves. For example, both efficiency and speed gains can be obtained by doing the following.

- Adopting and enforcing standards for technology and applications that, for example, can reduce the cost and speed up the process of developing interfaces
- Hiring and training excellent IT implementation staff
- Avoiding the use of expensive consultants and concentrating on staff retention

- Avoiding reflexive replacement of systems because they are "old," since system replacement diverts energy and resources
- Minimizing implementation overhead that can result from excessive dependence on committees and consensus

In general, organizations may be able to sustain an IT-based or IT-supported competitive advantage because they have an established and exceptionally strong IT asset (e.g., talented IT staff, strong relationships between that staff and the organization, and an agile technical platform) (Ross, Beath, and Goodhue, 1996). This asset is able to consistently and efficiently deliver high quality applications that enable the organization to improve its competitive position. This asset and the ways that it can provide an advantage are discussed in the next chapter.

The Technology Is a Tool

IT can provide a competitive advantage. However, IT has no magic properties. In particular the technology cannot overcome poor strategies, inadequate management, inept execution, or major organizational limitations (e.g., a system that reduces the number of nurse staff may not make the salary savings gains desired if the average nurse salary is very high or the staff is unionized). Information systems are tools. If the objectives of the building are not well understood, its design flawed, the carpenter unskilled, and/or other tools are missing, the quality of the hammer and saw are irrelevant. In the three cases described earlier, superior strategy, deep understanding of the business, the ability to execute complex transformations of the business, and its core processes and organizational ability to capitalize on their IT prowess, led to the gains discussed. IT was necessary but not sufficient.

In a large number of the cases of IT use as a competitive weapon, the system leverages an existing capability of the organization (Freeman, 1991). If that capability is weak, IT may not be able to overcome the weakness. Organizations won't use, for example, a supply ordering system if the supplies are inferior in quality, too expensive, and the inventory has limited scope. Recent data from the use of the Internet (*Business Week,* 1998) to order books and music CDs suggest that people will not use these systems if the prices are too high or the convenience gains are marginal.

The referring physician won't use, or find valuable, a system that provides them access to hospital data if the consulting physicians at the hospital are remiss in getting their consult notes completed on time or at all. High quality, comprehensive data on care quality are diminished if the organization has limited ability or skill in improving the practice of care.

The pace of technology evolution is rapid, and new technologies arrive that enable new ways of supporting processes, gathering data, and differentiating and customizing products and services. In the cases reviewed earlier in this chapter, the organizations were quick to assess new technologies and thoughtful in their application. Incorporation of timesharing and the Web are examples of new, at the time, technologies that were effectively leveraged. This behavior suggests the following.

- Organizations should have a function that scans the industry for new technologies and engages in their evaluation and experimentation.
- Critical to the assessment of new technology is the development of an understanding of the key characteristics of the technology that provide value (e.g., what is it about the Web that might provide a significant improvement in organizational care delivery capabilities?). This assessment will be discussed further in Chapters 3 and 4.
- Organizations should be careful not to "fall in love" with today's technology but be able to ruthlessly jettison technology as its ability to provide a competitive distinction wanes.

Other risks which can limit the utility of the tool, that is IT, have been seen (Cash et al., 1992).

- Applications have been introduced too early and been unable to overcome "not ready for prime time" technology and an unreceptive customer environment. Some early computerized record implementations have suffered this fate.
- Inadequate understanding of buying dynamics across market segments. An academic medical center that hopes its consumer-oriented Web page will lead to increased admissions may not fully comprehend the referral process since, for that organization, 80% of the referrals are made by the patient's physician.
- Being too far ahead of the customers comfort level. For example, a very large percentage of the public today is uncomfortable with the idea of individually identifiable health data being transmitted

over the Internet. This discomfort has not been assuaged by the incorporation of advanced security and encryption technologies.

Singles and Grand Slams

When one looks back at organizations that have been effective at the strategic application of IT, over a reasonably long time frame, one sees what looks like a series of "singles" punctuated by an occasional leap (McKenney, Copeland, and Mason, 1995). One doesn't see a progression of grand slams or, in the parlance of the industry, "giant killer" applications.

Organizations, in the course of improving processes, differentiating services and gathering data, carry out a series of initiatives that improve their performance. The vast majority of these initiatives don't fundamentally alter the competitive position of the organization, but in aggregating these initiatives make a significant contribution. The difference between a great hotel and a mediocre hotel is not the presence of clean sheets or hot water. Rather it is one thousand "little things."

At various points in time, the organization has an insight that leads to a major leap in its application of IT to its performance. For example, airlines having developed their initial travel reservation systems continued to improve them. At some point, there was the organizational realization that the data, gathered by the reservation system, had enormous potency and frequent flyer programs resulted. American Hospital Supply having developed its supply ordering system continued to improve it. At some point it realized that it was in a materials management partnership with its hospital customers and not just in the supply ordering business.

No organization has ever delivered a series of giant killer or grand slam applications in rapid succession.

Organizations must develop the IT asset (discussed in the next chapter) in such a way that they can effect the types of continuous improvements that its managers and medical staff will see possible, day in and day out. For example, in an idealized world, the organization should be able to efficiently and effectively capitalize on the improvements in ambulatory scheduling that a middle manager may see. And be able to capitalize on one thousand such ideas and opportunities. The organization must also develop the "antenna" that senses leaps and the vision and focus that enable them to effect the systems needed to make the leap. This antenna is one of the key functions of the Chief Information Officer.

The resulting pattern may look like Figure 2–7, continuous improvement in organizational performance using IT (singles), punctuated by periodic leaps or grand slams.

It is also clear that organizations have limited ability to see more than one leap at a time. Hence, visions should be careful about being too visionary or having too long of a time horizon. Organizations have great difficulty understanding a world that is significantly different than the one they inhabit now or that can be only vaguely understood in the context of the next leap, let alone the leap after that. We might understand frequent flyer programs now. But they were not well understood, nor was their competitive value understood well, at the time they were conceived. Moreover, the organizational changes required to support and capitalize on a leap can take years, at times five to seven years (McKenney, Copeland, and Mason, 1995).

Competitive Baggage

The pursuit of IT as a source of competitive advantage can create baggage or a hangover. This baggage can occur in several forms.

FIGURE 2–7

Singles and Grand Slams

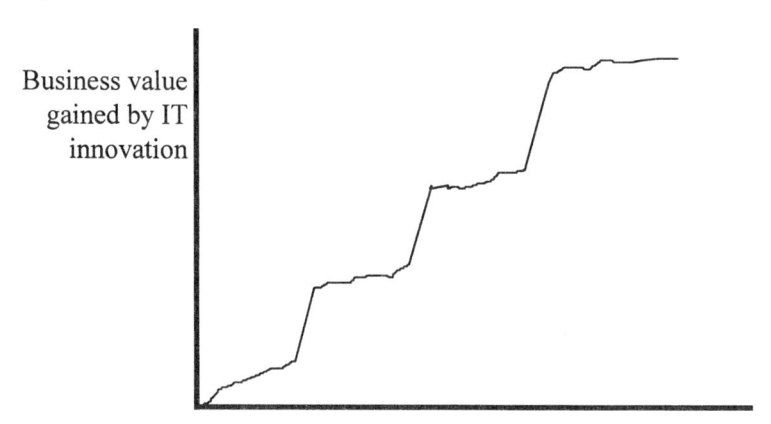

Significant investment in capital, creating an increase in capital costs and an increase in IS operating budgets (depreciation and interest), can erode margins. If several competitors are making similar investments, they may all arrive at a position where the customer sees better service or lower prices but none of the competitors have developed systems that truly differentiate themselves and enable them to reduce their margins in the process. ATMs are an example (Lake, 1998). No bank distinguishes themselves because of having ATM capabilities. Customers, however, are better off. The banks must now carry the cost of operating the ATM and funding periodic upgrades in ATM technology. The average ATM machine each has a net cost of $20,000 to $25,000 after subtracting fees charged to banks and customers for its use. For the healthcare provider, investment in an organizational home page for the Web may have a similar outcome.

Organizations can find themselves in an IT arms race in which prudence has fled, the conversation being replaced by the innate desire to "out feature" the competitor. The original thoughtfulness surrounding the use of IT to improve processes of care, expand market share, or reduce costs has been replaced by ego.

Governing concepts that were poorly constructed or which fail to evolve can blind organizations to new opportunities. (Governing concepts are discussed in more detail in Chapters 3 and 4.) For example, a concept or belief that personal computers were only for hobbyists and had no major role in a large organization, which was true in 1978, had become dead wrong by 1984. A belief that the Internet was a realm meant solely for hackers, voyeurs, and academics became wrong very quickly. Organizations often hold to beliefs and concepts long after they should be buried. This is particularly problematic when the initial belief led to an IT innovation that was very successful. People and organizations are loath to jettison beliefs that "got them here."

Rigidity of IT can be created by poor architecture design or poor partnership selection. Many hospitals have seen, belatedly, the consequences of failure to design for application integration as they attempt to implement the integration of years of a best-of-breed strategy. The pursuit of the advantage of each department implementing the best product on the market failed to consider properties of the infrastructure (the ability to integrate applications efficiently) that would be needed to enable the organization to continue to innovate efficiently.

Organizations, overly sensitive to the IT market and grasping for an advantage, can pursue new technologies and ideas well before the utility of the idea, if any, is known. These organizations do not want to be left behind as the only organization not pursuing, and as a result of this nonpursuit destined for the dust bin of also-rans, the latest technology or idea. A very large number of ideas, technologies, and management techniques fail to live up to their initial hype. Examples include patient focused care, total quality management, bed-side terminals, executive information systems, network computers, CASE tools, and client server technology. This should not imply that these techniques and technologies have no utility. Rather their utility has not lived up to their press releases. (This is discussed further in the next chapter.)The desire to achieve a competitive advantage can cause organizations to lose their senses, perspective, and, at times, appropriate caution.

Extensive use of IT results in organizations becoming quite dependent on IT. This dependence can range from staff to infrastructure performance. In several areas, e.g., Peoplesoft implementers and network engineers, IT talent is scarce and expensive. Organizational investment in these technologies leaves them dependent on their ability to continue to attract and retain this talent. Failure to plan for this dependency can leave the organization exposed if (or perhaps when) staff turnover occurs. Similarly, organizations that have become very reliant on a computerized medical record are now very dependent on having a high reliability and high performance technical infrastructure. Tolerance of downtime evaporates. Pursuit of a competitive advantage needs to plan for the dependence that will be incurred.

SUMMARY

IT planning has several objectives: the alignment of IT with the strategies, plans, and initiatives of the organization, the development of support for the plan, and the preparation of tactical plans. Several methodologies have been developed that improve the organization's ability to develop a comprehensive, accurate, and supportable plan. There are two forms of these methodologies: those that are derived directly from the organization's plans and strategies and those that originate from more fundamental views of organizations and competition.

IT planning is a very important organizational process. However, alignment of IT with the organization has been and remains a major organizational IT concern. This process is quite difficult. IT planning prowess cannot guarantee organizational excellence in applying IT. That excellence is significantly influenced by other factors to be discussed in the next chapter.

IT can be very effective in supporting an organization's effort to improve its competitive position. This support generally occurs when IT is utilized to leverage core organizational processes, support the collection of critical data, customize or differentiate organizational products and services, and transform core organizational characteristics and capabilities.

IT is incapable of providing these advantages by itself. Its utility occurs when it is applied by intelligent and experienced managers and medical staff in the pursuit of well-conceived strategies and plans. IT cannot overcome weak leadership, inadequate strategies and plans, or inferior products and services.

The pursuit of an IT supported advantage should be careful of incurring some of the baggage that can result: reduced margins with no improvement in position, process ossification, and nonrational pursuit of mirage technologies.

REFERENCES

Bensaou, M., Earl, M. (1998). The Right Mind-set for Managing Information Technology. *Harvard Business Review* 76(5):119–128, September–October.

(1998). Doing Business in the Internet Age: Information Technology Annual Report. *Business Week,* June 22.

Cash, J., Konsynski, B. (1985). IS Redraws Competitive Boundaries. *Harvard Business Review* 63(2):134–142, March–April.

Cash, J., McFarlan, W., McKenney, J. (1992).*Corporate Information Systems Management: the Issues Facing Senior Executives.* Chicago: Irwin.

Cecil, J., Goldstein, M. (1990). Sustaining Competitive Advantage from IT. *The McKinsey Quarterly* 4:74–89.

Clemons, E., Row, M. (1991). Sustaining IT Advantage: The Role of Structural Differences. *MIS Quarterly* 15(3):275–292, September.

Earl, M. (1993). Experiences in Strategic Information Systems Planning. *MIS Quarterly* 17(1):1–24, March.

Freeman, D. (1991). The Myth of Strategic I.S. *CIO Magazine,* July.

Harris, C. (1985). Information Power. *Business Week,* October 14.

Henderson, J., Venkratraman. (1993). Strategic Alignment: Information technology for Transforming Organizations. *IBM Systems Journal* 32(1):4–16.

Hopper, M. (1990). Rattling Sabre—New Ways to Compete on Information. *Harvard Business Review* 68(3):118–125, May–June.

Ives, B., Learmonth, G. (1984). The Information System as a Competitive Weapon. *Communications of the ACM* 27(12):1193–1201, December.

Keen, P. (1997). *The Process Edge.* Boston: Harvard Business School Press.

Kissinger, K., Borchardt, S. (1996). *Information Technology for Integrated Delivery Systems.* New York: John Wiley and Sons.

Konsynski, B. Vitale, M. (1991). *Baxter Healthcare Corporation: ASAP Express.* Harvard Business School.

Lake, K. (1998). Cashing in on your ATM Network. *McKinsey Quarterly* 1:173–178.

Malone, T., Rockart, J. (1991). Computers, Networks and the Corporation. *Scientific American* 265(3):128–136, September.

Martin, J., Wilkins, A., Stawski, S. (1998). The Component Alignment Model: A New Approach to Health Care Information Technology Strategic Planning. *Topics in Health Information Management* 19(1):1–10.

McFarlan, F.W. (1984). Information Technology Changes the Way You Compete. *Harvard Business Review* 62(3):98–103, May–June.

McKenney, J., Copeland, D., Mason, R. (1995).*Waves of Change: Business Evolution Through Information Technology.* Boston: Harvard Business School Press.

Minard, B. (1991). *Health Care Computer Systems for the 1990s.* Ann Arbor: Health Administration Press.

Porter, M. (1980). *Competitive Strategy.* New York: The Free Press.

Porter, M., Millar, V. (1985). How Information Gives You a Competitive Advantage. *Harvard Business Review* 63(4):149–160, July–August.

Ross, J., Beath, C., Goodhue, D. (1996). Develop Long–Term Competitiveness through IT Assets. *Sloan Management Review* 38(1):31–42, Fall.

Short, J.E., Venkatraman, N. (1992). Beyond Business Process Redesign: Redefining Baxter's Business Network. *Sloan Management Review* 34(1): 7–21.

Weill, P., Broadbent, M. (1998). *Leveraging the New Infrastructure.* Boston: Harvard Business School Press.

CHAPTER 3

Internal Capabilities and Characteristics

In the previous chapter we discussed issues, observations, and techniques associated with aligning healthcare organization strategies with IT initiatives and applying IT to improving an organization's competitive position. Chapter 2 was largely externally focused (i.e., defining the IT initiatives necessary to respond well to strategies and plans directed toward markets, patients, and competitors).

In Chapter 3 the focus is internal to the organization. Specifically Chapter 3 discusses the IT asset that includes technology, IS staff, data, IT governance, and applications. The chapter also reviews several studies that have examined factors associated with organizational excellence in the application of IT. Such factors include the relationship between the CEO, CIO, and the technical team and organizational politics.

This focus and these topics are critical for several reasons.

- IT strategic plans often call for changes in the asset in order to achieve organizational objectives. An objective to improve care may call for changes in applications, infrastructure, data, and IT staff. One needs asset strategies to ensure that the execution of those changes is guided by well-crafted thought and concepts. For example, what strategies will guide our efforts to integrate the IDS? What organizational group(s) will be responsible for

identifying those care processes that could be most improved by IT?
- Strategies for improving the IT asset and the factors that have been shown to improve IT effectiveness may be desirable in order to leverage a wide range of current and future IT plans. For example, improving infrastructure reliability may enhance the effectiveness of a series of IT initiatives. Improving the ability of the organization to prioritize IT initiatives or to evaluate the initiatives may similarly enhance a range of initiatives. Enhancing the relationships between IS and the rest of the organization should advance the organization's ability to effect IT alignment and improve project execution.

While strategic IT plans frame the initiatives necessary to improve organizational competitive performance, the strategies discussed in this chapter improve the ability of the IT function and the organization to execute those plans. Chapter 2 was, in effect, a discussion of formulation: what IT initiatives should we undertake. Chapter 3 will be a discussion of implementation: what IT capabilities and factors need to be in place to carry out these initiatives.

The following areas will be discussed in this chapter.

- The composition and characteristics of the IT asset, including a brief discussion on the role of the CIO
- Lessons learned and observations of the asset
- Strengths and limitations of factors that often influence organization choices regarding their assets, specifically
- The approach to the evaluation of IT investments
- The problem of "fads"
- The utility of surveys
- The results of studies that have examined organizational factors, including the IT asset, which contribute to highly effective use of IT (These factors will be referred to as IT-centric organizational attributes.)

ASSET COMPOSITION AND OVERVIEW

The information technology asset is composed of the following.

- *Application systems* are composed of the software that is used to support the work performed by organizational staff and,

potentially, organizational affiliates, and business partners. Examples include provider order entry, outpatient scheduling, managed care applications, and office automation.
- *Technical architecture* which is comprised of the base technologies (e.g., networks, programming languages, operating systems, and workstations), which form the foundation for applications and the manner in which these base technologies are "put together."
- *Data* are composed of the organization's data and analyses and access technologies.
- *IS staff* are the analysts, programmers, computer operators, and so on, who manage and advance information systems in an organization, the way in which the staff are organized, and the attributes of the organized staff (e.g., is the IS function agile or responsive?).
- *IT governance* is the organizational mechanism (committees, policies, procedures, and work methodologies) by which IS strategies are formed, priorities are set, standards developed, and projects managed.

These assets, designed, developed, and managed under the leadership of the CIO, are the organizational IT resources that can be (should be) directed to furthering organizational strategies and advancing the organization's abilities to achieve its goals. The differences between a strong asset and a weak asset can be significant. Applications that provide superior support of organizational processes are more of an asset than those that do not. IS staff who are skilled, motivated, and well organized are more of an organizational asset than staff who are not. Efficient and thoughtful procedures for prioritizing IS activities are more of an organizational asset than procedures that resemble armed conflict.

Each asset contributes to the overall effectiveness of IT in different ways. Strategies and plans are required to ensure that the asset is thoughtfully conceived, well developed, robust, sustained, and making significant contributions. For example, consider the following.

- Due to significant environmental uncertainty, we may need to have more agile applications and infrastructure. Hence our agility strategy will involve creating a loosely coupled technical architecture with well-defined interfaces between layers and components.
- We need to create a more responsive and service-oriented IS organization. Hence our strategy will be to decentralize our

development and implementation teams and locate them at our affiliated hospitals.
- We need to measure the quality and cost of our care across our delivery system. Hence we will develop standard definitions of a small set of quality measures and create an IS department to provide analysis support of that data.

ASSET DISCUSSION

In the following sections, each asset will be defined, asset characteristics will be described that can serve as a measure of asset strength, and a series of considerations will be presented that can be used to guide organizational definition of asset strategies.

Application Systems

Application systems are the software used by the organization in the course of performing organizational activities. There are two major types of application software. Specialized application software is intended for use by a reasonably narrow set of workers performing a reasonably narrow set of tasks. Examples of specialized application software include scheduling, clinical laboratory, managed care contract analysis, and computerized medical record systems. General purpose application software is intended for use by a broad set of workers or users, although the intended use can be narrow. Examples of general purpose application software include word processing, spreadsheets, and electronic mail.

Application Asset Characteristics

Application systems should exhibit several characteristics.

- *They should improve existing operations and activities.* Processes and activities should be more efficient and effective as a result of the implementation of application systems. Accounts receivable days should be lower. Medication errors should be fewer. Laboratory test turnaround should be faster.
- *They should provide superior support to critical processes and activities.* Not all processes are created equal, nor are they as important strategically. For those processes and activities that contribute more to organizational prowess than others, the

application systems support should be more than good, it should be superior.
- *These systems should behave with integrity.* The systems should perform as expected, consistently, and quickly. Errors in the application software should be few, if any. System performance (e.g., response time), should enhance and not interfere with work.
- *The application systems should have some agility.* In other words, it should be reasonably efficient, effective, and timely to alter the application to respond to the needs for evolution. This response can be in the form of frequent vendor upgrades or tools that enable the organization to safely change the application.

Assessing the Value of the Application Asset

Organizations will ask themselves "Do we have a good pharmacy system? Or scheduling system? Or patient care system?" To a large degree, the answer depends on how well the system fares when measured against the characteristics outlined above.

The characteristics of most importance are the degree to which the application enables and supports the improvement of organizational processes. In most cases we should be able to measure the impact of the application on the organization, and that impact should serve as a rough assessment of how well this asset is performing. At times this measurement is difficult or misleading (e.g., "What is the measurable value of electronic mail?"). We also recognize that the system by itself does not cause improvement. The system must be implemented well and related organizational changes may need to occur (e.g., reengineering the processes to be supported by the system). Nonetheless, it is the impact on the organization that serves as the best measure of this asset. A comparison of an application's features with those of another application or an idealized application is not an appropriate measure of application's worth, unless that comparison is clearly linked to value to the organization. The evaluation of IT investments, including applications, is discussed in more detail later in this chapter.

Organizations should exercise appropriate skepticism when confronted with the hyperventilation that is often associated with the introduction of new applications, or applications for which there is little experience with their implementation, operation or demonstrated value. The landscape is littered with examples (e.g., bedside terminals and enterprise-wide scheduling), of the hype to value ratio being a very large number. That is not to say that these applications have no value or that one cannot find settings that have happy users. However, some of these applications do not leverage critical processes. Moreover, organizations should look carefully, thoughtfully, and with some wariness at the precursors or assumptions that will determine the value of major applications. Some reasons follow.

- The value of executive information systems is directly related to having clear information needs on the part of senior management, senior management interest in conducting ad-hoc analyses, and queries with reasonable frequency and a base of high quality, well integrated data. None of these precursors are inherently present in a large number of organizations.
- Enterprise-wide scheduling presumes that a patient (or a provider's staff) in one locality is as likely to schedule an appointment with a local specialist as they are to schedule an appointment with a specialist in a locality 20 miles away. This presumes a series of factors are present: some degrees of freedom of patient movement, some knowledge on the part of the referring provider of the skills and existence of a wide range of specialists (and assessment that all of these specialists are of equivalent skill and deliver equivalent levels of care and service), and/or some exceptional rationalization of care by the IDS.

The replacement of an existing, working application should occur as a "last resort." The industry appears to replace applications too frequently, often citing new technologies and application features. Clearly technologies advance, as do applications, and become better over time. However, application replacement is expensive, time-consuming, and has opportunity costs that are not well assessed or value gains that are insufficient. Replacement will occur but the rationale for replacement must be very compelling. A replacement cycle that is too frequent actually retards organizational advancement because it diverts resources to areas where the gain is marginal.

The application asset can be evaluated as a portfolio of applications (Weill and Broadbent, 1998). An organization can array its applications across a matrix with the Y-axis being a measure of "current business value," and the X-axis being an assessment of "technical quality." Each application can be plotted and given a circle that represents the size of the investment being made in the application and the color of the circle representing strategic importance (See Figure 3–1).

If the resulting patterns show strategically critical applications being underfunded and of poor technical quality, the organization has a problem. If the resulting pattern shows too many applications being well funded and of high technical quality, but having little business value and little strategic importance, the organization has a problem.

Each application can be valued and the set of applications can be valued.

Application Acquisition

The world is full of companies that develop applications, and a large number of them do a very good job. So, how do you decide whether to buy software from them or build it yourself? The decision is subjective at times. However, several criteria guide a decision to build.

- *The software one can buy isn't very good.* This is more common with niche application software, for which there are few or weak competitors, than it is for software that has a large market.

FIGURE 3–1

Application Portfolio Assessment

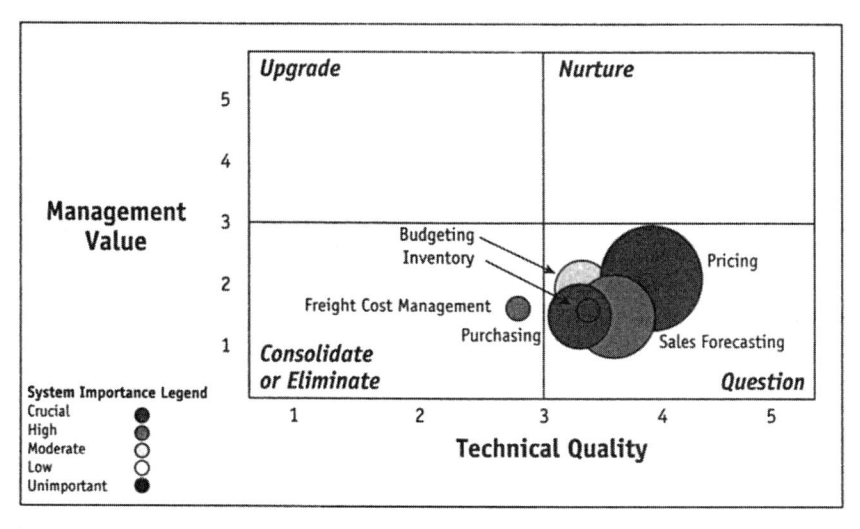

Source: Weill, P., Broadbent, M. (1998). *Leveraging the New Infrastructure.* Harvard Business School Press.

- *The organization's needs are unique.* There are times when needs are so unique that the existing market offerings don't adequately support the work that the organization needs to perform. One has to be careful about claiming to be more unique than one really is.
- *Needs are volatile or uncertain.* At times an organization can be quite certain about the features that the application must possess. At times the organization is uncertain since it needs to garner experience with the use of the application before it can fully understand the complete set of capabilities it will need. As this learning occurs the organization would like to alter the application. Or the environment in which use is occurring is very volatile and, hence, needs will change constantly and significantly.
- *It is important to the organization that it deliver better applications than its competitors can buy.* There are times when an organization's competitive performance will rest to a large degree on it having implemented an application system that is materially better than its competitors are able to implement.
- *The organization needs it now.* The development of an application can be (not always) faster to effect than the purchase of an application. Development can enable the delivery of the "crucial 30%" faster than the implementation of the "full 100%."

Few delivery systems engage in significant internal development of application systems. However, improved vendor-supplied tools and advances in programming languages and techniques are enabling organizations to use internal resources to supplement or extend an application's capabilities.

Healthcare organizations have several general strategies for acquisition.

- *The organization may commit itself to the product line of a vendor or engage in a "best of breed" strategy, or some mixture of the two* (e.g., all financial systems from Peoplesoft with ancillary systems being purchased from niche vendors). A single vendor commitment enhances the likelihood of integration of systems and reduces the complexity of vendor management. However, the vendors offerings may be uneven across

applications and, once the commitment has been made to the vendor, organizational leverage over the vendor may decline.
- *Some organizations and vendors have entered into agreements in which they share business risk and reward.* If the system is intended to reduce costs in the outpatient clinic, both the organization and the vendor can share in the savings. While such an arrangement may enhance vendor commitment to a successful implementation (with a broad definition of implementation) and assist in ensuring that critical system capabilities are present, such arrangements can be complex and require that the organization give the vendor some of the management responsibility formerly possessed exclusively by the organization.

Common Systems Across the Enterprise

Having the same application system across the enterprise has the same inherent value as having one's children dress identically. Sameness has no per se value. However, there can be compelling reasons for having common systems.

- One might be able to reduce the unit cost of each system by amortizing resources (e.g., support staff and hardware), across multiple systems.
- A common system can be a catalyst for developing common organizational processes and common data across the enterprise, and may be necessary to consolidate a function across multiple organizations. It should be clear, however, before one pursues commonness, that the value of commonness is compelling. Developing common processes and data across several organizations is very hard work. Several IDS have also found that the organization-wide consolidation of functions has resulted in fewer cost savings than planned, a degradation in function service performance, and a reduction in function responsiveness. This should not mean that consolidation or common processes is bad. Rather it means that the rationale should be quite compelling, stripped of naivete.

Finally, we should remember that a common application does not actually lead to common processes and data.

Technical Architecture

Technical architecture is often discussed by IT vendors and their customers. One hears statements such as the following.

- We utilize a three-tiered architecture.
- Our products are based on a client–server architecture.
- Our organization uses a best-of-breed architectural strategy.

These statements, and others like them, confuse architecture with architecture. All information systems have been designed and their design can be presented, discussed, and classified. One can talk about the location of the database in the system or the distribution of the application processing across computers. One can label different classes of designs with the term "architecture." For example, applications that separate processing power between a "master" and a "slave" processor can be called a client server architecture.

While these classes of designs can be very important, and at times demonstrate insight and progress, they have no context. An organization doesn't know if client–server or object-based architectures, for example, are good or bad or indifferent. IS professionals at times equate the column inch in the trade press, trade show decibel levels, or quality of vendor booth trinkets devoted to a class of designs with "goodness."

A more helpful definition of architecture is as follows: technical architecture is the set of organizational, management, and technical strategies and tactics utilized to ensure that platforms have critical, organizationally defined characteristics and capabilities.[1]

There are two major types of platforms: infrastructure and clusters of applications.

Infrastructure is composed of the base technologies used by an organization (e.g., servers and networks, and the manner in which they are "put together"). Clusters of applications are suites of applications that are generally viewed as being part of an integrated package (e.g., Microsoft Office, Peoplesoft financial applications, or Eclipsys clinical information

---

[1] Weill and Broadbent (1998) note that the goals of an architecture are to enable an enterprise-wide infrastructure to achieve compatibility between various systems, specify the policies and mechanics for delivering the information technology strategy, describe the technological model of the organization, and cut through the multi-vendor chaos and move toward vendor independence.

systems). The suites have components and are put together in specific ways.

Architecture Characteristics and Capabilities
For both types of platforms (although the remainder of this section focuses on infrastructure), an organization may decide that the critical characteristics are the following.
- *Supportability.* The organization can efficiently and effectively provide day to day support of the platform (e.g., answer user questions, troubleshoot problems, perform backups, make minor enhancements, and run batch jobs).
- *Reliability.* The platform has excellent up-time, is fast, and behaves predictably.
- *Potency.* The platform utilizes technologies that allow the organization to buy lots of bandwidth, storage, and processor power for as little capital per unit of MIP, Mbs, or GB as possible. Potency also means that the tools the organization has to develop applications and manage the infrastructure are powerful.
- *Agility.* The organization can replace major components of the platform easily and with minimal disruption to other components. For example, the organization could change its server vendor and not have to change its server operating system or applications. At its extreme, agility would mean that the organization that wants to replace one component can ignore or need not be aware of other components. For example, an application that runs in Windows Internet Explorer may be able to ignore the workstation, or a standardized transaction interface can ignore the specific technology of the receiving application. For some organizations this may be the definition of "open systems." Agility also means that we can respond to the needs of organization relatively rapidly and efficiently (e.g., add a new remote site, change application functionality, or add new fields to the database).
- *Integratibility.* The infrastructure and application eases, as much as possible, the integration of other applications, data, and components of the infrastructure. Techniques such as having a common organization-wide workstation, the utilization of

object-oriented concepts in the development of applications, the incorporation of industry messaging standards, and the implementation of a common network protocol support integratibility.

Capabilities are attributes of the architecture that can be utilized by a wide range of applications or represent a narrow, but significant, addition to "what one can do." Capabilities can generally be stated with sentences that begin with "we can" or "we will be able to." Example sentences include the following.

- We will be able to provide access to radiology and pathology images from any workstation in the organization.
- We can offer access to our clinical information systems using mobile, small-form factor devices.
- We will be able to extend access to our systems to any part of the globe.
- We can provide context-sensitive access to knowledge resources.

In the context of the above discussions of characteristics and capabilities, is the fact that an application is "client server" good or bad? It depends whether that design in general, and the application's specific implementation of it, enhances or detracts from the organization's ability to achieve the goals cited above. If the application uses a database management system that is different from the organizational standard and, hence, reduces the ability to integrate the application with other applications or to support the application, then client server can be bad. If the application, despite being client server, is unstable, then it is bad. If the application requires that most of the program code run on the client then extending access to our systems to anywhere in the globe may be a problem. If the application conforms to the standards, is highly reliable, and utilizes commodity technology (e.g., Intel-class machines, which enhance its potency), then it may be good.

Technical Architecture Strategies

Architectural strategies are composed of four major elements.

The first element is *statements of desired characteristics* that are clear and, where possible, measurable. How do we define reliability or agility? How would we know if reliability or supportability has been improved? The statements should be robust. In other words the statement will endure as the specific products change and evolve (e.g., an organization's definition of supportability should survive the industry's movement from Windows 95 to NT). The changes in products hopefully enhance the ability of the organization to realize the desired characteristic but the definition of the characteristic doesn't change.

The second element is statements of *desired capabilities* that are clear. To how much of the globe do we want to provide access and is this access to all of our applications or some of them? Does image access need to ensure diagnostic quality images or not? Capability statement should also have an associated statement of value. Why would one want to invest the time and energy to provide these capabilities? How will care or administrative effectiveness be improved?

The third element is the *statement of specific components* (e.g., Cisco routers), or classes of components (e.g., source routing), that will form the building blocks of the architecture. These components have features that enable them, by themselves to provide the capabilities or be more reliable, supportable, and so forth. These components are "put together" or engineered so that the whole achieves the characteristics and capabilities. One can engineer a very unreliable source routing network or a very reliable one. One can engineer a network such that the movement of images cripples the performance of other applications or is not noticeable by the users of the other applications. The same components may also be engineered to arrive at different designs such that the resulting system is client server or not.

The fourth element is the *approaches to "putting together" or "fitting" such that the whole achieves the desired characteristics and delivers the desired capabilities.* These approaches can be very diverse. Some examples follow.

- The organization can standardize upon a workstation (or database or development language) to enhance supportability.
- Fault tolerance, disk mirroring, and rigorous application testing methodologies all can improve reliability.
- Internal development of applications, standardized interfaces, and the selection of market standard operating systems can all enhance agility.
- The choice of commodity technologies (e.g., the processors based on the Intel chip set) or an aggressive technology replacement cycle (e.g., 40% of the workstations are replaced every year) can improve potency.
- Network segmentation can enable image movement.

- A virtual private network service or the Internet can provide some forms of global access.

The approaches for "fitting" run the gamut from choices of technology to adoption of standards to engineering of component relationships to staff support mechanisms to technology obsolescence tactics to organizational policies.

Changes in Characteristic Importance

The importance of architectural characteristics can change or vary. If an organization has significant reliability problems, that attribute will be viewed, appropriately, as deserving the full attention of IS management even if that attention detracts from efforts to improve agility.

The rate of business change and technology change will also influence the importance of these attributes (GartnerGroup, April, 1998). If the technology is to support volatile and critical business activities then agility is paramount. If the technology is to support core transaction activities that are used directly by customers (e.g., airline reservations), then reliability and supportability become paramount.

Technology change is, in general, continuous and accelerating. However, the technology change that matters to an organization is the change that surrounds the technologies it is using or intends to use. An organization may see little relevant technology change in some segments despite a changing technology industry.

Component choices and "fit" approaches will also change as new technologies and techniques enable the organization to consider new architectural strategies. The World Wide Web, component-based architectures, and high performance, high availability servers are examples of such technologies. New technologies often present characteristic tradeoffs (e.g., agility may be improved but reliability is a problem), and capability tradeoffs (e.g., providing global access may hinder the development of a highly secure environment).

While the choices will change, the definitions of technology architecture characteristics and capabilities, adopted by an organization, tend to be static for long periods of time.

Architecture Representation

There is utility to expressing architecture in terms that a non-technical audience can understand (e.g., during the budget development process). This expression is generally easier for application architectures than for technical architectures.

Internal Capabilities and Characteristics

Applications architectures can be well presented by diagrams of components and their interrelationships and by narrative descriptions of work flow. Figure 3–2, for example, depicts the components and fit for Partners clinical information systems.

Figure 3–3 presents a paragraph from a narrative description of clinical information systems workflow.

Drazen and Metzger (1998) present very well-developed and thoughtful descriptions of the application architecture to support enterprise-wide processes for an IDS.

Representing technical architecture is more difficult. At times, organizational leadership will be presented with a diagram that shows multiple boxes, some squiggly lines and an oval or two. The diagram may be a 400% reduction of a large piece of paper to an 8 X 11 piece of paper, making the whole thing illegible. This diagram will have a title "Our Technical Architecture." Figure 3–4 presents a typical architecture diagram for a hospital information system.

FIGURE 3–2

Architecture for Clinical Information Systems

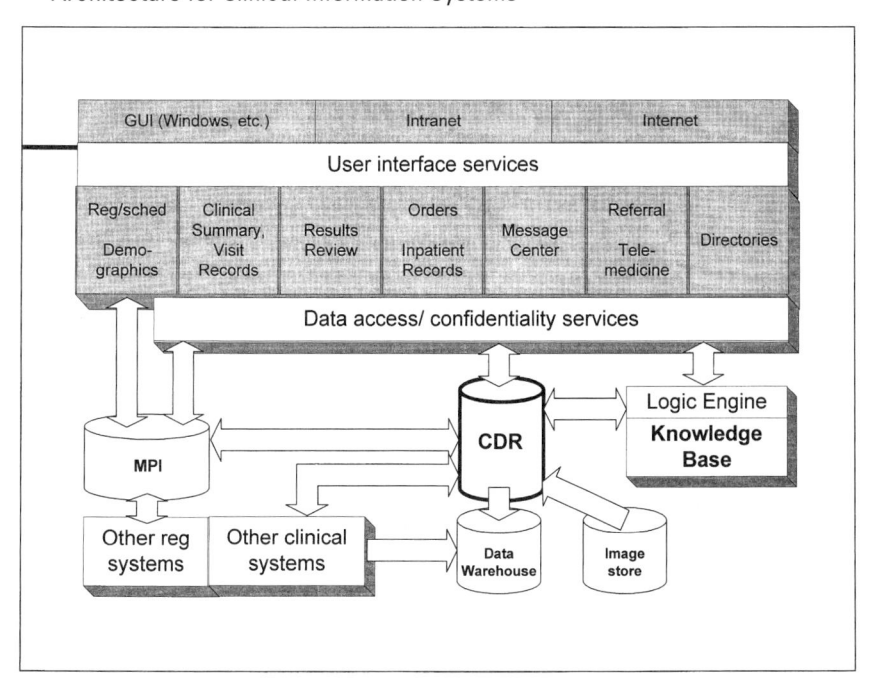

Source: Teich, J., Internal document. Partners HealthCare System, 1997.

FIGURE 3–3

A Day in the Life of a Clinician—A Primary Care Provider Starting the Day

> Dr. Smith is a primary care physician at a community practice outside of Route 128. She has a workstation at her desk connected to the Partners network. She arrives at her practice on a weekday morning, ready for a full day of primary patient care. Upon arriving at her desk, she checks her workstation and finds several items waiting in its electronic in-box.
>
> The computer first reports on the status of the two patients in Dr. Smith's practice who are currently hospitalized. The report shows the narrative status and current plan for each, as well as a summary of the patient's most recent test results, medications, and procedures. The screen also displays the phone number of the patient's floor, as well as the name and beeper of the inpatient physician. By selecting a button, Dr. Smith can page the doctor, call the nurse on the floor, or leave electronic mail, or both.
>
> The in-box also indicates that there is news about two of the five patients who are in active consultation referral. One, sent to an orthopedist, has had an MRI; the results are available by selecting a View button. Another, sent for neurology consultation, has finished the consultation; the screen displays the summary report.
>
> Dr. Smith next proceeds to the Results Manager section of the in-box. It shows her all new results of tests and diagnostics studies on her patients. Dr. Smith selects the first patient and notes a normal mammography result. Choosing from the available options, she opts to send a letter to the patient, informing her of the result. The computer automatically updates the patient's health-maintenance profile.

Source: Teich, J., Internal document. Partners HealthCare System, 1997.

Or an organization may see an oval that has lines from it to clip art pictures of hospitals, pharmacies, nursing homes, and physician offices with the title "Our IDS Architecture." Figure 3–5 presents a typical architecture diagram for an IDS system.

These diagrams may help leadership understand some of the concepts behind the architecture. However, architectures are strategies and tactics to achieve goals and not diagrams. This paragraph is not intended to denigrate the utility of such diagrams but rather to ensure that we, who put them up on the slide projector, remember that these diagrams in and of themselves are insufficient statements of architecture.

Internal Capabilities and Characteristics

FIGURE 3-4

Typical Hospital Information System Architecture

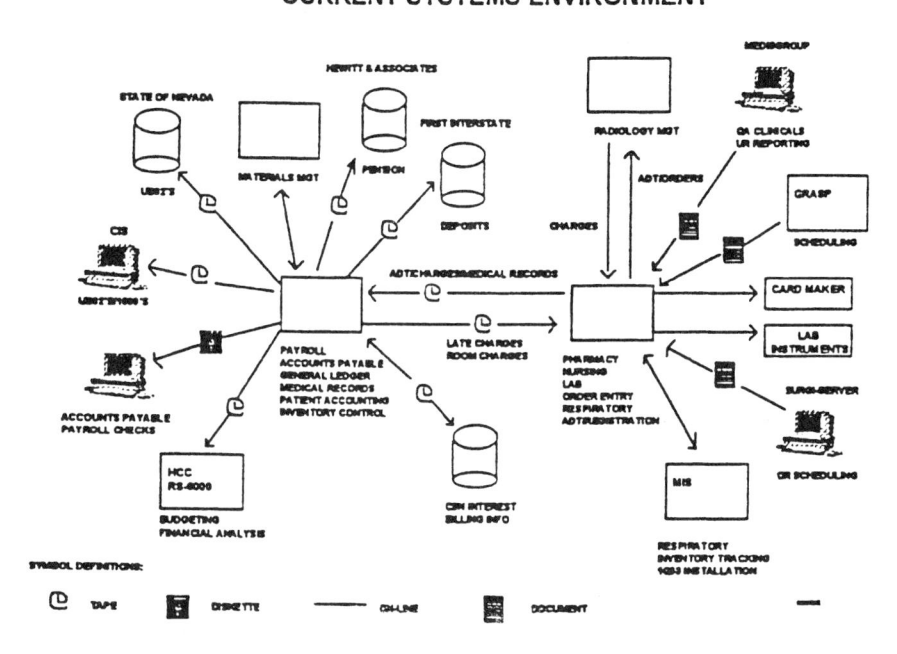

In Chapter 4 an example of developing strategies and tactics, to achieve the architectural objective of the integration of applications across an integrated delivery system, is presented in more detail.

Data

The data asset is composed of the following.

- Data recorded on some media
- Organizationally defined data coding conventions, standards, and definitions (e.g., ICD-9 codes, zip codes, and standards for identifying whether a physician is a primary care provider or not)
- Policies, procedures, and management mechanisms that guide the capture, "cleaning," and use of data

FIGURE 3-5

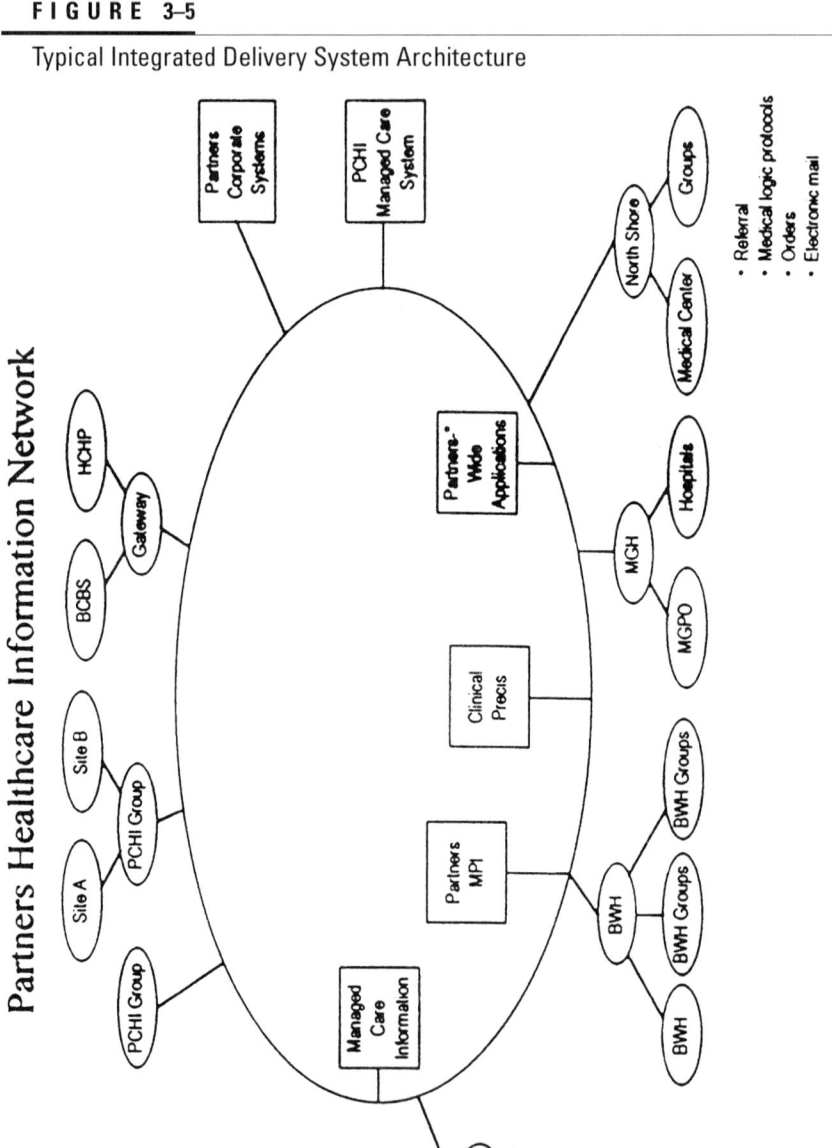

Typical Integrated Delivery System Architecture

- Technologies that capture, store, and support the access and analysis of data (e.g., database management systems and reporting packages)

Data Characteristics
Organizational data has five critical characteristics.
- *Accurate.* Data that is accurate captures, with tolerable error, the "true" state of some phenomenon, activity, or thing. If the data say that 24% of a provider organization's patients are subscribers of one HMO, then that should be a fair reflection of the truth.
- *Timely.* The interval between the time or period when someone wants to make a decision or check the status of an activity and the time of the availability of the data should be short relative to factors such as the pace of change, the organization's ability to move with a certain speed, and the urgency of dependent decisions.
- *Understood.* Data should have a definition that is consistent and comprehensively understood by all users of those data. An "encounter," for example, should have a common definition across the enterprise.
- *Accessible.* Decision makers should be able to access, with modest difficulty, the data that are needed to make decisions and monitor activities.
- *Efficient.* The capture, transformation, and reporting of data should be efficient.

These desired characteristics are not particularly controversial. One can develop other characteristics but one doesn't generate extensive arguments over whether there is utility to accurate, timely, well-understood, accessible, and efficiently gathered data.

Despite this lack of argument, the quality of data in most organizations is relatively poor. The major contribution of Executive Information Systems and Decision Support Systems, quite the fad and rage several years ago, was, for most organizations, to point out the exceptionally poor quality of organizational data. Executives found that they were able to bring forth, with the touch of a button, multi-color graphs of garbage.

Data, as discussed in the previous chapter, can be a very important source of competitive advantage and critical for organizational monitoring of performance and strategic progress. Data may be the most unforgiving component of the asset. If the organization implements a lousy application system or unreliable technology, it can replace them. If the organization hires someone who is incompetent, they can remove them. If the organization allows poor quality data to enter into its systems or develops an ill-conceived coding scheme, it may not be able to correct the problem.

Data Strategies

There are four major areas where strategies regarding data are necessary.

The first area is the *definition of what data to collect.* This is a complicated problem where the answer depends, to a very large extent, on organizational definitions of strategy, critical success factors, key environmental variables, and essential performance areas. Data can be gathered to assess market share, fiscal performance, care outcomes, cost of care, conformance of care to protocols, appointment availability, and patient satisfaction. All of these areas, and others, involve discussions of specific data elements, data definition, sources of data, acceptable data error rates, users of data, and confidentiality of data.

The second area involves the *definition of which data should be standardized across the enterprise and which standards should be utilized.* In some areas, the standardization choices are constrained (e.g., General Accounting Practices have a significant influence on the definition of data on fiscal performance). In other areas, a small number of choices exist but the choices have quite different ramifications and limitations (e.g., schemes for coding patient problems). And, in some areas, the organization may have great latitude (e.g., the definition of market share), although the choices, again, have very different ramifications.

The third area is *the identification of data management and access technologies.* Technologies and techniques are varied and the industry is currently awash in discussions on data management technologies. This discussion is complete with new buzzwords and terms such as data mining, data warehouses, data marts, OLAP (On-line Analytical Processing) tools, and operational data stores (Marietti, 1998; GartnerGroup, September, 1998). Despite the buzzword frenzy, these techniques and technologies do have important distinctions and contributions.

The fourth area is the *development of organizational mechanisms and functions to manage data and perform activities designed to improve the characteristics of the data asset.* These mechanisms are often decentralized. For example, Finance manages data on fiscal performance,

Marketing may manage data on market share and patient satisfaction, Health Information Management is responsible for coding of procedure and disease data and Quality Assurance may manage data on outcomes.

Regardless of the responsibility distribution, organizational leadership should recognize that developing and maintaining high quality data requires (Glaser and Ashman, 1990) the following.

- *Staff who are responsible for managing data quality.* These staff document data meaning and ensure data integrity by developing and enforcing data management techniques such as data dictionaries, initial and retrospective data entry checks and edits, and supporting "official databases." Responsibility means that their job descriptions are explicit about these tasks. These staff can be asked to oversee data generated externally and used by the organization.
- *Senior management support.* Data quality involves changes in applications systems and work processes, and budgets to support the data quality and management function.
- *A recognition that while technology can be sexy, managing data quality is generally not.* Trying to determine how an organization managed to perform a hysterectomy on a 20-year-old male, which the data indicate, requires the skills of a good detective and often involves the drudgery of a stakeout. Nonetheless, sexiness has never been a good predictor of importance.

Data management should also include the following (Levitin and Redman, 1998).

- Developing, maintaining, and making widely available the inventory of data resources
- Specifying the terms and conditions under which one organizational unit may have access to another's data

IS Staff

The IS staff asset has three major components.

1. Attributes of the staff
2. Core staff capabilities and competencies
3. Organization of the staff

Staff Attributes

A high-performing IS staff has several general characteristics.

- *They execute well.* They deliver applications, infrastructure, and services that are a sound understanding of organization needs. These deliverables occur on time, on budget, and leave those who were involved in the project giving the project team high marks for professional comportment.
- *They are good consultants.* They advise organizational members on the best approach to the application of IT, given the organizational problem or opportunity. They advise when IT may be inappropriate or the least important component of the solution. This advice ranges from help desk support to systems analyses to new technology recommendations to advice on the suitability of IT in furthering an aspect of organizational strategy.
- *They provide world class support.* Information systems require daily care and feeding and problem identification and correction. This support needs to be exceptionally efficient and effective.
- *The staff stay current with their expertise* keeping up to date on new techniques and technologies that improve the ability of the organization to apply IT effectively.

A wide variety of techniques exist that can assist IS management in their efforts to improve staff attributes (e.g., the ability of staff to manage projects and to ensure staff are current in their expertise).

Currently, there appears to be two major strategic issues regarding staff.

The first involves the *attraction and retention of staff*. The market for talented and experienced IS staff will be competitive for some time (King, 1997). Organizations clearly need to ensure that their salary structures, merit programs, benefits, educational offerings and job titles are competitive. A variety of strategies and tactics have been developed to improve an organization's recruitment and retention abilities (Wible, 1997; Scheier, 1997) (e.g., provide comfortable office space, remove petty rules, and improve performance reviews).

These steps are important. However, fundamentally, people work at organizations where the work is challenging and meaningful. They work at places where they like their co-workers and respect their leadership.

They work at places where they are proud of the organization, its mission, and its successes.

The second strategy surrounds the *potential for outsourcing or task sourcing to provide access to needed expertise and experience.* In a way, this topic is not new. Facilities management has been around for a while, as has consultant support of implementations and technical architecture development.

Full outsourcing experiences have been mixed (Strassman, 1997) with a significant number failing to deliver expected cost reductions and service improvements. Partial outsourcing or task sourcing (e.g., deployment of workstations or Year 2000 remediation work), appears to be more effective. These partial outsourcing arrangements enable organizations to obtain expertise and competence that is not critical to the organization or for which the organization cannot afford to replicate the competencies of others. Lacity and Willcocks (1998) provide an overview of practices that enhance the effectiveness of IT sourcing. Example practices include selective rather than total outsourcing, sourcing decisions jointly made by IT managers and senior leadership, and inviting internal bids for the "sourcing business."

Core Capabilities and Competencies

IS staff who execute well, provide terrific consulting support, and carry out world class support are very important. However, organizations should identify a small number of areas that constitute core IS capabilities and competencies. These are areas where getting an "A+" matters. The strategic question involves the definition of these core capabilities and the development of plans to establish A+ competencies.

For example, in 1998, Partners HealthCare System defined three areas of core capabilities: base support and services, care improvement, and technical infrastructure.

Base Support and Services This category of core capabilities included three sub-categories.

1. Operational management and support of a high performance technical infrastructure
2. Front line support (e.g., PC problem resolution)
3. Project management skills

While skills in these areas are probably always very important, they reflect a particular emphasis, across all Partners' centralized services in 1998 (e.g., Finance and Human Resources), on improving service quality. These departments had seen their service suffer as a result of their efforts to integrate their function across the organizations in the delivery system. Restoring the groups to prior levels of service, and exceeding prior levels, was judged to be a critical Partners' strategic emphasis.

Care Improvement Central to the Partners' agenda was the application of IT to improve the process of care. (A series of strategies surrounding this emphasis are discussed in more detail in Chapter 4.) One consequence was to establish, as a core IS capability, the set of skills and people necessary to innovatively apply IT to medical care improvement. An applied Medical Informatics function was established to oversee a research and development agenda. Staff skilled in clinical information systems application development were hired. A group of experienced clinical information system implementers was established. An IS unit of health services researchers was formed to analyze deficiencies in care processes, identify IT solutions that would reduce or eliminate these deficiencies, and assess the impact of clinical information systems on care improvement. Organizational units, possessing unique technical and clinical knowledge in radiology imaging systems and telemedicine, were also created.

Technical Infrastructure Recognizing the critical role played by having a well-conceived, executed, and supported technical architecture, infrastructure architecture, and design continued to serve as a core competency. A Partners IS unit is responsible for identifying major technology trends and developing strategies to capitalize on those trends. The group is responsible for developing architecture strategies and monitoring strategy implementation. This group also addresses issues and questions such as "How do we improve the security of our systems?" and "How do we reduce the total cost of ownership of the infrastructure?" Significant attention was paid to ensuring that extremely talented architectural and engineering talent was hired along with staff with terrific support skills.

IS Organization
There are three aspects of the IS organization for which strategies must be developed.

1. The definition and formation of departments or major functions
2. The form of the IS structure (e.g., matrixed or flat)
3. Properties of the IS organization as a whole (e.g., agility)

Major Departments   There are multiple considerations in defining the departments or major functions within an IS organization. Example functions include financial application implementation and support, telecommunications, Telemedicine, and decision support. One of the primary strategic considerations is the "organizing unit or concept."

One can organize around the following.

- Sites or members of the IDS (e.g., dedicated IS staff to support each organizational member of the IDS with a site CIO)
- Platforms and platform support (e.g., a unit of staff responsible for implementing and supporting a common IDS-wide e-mail system or workstation configuration)
- Applications or application suites (e.g., financial systems or patient care systems)
- Processes (e.g., a unit of IS staff responsible for systems support for all outpatient scheduling and registration activities across the IDS)
- Classes of care (e.g., inpatient, sub-acute, and primary care)
- IT research and development (e.g., the investigation of new technologies)

An IS organization is likely to organize around more than one concept (e.g., have site IS organization staff and CIOs and central support of some platforms). And an IS organization is unlikely to try to adopt all of the concepts since some form of dysfunction and chaos would follow quickly.

The IS organization should organize in a manner that mirrors the overall organization of the IDS. The IS organization should adopt the organizing concepts of the IDS, and the IS organization should be a reflection of the IDS. For example, if the IDS has CEOs for each member hospital, the IS organization should have organization CIOs. If the IDS has centralized Finance, then the IS organization should have a function responsible for systems support of Finance.

Each major IS department should have the following.

- A senior IS manager who has an IS reporting relationship and a business unit reporting relationship. This business unit reporting relationship could be the COO of a hospital, the CFO for centralized Finance or, in the case of areas such as infrastructure, a committee of IDS representatives.
- A business unit IS decision making and priority setting body, which may be the same as the reporting relationship, but may also be a hospital IS steering committee.

Form of the IS Organization IS organizations in an IDS are invariably matrixed. Kilbridge et al. (1998), in their study of IDS IS organizations, found three dimensions that defined the matrix. The functional dimension was devoted to IDS-wide infrastructure (e.g., communications network and enterprise master person index), and the support of IDS-wide consolidated functions (e.g., Finance). The geographic dimension was devoted to supporting distinct geographic sites or logically separate provider sites (e.g., one of the IDS community hospitals). The cross-continuum process oriented dimension might support acute care in general or a "carve out" such as oncology services. Figure 3–6 depicts a two-dimensional structure based on function and geography.

FIGURE 3–6

Two-Dimensional Organizational Structure: Geographical/Functional

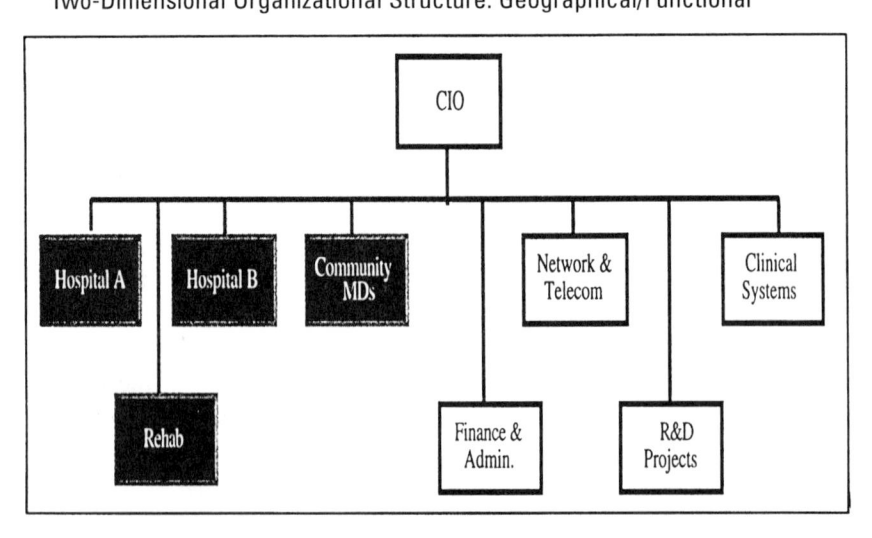

Source: Kilbridge, P. (1998). *Information Systems for IDNs: Best Practices and Key Success Factors.*

Internal Capabilities and Characteristics

Figure 3–7 shows a two-dimensional structure based on function and process.

Within a particular type of matrix (e.g., functional and geographic), one might find different IS functions across different IDS, and find some functions listed on the functional axis for one IDS and the geographic axis for another IDS.

The matrix form of IS is largely a reflection of the matrix structures of most IDS. IDS have evolved to some form of central control and functions and local autonomy. The degree of centralization may vary but it is unusual to find a pure hierarchy in an IDS or an IDS with no central management.

There is no single way to organize. IDS will differ in their efforts to consolidate some functions and not others. IDS will vary in their efforts to create "lines of business" (e.g., diabetes care or women's health) that cut across its member organizations. And most organizations experiment, over time, with changes in the degree to which they centralize and decentralize, as they discover the limitations of the current structure and forget about the limitations of prior structures.

Matrices are very hard to manage. In any matrix, there are a small number of core organizational processes that must be managed well if the IS matrix is to function well.

- *Communication among IS units and between IS and the business units.* With a matrix structure, multiple centralized functional IS

FIGURE 3–7

Two-Dimensional Organizational Structure: Functional/Process

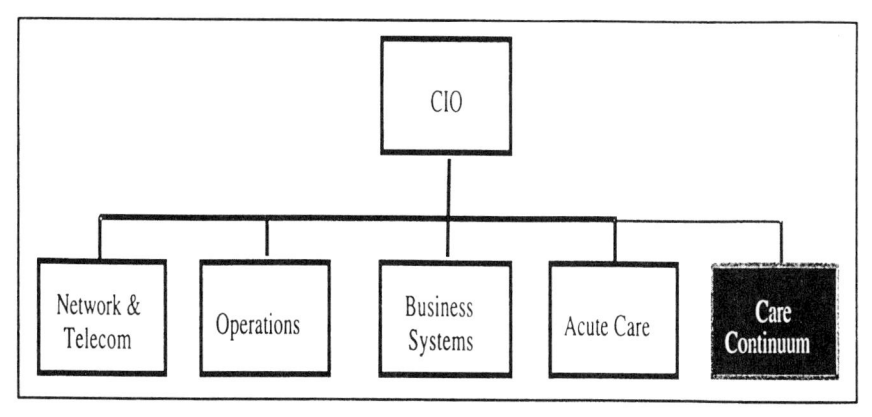

```
                    ┌─────┐
                    │ CIO │
                    └──┬──┘
      ┌──────────┬─────┼──────┬──────────┐
┌─────────┐ ┌──────────┐ ┌──────────┐ ┌──────────┐ ┌──────────┐
│Network &│ │Operations│ │ Business │ │Acute Care│ │   Care   │
│ Telecom │ │          │ │ Systems  │ │          │ │Continuum │
└─────────┘ └──────────┘ └──────────┘ └──────────┘ └──────────┘
```

Source: Kilbridge, P. (1998). *Information Systems for IDNs: Best Practices and Key Success Factors.*

units may be engaged in projects or support at any individual member organization. The site CIO must coordinate and communicate with the managers of those groups, most of whom will be peers rather than superiors or subordinates.
- *Priority setting.* Large, strategic priorities can be defined by an IDS IS steering committee. However, tactical priority setting will occur daily. If the centralized infrastructure group can deploy fifty workstations a day, and each of six sites has twelve workstations that they need tomorrow, who decides who gets the fifty? If the network has failed in two sites, who decides which site will get fixed first?
- *Conflict resolution.* Conflicts can occur over differences of opinion about priorities or member organization belief in the utility of different directions and IS strategies. If the site believes that a particular application package is the answer for it and the central infrastructure group believes that such a choice threatens the supportability of the architecture, how are such issues resolved?

Communication, priority setting, and conflict resolution are problems that confront all organizations and all IS organizations. One need not be an IDS to have these issues. However, these processes become more difficult to manage when the organization's structure is a matrix. The lines of authority are less clear and priority setting, for example, may have to be done through negotiations among peers rather than reliance on a chain of command. Organizations that have recently joined an IDS discover that their chain of command reflexes or their sense of negotiation based on their own internal organization is no longer valid when they have to fit in with the rest of the IDS. Such a discovery creates conflict and confusion. All of this occurs in the context of most new IDS still struggling to find the best ways to manage themselves, addressing complex issues such as capital budget development, rationalization of board structures, and the creation of coherent medical management processes, which are consistent and embraced across the IDS medical staff.

Organizational Attributes   IS organizations, like people, have characters. They can be agile or ossified. They can be risk tolerant or risk averse. The characteristics can be stated and strategies to achieve desired characteristics can be defined and implemented. While there are many characteristics

Internal Capabilities and Characteristics

that organizations can have, this section will briefly discuss three: smart, agile, and innovative. These three are illustrative of any organizational characteristic and are generally viewed as desirable.

A *smart* IS organization would probably have several attributes, including the following.

- Largely composed of smart people who are not only natively smart (high IQ), but are also smart in the sense that they are skilled, knowledgeable, and experienced. The organization clearly values smart people, perhaps rewarding them, in addition for their performance, for being smart.
- Effective at sharing knowledge. Knowledge sharing is rewarded, mechanisms to promote sharing are in place and means exist to identify that knowledge to be shared and with whom it should be shared.
- Efficient and effective at institutionalizing knowledge. New knowledge appears in changes in procedures and processes, documentation and the implementation of tools that incorporate that knowledge (e.g., the introduction of new application development tools)
- Focused, sensitive external sensors that detect and evaluate promising new areas of knowledge. These sensors can consist of sending people to conferences and school and dedicated research and development functions.
- Able to forecast changes in the internal and external environments and evaluate alternative scenarios of the future. The organization would be able to, for example, forecast the implications of a younger workforce that is more "computer literate" or understand the information systems implications of a rapid shift to capitation.

An *agile* organization would probably have several attributes that could include the following.

- The ability to form teams quickly. This implies some level of "slack" in resources and the ability to "park" initiatives currently in progress, as members of that initiative are included in the new team.
- Appropriate "chunking" of initiatives such that there are multiple points along the initiative during which the project could be

stopped and still deliver value in its stopped state. For example, the rollout of a computerized medical record, which may call for ten clinics per year, could be stopped temporarily at four and still deliver value to those four.
- Decision making forums (e.g., IS steering committees) that are able to make decisions and encumber resources quickly.

An organization that emphasizes agility will also attempt to create agile platforms (e.g., select and implement applications that have potent tools that enable the organization to rapidly enhance the applications). They would also try to create loosely coupled architectures (e.g., architectures that provide efficient and standard interfaces between applications), which enable applications to be replaced without causing significant changes in other applications (almost "plug and play").

An organization that is *innovative* could have characteristics such as the following.

- Reward systems that encourage new ideas and successful implementation of innovative technologies and applications
- Punishment systems that are loath to "punish" those involved in experiments that failed
- Small "grants" that can be obtained outside of the normal budget process to fund the pursuit of interesting ideas
- Dedicated research and development groups within IS

The above discussion of organizational characteristics does not cover all characteristics (e.g., a service-oriented IS organization). Moreover, there is a wealth of literature and experience on the topic of molding and creating organizational cultures that have desired characteristics.

Healthcare organizations and IS leadership should recognize that IS organizational attributes and cultures are created, whether intentionally or not, through the combined acts, speech, and behavior of its members. IS leadership molds culture every time it speaks or doesn't speak, acts or doesn't act, rewards or punishes, and whom it hires and doesn't hire.

IS organization will struggle if they attempt to create a culture or character that is different from that of the rest of the organization particularly if members of IS have to interact with other members of the organization on any routine basis. The two different cultures are at risk of rejecting each other, often for reasons no more solid than "they are different."

Governance

Governance refers to the principles and organization that governs the IT resources (Drazen and Staisor, 1995). Strategies regarding governance must address several issues.

- Who sets priorities for information systems, and how are those priorities set?
- Who is responsible for implementing information systems plans, and what principles will guide the implementation process?
- What organization structures are needed to support the linkage between information systems and the rest of the organization?
- How are information systems responsibilities distributed between IS and the rest of the organization, and between central and "local" information systems groups?
- How are IS budgets developed?
- What principles will govern the IT asset?

At its core, governance involves determining the distribution of the responsibility for making decisions and the scope of the decisions that can be made. Developing answers to the above questions can be a complex exercise. Answers should be derived from basic strategic objectives (e.g., a desire to be integrated), and answers should be consistent across the questions. Some examples of answers, derived for a strategic objective, are presented below.

Governance answers to support the *integration* of an IDS may be as follows.

- Priorities should be developed by a central IDS IS committee to help ensure the perspective of overall integration, and initiatives that support integration should be given a higher priority than those that do not.
- IS budgets that are developed locally are subject to central approval.
- The IS plan must specify the means by which an integrated infrastructure and application suites will be achieved and the boundaries of that plan (e.g., local organizations are free to select from a set of patient care system options but, whatever the selection, the patient care system must interface with the IDS clinical data repository).

- A centralized IS group needs to exist and it has authority over local groups.
- Members of the IDS are constrained in their selection of applications to support ancillary departments to those that are on an "approved" list.
- Certain pieces of data (e.g., payor class or patient problems), and certain identifiers (e.g., patient identifier and provider identifier) have to utilize a common dictionary or standard.
- All IDS members must use a common electronic mail system.

Answers to support the ability of the IDS member organizations to be *locally responsive* might include the following.

- A small central IS group will be created to assist in local IS plan development, develop technical data and application standards, and perform technical research and development. This group will have an advisory and coordination relationship with the local IS organizations.
- Local IS steering committees will develop local IS plans according to processes and criteria defined locally. A central IS steering committee will review these plans, in an advisory role, to identify areas of potential redundancy or serious inconsistency.
- IS budgets are developed locally according to overall budget guidelines established centrally (e.g., the rules for capitalizing new systems and the duration to use for depreciation).
- Certain pieces of data will be standardized as appropriate to ensure the ability of the IDS to prepare consolidated financial statements and patient activity counts.
- Local sites are free to, for example, select any electronic mail system but that system must be able to send and receive messages using SMTP and the electronic mail system directory should be able to expose itself to other electronic mail directories.

Developing governance structures and approaches requires strategies that are driven by the need to achieve certain organizational objectives. There should not be governance development purely for the reasons of performing some normative task (e.g., all organizations have IS steering committees composed of a broad representation of senior leadership and hence so should we). An organizational objective of being locally responsive may mean that no central steering committee would exist or its powers would be limited.

The Chief Information Officer

The chief information officer (CIO) role, and the need for one, has been much discussed in the IT and management literature and conferences over the last two decades. The CIO is seen as the executive who would successfully lead the organization in its efforts to apply information technology to advance its strategies and can be viewed as a critical component of the IT asset.

In healthcare surveys, such as those conducted by the College of Healthcare Information Management Executives (CHIME), have chronicled the evolution of the healthcare CIO (CHIME, 1998). This evolution has included debates on CIO reporting relationships, salaries, titles, pedigrees (from outside healthcare or not), and the role of the CIO in organizational strategic planning.

The CIO community can be too shrill in its demand for respect, and legitimate concerns can, and need to, be raised by organizational leadership about the hype surrounding and the contribution of the CIO (Freeman, 1993). Nonetheless, a good CIO can be a significant asset to an organization. The CIO can do the following.

- Be a major contributor to organizational strategy development and apply business thinking and strategy formation skills that extend beyond their IT responsibilities
- Help the organization understand the potential of IT to make real and significant contributions to organizational plans, activities, and operations
- Be a leader, motivator, recruiter, and retainer of superior IS talent
- Ensure that the IT asset is robust, effective, efficient, and sustained
- Ensure that the IS organization runs effectively and efficiently

Earl and Feeney (1995) conducted a study of CIOs who "added value" to their respective organizations. They developed a set of attributes of those CIOs and a set of characteristics of their organization's views of IT. Specifically, they found that the "value add" CIOs do the following.

- Obsessively and continuously focus on business imperatives so that they focus the IT direction correctly
- Have a track record of delivery that causes IS performance problems to drop off of the management agenda
- Interpret, for the rest of the leadership, the meaning and nature of the IT success stories of other organizations
- Establish and maintain good working relationships with the members of the organization's leadership
- Establish and communicate the IS performance record
- Concentrate the IS development efforts on those areas of the organization where the most leverage is to be gained
- Work with the organization's leadership to develop a shared vision of the role and contribution of IT
- Make important general contributions to business thinking and operations

Earl and Feeny (1995) found that the "value add" CIO, as a person, has integrity, is goal directed, is experienced with IT, and is a good consultant and communicator. Those organizations that have such a CIO tend to describe IT as critical to the organization, find that IT thinking is embedded in business thinking, note that IT initiatives are well focused, and speak highly of IT performance.

Organizational excellence in IT doesn't just happen. It is managed and led. If the organization decides that the effective application of IT is a major element of its strategies and plans, they will need a very good CIO. Failure to have such talent will severely hinder the organization's aspirations.

While CIOs can be of great value, the healthcare CIO community, and some of its members, can hinder themselves and their potential for contributing to the organization by directing the conversation into areas of concern that do little to advance the organization. The healthcare CIO community often expresses concerns:

- *About the reporting relationship of the CIO.* Not everyone will report to the CEO (which is merciful to the CEO). The CIO needs access to the CEO but the CIO also needs a boss who is a good mentor, provides appropriate political support, and who is genuinely interested in the application of IT. CFOs and COOs can be terrific in these regards.

- *That the organization doesn't understand how hard the management and the implementation of the technology can be, and how nefarious the vendor and consulting community can be.* All members of the organization can drag out litanies that portray the general difficulty of life, or the problems of changing large, unruly organizations, or the failure of the rest of the world to appreciate the complexities and value of their profession. Part of the problem is that the organization, to a degree, doesn't care about the woes of a profession—it just wants the job to get done. And part of the problem is the CIOs failure to communicate well about the challenges posed by IT.
- *About the lack of senior management interest in technologies and applications* such as the clinical data repository, client server technology, and object-oriented development environments. Management will care if it understands why it should care. Management is no more interested in CIO discussions of seemingly arcane and irrelevant aspects of the IT arena then they are of CFO monologues on murky Medicare rulings or medical staff ramblings on the nuances of new clinical findings.

ASSET LESSONS LEARNED AND OBSERVATIONS

In addition to the lessons and observations discussed above, there are two overall observations of the IT asset: the need for asset plans and caveats regarding asset investments.

Plans for the Asset

IT strategic plans invariably center on the applications that need to be implemented to further organizational goals. While that focus is not inappropriate, these plans often give insufficient attention to describing the plans, activities, and resources needed to advance the non-application portion of the asset.

One shouldn't conclude that a solid infrastructure, terrific staff, a well-crafted infrastructure, and high quality data are a replacement for the need to deliver applications. On the other hand, it is difficult to deliver applications well and consistently well if the asset is in poor shape. In an analogous fashion, one may be able to force one's dreadfully out-of-shape body to hike twenty miles, but one might not be able to hike twenty miles day after day until the body's fitness is improved. A dollar invested in enhancing the asset can deliver more of a return than a dollar invested in an application.

Information systems plans need to devote serious attention to the steps that will be taken, for example, to improve infrastructure agility, improve staff skills, enhance data quality, and streamline governance processes. These plans require serious strategic thinking. Ill-conceived analyses or half-baked strategy surrounding plans for IT governance or technical architecture, for example, can severely hinder organization progress.

Asset Investment

A study by Strassman (1990), using data from *Information Week,* examined the relationship between information systems expenditures and organizational effectiveness. Data from *Information Week's* survey of the top 100 best users of information technology were used to correlate IT expenditures per employee with profits per employee (Figure 3–8). Strassman concluded that there is no obvious direct relationship between effectiveness or expenditure and organizational performance. This finding has been observed in several other studies (Keen, 1997).

This finding leads one to several conclusions.

- *Just because you spend more, there is no guarantee that the organization will be better off.* There has never been a correlation between spending and outcomes. Paying more for care doesn't give one better care. Clearly one can spend so little that nothing effective can be done. And one can spend so much that waste is guaranteed. But moving IT expenditures from 2% of the operating budget to 3% of the operating budget does not inherently lead to a 50% increase in desirable outcomes.
- *Information technology is a tool and its utility as a tool is largely determined by the tool user and the task.* Spending a large amount of money on a chainsaw for someone who doesn't know how to use one is a waste. Spending more money for the casual saw user who trims an apple tree every now and then is also a waste. On the other hand, a skilled logger might say that if the blade were longer and the engine more powerful, it would be possible to cut 10% more trees in a period of time. The

Internal Capabilities and Characteristics

FIGURE 3-8

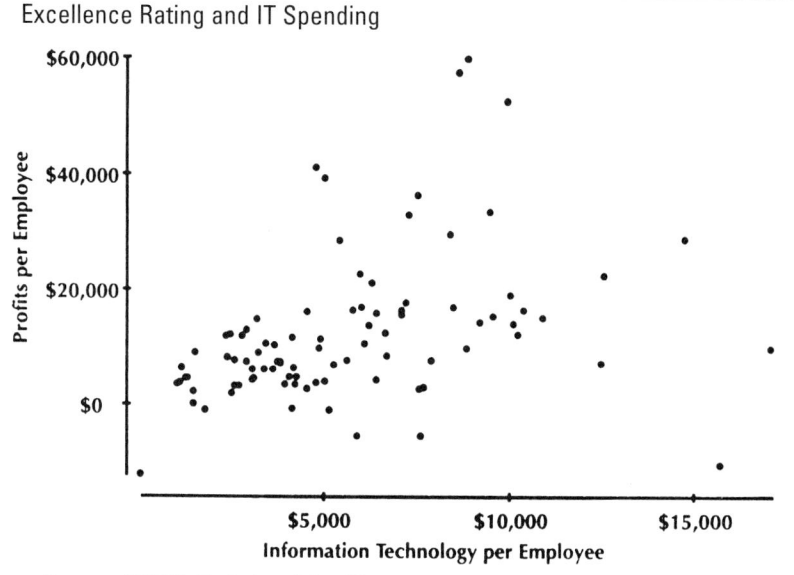

Excellence Rating and IT Spending

[Scatter plot: Profits per Employee (y-axis, $0 to $60,000) vs. Information Technology per Employee (x-axis, $5,000 to $15,000)]

Source: Strassman, P. (1990). *The Business Value of Computers.*

investment needed to enhance the saw might lead to superior performance. Organizational effectiveness at applying IT has an enormous effect on the potential for a useful outcome from increased IT investment.

- *Factors other than the appropriateness of the tool to the task influence the relationship between IT investment and organizational performance.* Example factors include the nature of the work (e.g., IT is likely to have a greater impact on bank performance than the performance of a consulting firm), the basis of competition in an industry (e.g., cost per unit of manufactured output versus prowess of marketing), and an organization's relative competitive position in the market.

In healthcare we often decry that while banks spend 8% to 10% of their revenue on IT, we, in healthcare, spend only 2% to 3%. One can offer several reasons why that difference in percentage exists: healthcare has been competitive only recently, healthcare organizations have only recently hit a scale where IT investments can have great leverage over organizational processes, and/or the nature of information processing at a bank is less complex than healthcare and more amenable to today's IT solutions. Regardless, there is no evidence that healthcare would be more effective and efficient if it spent four times as much on IT as it does now. Certainly Strassman's analyses wouldn't support a conclusion of more money equals greater performance.

FACTORS THAT INFLUENCE ORGANIZATIONAL IT ASSET DECISIONS

A variety of factors influence how organizations make choices regarding the type and level of asset investment and the manner in which they manage the asset (e.g., organizational risk tolerance, previous experiences with IT, availability of capital, the IT inclinations of the board, and the actions of competitors). This section focuses on three factors.

1. The approach to the evaluation of IT investments (or costs)
2. The influence of "fads" in the industry
3. The influence and meaning of surveys of top IT issues and IT adoption

Evaluation of IT Investments[2]

As they evaluate information system investment opportunities, healthcare executives search for techniques and tools that will help to frame the alternatives and guide funding decisions. Organizational committees are often formed to prioritize and comment on the proposed information systems projects.

Recently there has been much discussion across all industries about how one identifies the return on investment (ROI) of the IT investment. For example, what is the ROI of the computerized patient record? It is hard to argue against a position that says that organization should evaluate and assess the degree to which an IT investment (or any investment) is likely to lead to whatever returns are viewed as important.

---

[2] The following section originally appeared as Glaser, J. (1997). Beware Return on Investment. *Healthcare Informatics,* June.

Evaluation Lessons

In determining how they will evaluate IT investments, organizational leadership should bear in mind several lessons learned from IT investments in healthcare and other industries. These lessons are discussed below.

The questions should be the same regardless of the type of investment. IT investment decisions must be considered in the context of a broad array of questions and answers to those questions. Are the overall organizational strategies, plans, and proposed tactics sound? Do they appear to be a thoughtful assessment of what needs to occur to further the organization? Is management capable of executing well? Do the proposed investments in people, organizations, medical technology, and IT link clearly and convincingly to the plans, and does the level of investment and risk seem appropriate given organizational goals? Are the relationships between the various types of investments clear?

The questions are the same regardless of whether the potential investment is in IT or something else. Similarly the answers need to be crisp and convincing regardless of the nature of the investment. If the answer regarding the linkage between the investments and strategies and plans is murky or unconvincing, or management's wherewithal to execute is a cause of concern, the investment is problematic. Asking and receiving good answers to the questions listed above are essential before any investments should be approved. The IT investment is no different in that regard than a proposal to acquire five primary care practices in an effort to increase the volume of referrals to an academic medical center.

The orientation of the questions must be right. IT has no value outside of the context of strategies and plans. It must clearly support these strategies and plans and the specific needs for IT should be drawn from the plans and strategies. One should ask, for example, if we intend to improve the quality of our care, what information system capabilities, and related investments, are necessary to support this objective? This is a more appropriate orientation of the question than, what is the return on an investment for a computerized record? The former question helps to ensure that IT investments are specifically targeted to organizational initiatives. The latter question smells like a solution looking for a problem.

IT is one investment component. IT is invariably one of several investments that must be made for an initiative to succeed. Hence management needs to believe that all investments have been identified, their application well defined and their interrelationships well understood. If information systems are being proposed as an approach to reduce the cost of care, what other investments must be made in order for this reduction in cost to occur? Failure to identify and plan for the full scope of investments jeopardizes the likelihood that the initiative will succeed. If there is a need for a ROI, the ROI should be applied to the full set of the investments, in aggregate, and not to just one component.

Thoughtfully identify major contributors to investment performance failure. The following are major contributors to failure to achieve a solid return on IT investments (Quinn et al., 1994).

- A sub-optimal organizational strategy or organizational assessment of its competitive environment. Insufficient return occurs because the overall strategy is wrong.
- The strategy is fine but the associated IT capabilities are not defined appropriately. The information system, if it is solving a problem, is solving the wrong problem.
- Failure to identify and draw together well all investments and initiatives necessary to carry out the organization's plans. The IT investment falters because other changes, such as reorganization or reengineering work, fail to occur.
- Failure to execute the plan well. Poor planning or less than stellar management can diminish the return from any investment.

These factors account for more failure to achieve desired outcomes with information systems than can be accounted for by less than rigorous return analysis or the selection of the wrong analytical technique. IT should not be assessed in isolation.

The more strategic the IT investment the more its value can be diluted (Weill and Broadbent, 1998). An IT investment directed to increasing market share can have its value diluted by non-IT decisions and events (e.g., pricing decisions, the actions of competitors and the reaction of customers). The IT investment can be diluted by factors internal to the organization and external to it. IT investments that are less strategic but have business value (e.g., improve the utilization of the operating rooms) can also be diluted (e.g., by the failure to provide adequate OR nurse staffing), but the dilution can be due to internal factors. The value of an IT investment directed toward improving the characteristics of the infrastructure has less opportunity to be diluted by factors outside of the IS organization (although it can be diluted by the immaturity, for example, of the technology).

Categories of Information System Investments

There are times when the ROI is the appropriate investment analysis technique. If a set of investments, including the IT component, is intended to reduce clerical staff, an ROI can be calculated. However, there are times when the ROI is clearly inappropriate. What is the ROI of electronic mail or word processing? One could calculate the ROI but it is hard to imagine an organization basing its investment decision on that analysis. Would an ROI analysis have captured the strategic value of the American Airlines SABRE system or the value of automated teller machines? Few strategic IT investments have impacts that are fully captured by an ROI. Moreover, the strategic impact is rarely fully understood until years later. Whatever ROI analysis might have been done would have invariably been wrong.

The techniques used to assess IT investments should vary by the type of initiative or objectives that the IT investment intends to support. One technique does not fit all IT investments. According to Quinn et al. (1994), there are six categories of IT investments.

Infrastructure   IT investments can be infrastructure that enables other investments or applications to be implemented and deliver desired capabilities. Examples of infrastructure include data communication networks, personal computers, and clinical data repositories. A delivery system-wide network enables one to implement applications to consolidate clinical laboratories, establish organization-wide electronic mail, and share patient health data between providers.

It is difficult to quantitatively assess the impact or value of infrastructure investments.

- *They enable other applications.* Without those applications, infrastructure has no value. Hence infrastructure value is indirect and depends on application value.
- *The ability to allocate infrastructure value across applications is difficult.* Of the millions of dollars invested in a data communication network, how much of that investment can be allocated to the ability to create delivery system-wide electronic medical records may be difficult or impossible to determine.
- *A good information system's infrastructure is often determined by its agility, potency, and ability to facilitate integration of applications.* It is very difficult to assign ROI numbers or any meaningful number to some of these characteristics. What's the

value of being able to, because of agility, speed up the time it takes to develop and enhance applications?

Information system infrastructure is as hard to evaluate as other organizational "infrastructure" such as having talented, educated staff. As with other infrastructure:

- Evaluation is often instinctive and experientially based.
- In general, underinvesting can severely limit the organization.
- Investment decisions are made between alternatives that are assessed based on their ability to achieve agreed upon goals. These goals may be difficult to quantify. Example goals include moving images across the system, high availability of information systems, and rapid application development.

Mandated Information system investment may be necessary because of mandated initiatives. Examples of mandated initiatives may include reporting of quality data to accrediting organizations or required changes in billing formats.

Assessing these initiatives is generally approached by identifying the least expensive, and the quickest to implement, alternative while achieving some level of compliance.

Cost Reduction Information system investments directed to cost reduction are generally highly amenable to ROI and other quantifiable dollar impact analyses. The ability to conduct a quantifiable ROI analysis is rarely the question. The ability of management to effect the predicted cost reduction or avoidance is often a far more germane question.

Specific New Products and Services Information systems can be critical to the development of new products and services. At times, the information system delivers the new service or is itself the product. Examples of information system-based new services include bank cash management programs and credit card/airline mileage linkage programs. In healthcare, a new service may be World Wide Web access, by patients, to guidelines and consumer-oriented medical textbooks.

For some of these new products and services one can quantifiably assess these opportunities in terms of return. These assessments include analyses of potential revenues, either directly from the service or service-induced utilization of other products and services. An ROI analysis will need to be supplemented by techniques such as sensitivity analyses of consumer response.

Despite the analyses, the value of the investment usually has a speculative component. This component includes consumer utilization, competitor response, and impact on related businesses.

Quality Improvement Information system investments are often directed to improving the quality of service or medical care. These investments may intend to reduce waiting times, improve ability of physicians to locate information, improve treatment outcomes, or reduce errors in treatment.

Evaluation of these initiatives, while quantifiable, is generally done in terms of service parameters that are known or believed to be important determinants of customer satisfaction and, hence, revenues. These parameters are usually measures of aspects of organizational processes that customers encounter and are used by them to judge the organization (e.g., waiting times in the physician's office).

A quantifiable dollar outcome of service quality improvement can be very difficult to predict. Service quality is often necessary to protect current business and the effect of a failure to continuously improve service can be difficult to project.

Major Strategic Initiative Strategic initiatives in information systems are intended to significantly change the competitive position of the organization or redefine the core nature of the enterprise. These are rare. Examples are automated teller machines and home banking, which have led to a remarkable decline in branch banking; and the use of universal product codes, bar code scanners, and customer cards by supermarkets, which are leading to their ability to personalize grocery shopping.

There can be an ROI core or component to these analyses since they often involve major reshaping or reengineering of fundamental organizational processes. However, assessing, with high degrees of accuracy, the ROI of these initiatives and related information systems can be very difficult. Several factors contribute to this difficulty.

- The initiatives usually recast the company's markets and its roles. The outcome of the recasting, while visionary, can be difficult to see with clarity and certainty.
- The recasting is evolutionary; the organization learns and alters itself as it progresses over what are often lengthy periods of time. It

is difficult to be prescriptive about this evolutionary process. Most integrated delivery systems are confronting this phenomenon.
- Market and competitor response can be difficult to predict.

Evaluation Summary

IT initiatives can be carried out for very different basic organizational purposes. The ability to quantifiably evaluate and the appropriate quantitative technique will vary as a result. One approaches the assessment of an initiative designed to reduce costs differently than an initiative designed to recast the organization. Some objectives, and the associated IT investment, lend themselves well to rigorous ROI analysis. Others do not. The use of an inappropriate analytical technique can mislead investment decisions.

For most service organizations, a formal ROI analysis is appropriate for a minority of IT investments (Quinn, 1994). A large number of IT investments in healthcare today focus on improving service quality, the creation of new services, or recasting the organization in an effort to create a continuum of care.

There are techniques that can be applied to each type of investment. There are also techniques that can be applied to evaluate a portfolio of investments. Examples include bench-marking or multi-attribute utility analysis, which scores each investment against strategic criteria such as increase market share, reduce costs or improve quality. See also (Figure 3–1.)

Assessment of the IS Function

A wide variety of analyses, academic study, and pontification have been directed to the question of "How do we assess the value of the IT?" This question generally is directed at assessing the value of the aggregate IT investment or the contribution of the IS organization. This is a different question than assessing the value of an initiative and, at times, a more complex question. Developing a definitive, accurate, and well-accepted way to answer this question has eluded the industry and may continue to be elusive. Nonetheless there are some basic questions that can be asked. Interpreting the answer is a subjective exercise making it difficult to derive numeric scores. Bresnahan (1998) suggests five questions.

1. How does IT influence the customer experience? Do patients and physicians, for example, find that organizational processes are more efficient, less error prone, and more convenient?

Internal Capabilities and Characteristics

2. Does IT enable or retard growth? Can the IS organization support effectively the demands of a merger? Can IS support the creation of clinical product lines (e.g., Cardiology), across the IDS?
3. Does IT favorably affect productivity?
4. Does IT advance organizational innovation and learning?
5. How well is IS run?

Glaser (1991) suggests the following.

- Ask the CIO how your level of information systems expenditures compares with the expenditures of comparable organizations. While one has to be careful of viewing expenditure percentage data as a guide to a specific organization's decisions, the fact that such data are known means that the function is worrying about its costs and comparing itself to others.

- Ask three members of the management team to identify the major IS initiatives for the next year. Inconsistent answers or blank stares indicate a failure in the IT planning process.

- Review the expectations that were set for the last two systems you purchased. Ask for an assessment of the extent to which the goals were met and whether the implementation was on time and on budget.

- Ask for information to support two upcoming decisions. See whether, how quickly, and at what costs the requests can be satisfied.

- Ask the personal computer support group if it can tell you how many trouble calls it received last month, the average time to correct the problem, and the number of repeat visits. A lack of such data indicates an orientation that still struggles to spell the word "service."

- Ask your CIO for his or her assessment of the role of object-oriented technology in the organization. Did you understand the answer? Does the response seem thoughtful?

Answers to these questions provide an indication, perhaps crude, of how well the IS function is being run and whether the aggregate IT investment is providing value. All of these questions come from common sense, management beliefs in what is involved in running an organization well, and tests of IT domain knowledge.

Fads[3]

Our industry is awash with slogans; magic phrases that imply Nirvana is close at hand and that some new technology or management technique has supernatural powers that can transform organizations and the care process.

Cynical about Slogans

Open Systems will provide unparalleled interoperability between applications allowing *Plug and Play* that rivals Lego sets. *Client Server* systems will solve the rigidity and cost problems of legacy systems enabling *Reengineering* and *Organizational Transformation*. *Data Mining* will allow us to discover relationships between data that will open up new and insightful understandings about how the world works (e.g., there is a correlation between light blue scrub laundry bills and surgery volume).

Total Quality Management will lead us all to an organization with all staff mumbling "Have a nice day" to their customers, and where we develop mission statements before we determine where to have lunch. The *World Wide Web* will allow us to engage in *e-commerce,* that will give us a *Competitive Advantage,* although we're not sure how but our home page gets lots of hits.

Slogan Tips

The above is cynical; too cynical. But at times the industry is not cynical enough. We do a disservice to our organizations, ourselves, and our professions by embracing slogans and buzzwords too quickly, which are presented as having the ability to be a major contributor to our asset strategies, and leverage IT's ability to further organizational strategies. A couple of thoughts and guidelines should help preserve a balance between cynicism and a too-ready acceptance of fantasy.

There Are Pearls Behind each of these slogans are pearls of truth, insight, and advancement. The pearls may be wrapped with tons of nonsense, but they are there nonetheless.

---

[3] The following section originally appeared as Glaser, J. (1996). The Siren Call of the Slogan. *Healthcare Informatics,* July.

Internal Capabilities and Characteristics

There is utility to having applications portable over a range of hardware platforms and to have operating system standards, set by the market, that support a very rich diversity of applications.

There is utility to sharing processing demands between processors as can occur in a client server model.

The impact of the World Wide Web is actually quite profound.

Acknowledge that behind each slogan there are pearls. Do not dismiss the apparent slogan out of hand, but rather look for the pearls. Having found the pearls, determine whether the implementations of the pearls have done a nice job of encapsulating the essence of the insight.

You Must Be Able to Explain to Others Who May Not Really Care. In the process of identifying the pearls, you must keep in the back of your mind that you have to be able to explain what you find to others. These others are usually organization board members, senior management, and medical staff. A great test of our ability to explain is if you can present it to your spouse or significant other in five minutes so that they understand what you have said and have not lapsed into a coma.

As you construct your explanation you have to be able to cover the following areas.

- *The root or fundamental concepts behind the pearls.* For example, fundamental concepts behind total quality management are that we should focus on organizational processes, be able to describe and measure them, continuously try to make them better (where better is defined by the "customers" of that process), and measure whether our intended improvements have actually happened.
- *How the concepts and the specific implementations of these concepts will solve current problems or allow us to pursue new opportunities.* In other words, why should we care if we do it at all? For example, what issues confronting a provider organization will the World Wide Web or three-tiered architectures solve? The answer may be "not many of the important issues." This is a reasonable conclusion that would cause you to lose interest in the slogan.
- *Describe the major steps that appear to be required if the organization were to pursue these pearls and their implementations.* In other words, how do we get there? Be sure

that the implementation can be grasped and is viewed as tractable and manageable.
- *How to "sell" the ideas.* Why would people get excited by the idea and view the steps as a reasonable series of activities to undertake in order to pursue this direction? For example, can I envision how I would get the VP of Managed Care excited about the movement to object-oriented systems? Selling requires that you complete the three areas outlined above, and also requires that you understand your audience and what makes them tick.
- *Determine hurdles, barriers, and risks that will confront the organization as it pursues the pearls.* Failing is low on our list of things to do on any given day. The organization deserves an honest appraisal of hurdles, barriers, and risks so that it can judge whether the rewards are commensurate with the impending effort and possibility of failure. In addition to describing potential problems determine if there are strategies that can reduce their likelihood and severity.

Critical thinking is an essential component of moving from pearl identification to an effort, if warranted, to move the organization to adopt the new concepts. The thinking needs to be applied, often iteratively and with multiple contributors, in each of the above areas.

If you cannot explain it well, you should abandon the slogan. The problem may lie in the communication but the slogan may have real merit. It doesn't matter. You won't be able to get the organization to embrace the initiative.

You Are Not Alone   At times you may walk away from conferences or the reading of industry publications believing that you and your organization are the only people who have not adopted and implemented the slogan. Moreover, everyone appears to be brilliantly successful at implementing the slogan except *you*. They're so good at it that they never have to comb their hair and their organization's staff must come from Mars since they don't seem like they behave at all like *yours*.

Don't be deceived. This work is hard, full of problems, and everyone has failures and partial successes. You have lots of company. Learn from the successes of others and be pleased for them. Recognize that people tend to gloss over difficulties, they find it hard to talk about failures, and that slogan enthusiasm often clouds pragmatic judgment. Also recognize that conferences and publications can only carry a small percentage of the experiences of the industry as a whole and, since they thrive on news, tend to highlight people trying new ideas; conferences and publications are not always representative of what is globally going on.

Be Aware of the Slogan Curve Each of these slogans, and we'll have many more throughout our careers, has a "life cycle" or "hype cycle." Figure 3-9 presents the cycle curve developed by the GartnerGroup, which depicts various technologies at different stages of "slogan-ness." Conference hot topics and publication column inch reflect the coming and going of slogans. We should recognize that slogans and technologies have a curve.

In the beginning, some group realizes that for monetary, organizational, or academic reasons that they are onto something. Word spreads and enthusiasm sets in, usually to a degree that is unwarranted. Often the original idea and its value become transformed into something that sort of resembles the original idea but has accrued some magical properties along the way (e.g., the gap between slogans that sometimes surrounds relational database technology today and the original Codd and Date work on the relational calculus). At other times, the idea is sound but the implementations of it are neophytes, unshaped yet by the reality of use.

People, excited by the slogan, begin to try to implement the idea. Sometimes those who try have been thoughtful about why they are doing so. Sometimes they are not. As real experience begins to be accrued, the enthusiasm is replaced by a pragmatic understanding of the real value of the pearl and the challenges of implementing it. In addition, the developers of the technology, obtaining feedback for those who have adopted it, improve the technology, which leads to greater acceptance. Finally, a mature understanding of slogans, pearls, and their implementations begins.

One should realize that this curve exists. One should recognize that the following occurs.

- Original ideas can become twisted in the early stages, at times intentionally, at times due to poor understanding of the original idea, and at times because it isn't clear to anyone whether this is an idea that should flourish or gracefully disappear.
- Early enthusiasm is often unwarranted.
- Reality will set in.

FIGURE 3-9

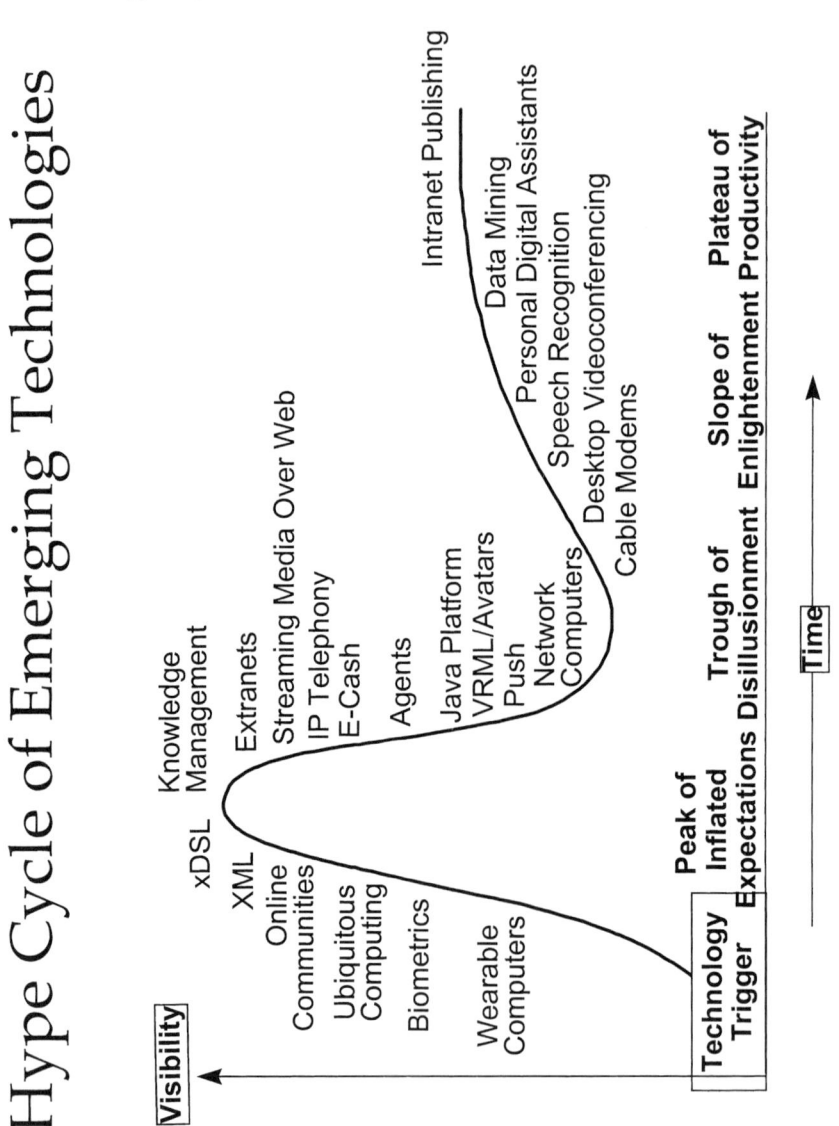

Technology Adoption Curve

Hype Cycle of Emerging Technologies

Visibility

- xDSL
- Knowledge Management
- XML
- Extranets
- Online Communities
- Streaming Media Over Web
- Ubiquitous Computing
- IP Telephony
- E-Cash
- Biometrics
- Agents
- Wearable Computers
- Java Platform
- VRML/Avatars
- Push
- Network Computers
- Intranet Publishing
- Data Mining
- Personal Digital Assistants
- Speech Recognition
- Desktop Videoconferencing
- Cable Modems

Technology Trigger | Peak of Inflated Expectations | Trough of Disillusionment | Slope of Enlightenment | Plateau of Productivity

Time

Source: Gartner.

- While one can be cynical during the early stages of this curve, one should also realize that there is likely to be real value accrued to the industry and its players. At the end of the curve, we are better off. Cynicism should not lead to unwarranted blanket rejection of the slogan since there are pearls, and the pearls will get implemented successfully by some set of people and organizations.

Surveys of Issues and IT Adoption

Surveys are regularly conducted on top IT issues in healthcare and across industries. Example cross industry surveys include those conducted by Computer Sciences Corporation (CSC) and the Society for Information Management/Management Information Research Center at the University of Minnesota. Examples of healthcare IT surveys include those conducted by the Healthcare Information and Management Systems Society (HIMSS) and Dorenfest Associates. Summary findings from the CSC and HIMSS surveys are presented and discussed below.

CSC Surveys

The CSC survey is designed to identify the top IT issues across a range of industries. The survey is highly regarded and widely quoted since it has a highly reputable methodology. For the 1997 survey, approximately 613 information executives from the world's largest companies from North America, Europe, and Asia/Pacific were surveyed. Table 3–1 presents the rankings of the top IT issues for the last 10 CSC surveys.

The responses, to the 1997 CSC survey, from healthcare IT executives are shown in Table 3–2. In this survey, healthcare includes providers, payors, pharmaceutical and healthcare supplier organizations.

HIMSS Surveys

The HIMSS survey results are widely reported in the healthcare IT industry. The survey data are gathered via computer-based questionnaires that are completed by attendees at the HIMSS annual conference.

Tables 3–3 through 3–6 contain the results for 1995 through 1998 to the HIMSS survey question, which asked the respondents to identify the two most important IT priorities for their organization. The choices of priorities are prepared by a panel of healthcare IT industry experts and vary from year to year.

TABLE 3–1
CSC Top IT Issue Surveys 1988–1997

Top IT Issues	97	96	95	94	93	92	91	90	89	88
Aligning IS and corporate goals	1	1	1	2	2	1	2	4	2	1
Organizing and utilizing data	2	2	3	3	4	4	5	7	6	7
Capitalizing on advances in IT	3	5	15	13	14	19	20	NR	17	NR
Using IT for competitive breakthroughs	3	4	13	15	15	14	12	8	1	4
Connecting to customers, suppliers, and/or partners electronically	5	7	7	16	16	20	15	19	NR	NR
Integrating systems	6	5	16	8	11	13	9	16	12	6
Improving the IS human resource	7	11	5	9	12	5	13	11	8	8
Creating an information architecture	8	9	8	5	7	3	8	9	5	5
Instituting cross-functional information systems	9	3	2	4	4	6	3	3	7	NR
Updating obsolete systems	10	8	9	7	8	18	NR	13	NR	18
Improving the systems development process	11	12	10	6	3	9	4	6	13	12
Cutting IS costs	13	13	11	18	18	16	14	2	3	3
Educating management on IT	14	10	4	1	1	2	1	1	11	NR

Source: Computer Sciences Corporation.

TABLE 3–2
Top IT Issues in 1997 from Healthcare Organizations

Top 10 Healthcare IT Issues	Percentage
Instituting cross-functional information systems	71.0
Aligning IS and corporate goals	64.5
Educating management on IT	64.5
Organizing and utilizing data	64.5
Capitalizing on advances in IT	61.3
Integrating systems	61.3
Creating an information architecture	58.1
Implementing business reengineering	51.6
Using IT for competitive breakthroughs	51.6
Connecting to customers, suppliers, and/or partners electronically	45.2

Source: Computer Sciences Corporation.

TABLE 3-3

HIMSS/HP 1995 Leadership Survey

IS Issues	#1 IS Priority	#2 IS Priority
Integrating systems across separate facilities	33%	16%
Implementing a computer-based patient record (CPR)	20%	18%
Reengineering to a patient-centered computing environment	10%	12%
Incorporating wireless/portable devices	1%	3%
Increasing use of technology among clinicians	6%	12%
Complying with JCAHO IM Standard	2%	2%
Upgrading network infrastructure	13%	14%
Upgrading application software	8%	8%
Integrating disparate departmental systems	6%	12%

Source: Healthcare Information and Management Systems Society.

TABLE 3-4

HIMSS/HP 1996 Leadership Survey

IS Issues	#1 IS Priority	#2 IS Priority
Upgrade IT infrastructure	32%	16%
Migrate to client-server systems	11%	17%
Integrate systems in a multivendor environment	27%	28%
Reengineering to a patient-centered computing environment	23%	21%
Outsource IT services	2%	3%
Mobile access for caregivers	3%	9%

Source: Healthcare Information and Management Systems Society.

Survey Lessons and Conclusions

Surveys, such as the above, are interesting and can even be useful. However, one should always be careful with the use of "normative" survey results or industry data.

The average experiences or sense of priorities are not necessarily the experiences and priorities of an individual organization. Being different is not equivalent to being inferior or superior, or wrong or right. Nor is being average an indication of being right.

TABLE 3-5

HIMSS/HP 1997 Leadership Survey

IS Issues	#1 IS Priority	#2 IS Priority
Upgrade IT infrastructure	28%	15%
Migrate to client-server systems	7%	10%
Integrate systems in a multi-vendor environment	25%	24%
Reengineering to a patient-centered computing environment	17%	17%
Outsource IT services	2%	1%
Mobile access for caregivers	4%	7%
Implement an Internet strategy	5%	8%
Develop an Intranet	5%	11%

Source: Healthcare Information and Management Systems Society.

TABLE 3-6

HIMSS/IBM 1998 Leadership Survey

IS Issues	Top Two IS Priorities
Recruit and retain high quality IT staff	17%
Integrate systems in a multi-vendor environment	15%
Implement a computer-based patient record	12%
Implement a Year 2000 conversion	11%
Implement clinical decision support tools	9%
Implement a data warehouse capability	6%
Implement an IT strategic plan	5%
Implement an intranet	4%
Enhance mobile or wireless access for caregivers	4%
Create or expand a Web site	2%
Outsource IT services	2%

Source: Healthcare Information and Management Systems Society.

Methodological Limitations Survey readers are often unaware of survey methodological weaknesses or approaches. The HIMSS survey captures data from a set of individuals who attend the HIMSS annual conference. While generally over 50% of the HIMSS respondents are senior IT managers, a large percentage are not. Hence the survey cannot claim to be based on a representative sample of healthcare IT leadership. The

Dorenfest 1998 Market Leaders Report survey (Anderson, 1998) of healthcare application adoption by 1,500 IDS noted that two-thirds of the surveyed IDS have one hospital. Hence if one is from a multi-hospital IDS, one should be wary of inferring that the application adoption percentages from the Dorenfest survey accurately capture the adoption by one's peers. Implementing a master person index in a single hospital IDS is a very different challenge than implementing one in a multi-hospital IDS.

Persistent Issues In the CSC survey, there are four issues that consistently appear in the top ten: aligning IS and corporate goals, organizing and utilizing data, creating an information architecture, and instituting cross-functional systems.

The consistent ranking of the alignment of IT in the top four issues reflects its obvious importance. This ranking also reflects the difficulty that organizations encounter in effecting this alignment. (Chapter 2 discusses the alignment problem in more detail.) If the alignment challenge had been solved (i.e., we knew how to do it in a quasi-mechanical fashion that represented a modest but known challenge), this issue would not continuously carry this high of a ranking. This alignment is hard and exceptionally difficult to effect well. It may always be so.

The organizing and utilizing of data reflect the importance of this component of the IT asset and the competitive role that data can play. The ranking of instituting cross-functional information systems depicts the importance of organizational processes both as a source of advantage and organizational efficiency. The ranking of information architecture, which leverages data and cross-functional systems, also highlights the contribution of the technical architecture component of the IT asset.

We see, in the CSC survey results, the core of the discussions in Chapters 2 and 3: the persistent focus on alignment and advancing the organization's competitive position and the improvement of the IT asset.

Healthcare IT Immaturity The CSC rankings by healthcare organizations of top IT issues provide some evidence of the IT strategic immaturity of healthcare. Immaturity can be crudely gauged by looking at those issues whose 1997 rank differs by five or more when healthcare is compared to the overall survey results.

Educating management on IT (3 in healthcare, 14 overall) indicates that the senior leadership in healthcare is less conversant, knowledgeable, and comfortable with IT topics than their counterparts in other industries.

If the leadership is not comfortable in this area it will be difficult for them to view IT as a critical strategic contributor.

Using IT for competitive breakthroughs (9 in healthcare, 4 overall) reflects a healthcare view of diminished IT contribution to organizational strategy. This ranking is likely to be related to the ranking on management education.

Connecting to customers, suppliers, and/or partners electronically (10 in healthcare, 4 overall) indicates embryonic healthcare understanding of the efficiencies that can be gained through provider/payor linkages and provider to provider linkages as required to support affiliations.

Emergent and Transient Issues Some issues would seem to be "permanent" (i.e., their rank, while changing, changes within a reasonably narrow boundary). Aligning IS and corporate goals and utilizing data are examples of permanent issues. Other issues appear to be emergent.

Connecting to customers, suppliers, and/or partners is an issue that is emerging, rising from a rank of 20 in 1992 to a rank of 5 in 1997. This issue's emergence is likely due to the rising interest in the use of the Internet as a means to connect and the well-publicized examples of effective use of the Internet to link to customers (e.g., Dell.com, Amazon.com, and Yahoo.com). The ascendance of the Internet has led to a resurgence in interest in using IT as a competitive weapon (issue 4) as it offers a new vehicle for competition. And it would appear that the Internet has sparked a renewed interest in capitalizing on advances in IT.

When data from surveys, such as CSC's, note a trend up or down in ranking, where such a trend leads to rank changes greater than 5 over the course of several years, then an organization would be prudent to ask what is going on. Something is being detected by enough organizations that the phenomenon bears some examination. One should be careful. A rise in an issue is not always an indicator that the issue has merit; it could be a fad as discussed earlier. Nor should the decline in ranking indicate that the issue has become irrelevant (e.g., the decline in cutting IS costs to a rank of 13 in 1997 from a rank of 2 in 1990). Surveys also pick up trends late (i.e., a significant move in rank indicates that a large number of organizations are pursuing the issue or idea).

The HIMSS survey captures more transient issues (i.e., issues that rise and fall rapidly in rank). To a very large degree this reflects the process whereby the HIMSS survey is constructed. HIMSS is a trade organization and the survey is conducted at a trade show. Hence the survey is directed toward hot topics; the type of topics that draw people to the exhibit floor or create overflow crowds at a presentation. Hot topics tend to be laden with buzzwords and buzzwords tend to have very short lives.

Client server as an issue lasted two years (1996 and 1997). Implementing a computer-based patient record emerged in 1995, disappeared and then reemerged in 1998. Recruiting and retaining a high quality IT staff surfaced in 1998. This apparent transient nature can be false. For example, if an organization is committed to implementing the computer-based record then it will find that this implementation is a major issue for many years. Implementing the computer-based record is complicated, hard, and takes many years to accomplish.

In fairness, not all of the HIMSS issues are transient. Integrating systems in a multi-vendor environment, upgrading the IT infrastructure, and reengineering to a patient-centered computing environment were consistently reported as issues. Moreover, the list of issues that one could choose changed from year to year and hence their persistence cannot always be determined.

Survey Summary

Survey results are often reported widely in the trade press and repackaged for presentation for internal IT discussions. Surveys do influence IT strategy and asset discussions and decisions.

Surveys can provide useful information. However, organizations should be aware of their limitations.

- *The survey data collection methodologies can have characteristics that make their representativeness limited.* The sample may not be comprised of decision makers or like types of individuals. Surveys can combine different types of organizations together, which blurs the relevance of the data to a particular type. And survey construction may be less interested in trends and more interested in how hot are certain topics.
- *Surveys can show trends but they are late in detecting trends.* In addition, the reascendance of a trend may also be for very different reasons than those that gave the issue an initial high rank (e.g., the high ranking of IT as a competitive weapon in the 1989 CSC survey was likely due to the industry discussion of the giant killer application while the high ranking in 1997 is likely due to the Internet).

- *Trends reflect the average* and the average experience may not be relevant to a specific organization.

IT-CENTRIC ORGANIZATIONAL ATTRIBUTES

Several studies have examined organizations that have been particularly effective in the use of IT. Determining effectiveness is difficult and the studies have defined it differently. Definitions have included organizations that have developed information systems that defined an industry (e.g., the SABRE system), organizations that have reputations for being effective, and organizations that have had instances of exceptional IT innovation.

These studies have attempted to identify those factors or attributes of these organizations that have led to or created the environment in which effectiveness has occurred. In effect, the studies have sought to answer the question "What are the organizational factors that result in some organizations developing truly remarkable IT capabilities?"

If an organization understands these attributes and desires to be very effective in its use of IT, then it is in a position to develop strategies to create or modify its attributes. For example, one attribute is the strength of the working relationships between the IS function and the rest of the organization. If that relationship in an organization is weak or dysfunctional, strategies and plans can be created to improve the relationship.

Summaries of these studies are discussed below.

Financial Executives Research Foundation

The Financial Executives Research Foundation sponsored a study, conducted by Sambamurthy and Zmud (1996), on factors that led to the development of visionary IT applications. Visionary applications are

> applications that help managers make decisions, introduce new products and services more quickly and frequently, improve customer relations, and enhance the manufacturing process. Visionary IT applications seek to transform some of a firm's business processes in 'framebreaking' ways. These applications create a variety of benefits to businesses that not only affect their current operations but also provide opportunities for new markets, strategies and relationships.

The study had several findings.

The nature of visionary applications. Visionary applications focused on leveraging core business operations, enhancing decision making, improving customer service, and/or speeding up the ability to deliver new products and services. These applications were "platforms" that enabled the business to handle multiple work processes. An example of such a "platform" in healthcare is the computerized medical record.

Roles associated with the justification process. Visionary projects required the participation of four key players. Envisioners conceptualized the initial ideas for a project. Project champions were instrumental in selling the envisioner's ideas and value to senior executives. Executive sponsors provided champions with seed funding and political support. IT experts supplied the necessary technical vision and expertise to ensure that the idea would work.

Facilitating investment in visionary IT applications. Several factors facilitate investment in visionary applications.

- A climate must exist that enables employees to have the power, and support, to undertake visionary applications, which often carry significant personal and organizational risk.
- Mechanisms need to exist to invest, continuously, in IT technical infrastructures.
- Coordinating mechanisms must be established to bring together envisioners, project champions, executive sponsors, and IT experts.
- The role of the CIO, in addition to that of an envisioner and IT expert, was to ensure that the envisioner's proposal furthered the interests of the business, architect, and advocate for the corporate IT technical infrastructure and serve as the architect of IT-related coordinating mechanisms.

Rationale for justifying visionary IT applications. Visionary IT applications were generally defended using two distinct strategies: their contribution to critical work processes or their support of a primary strategic driver. In addition to the discussion and analyses that would surround one of these two strategies, prototypes, best practice visitations, and consultants would often be used to further organizational understanding of the proposed initiative.

Ross, Beath, and Goodhue

Ross, Beath, and Goodhue (1996) examined those factors that enable organizations to achieve long-term competitiveness in the application of IT.

They identified the development and management of three key IT assets as being critical to achieving a sustained IT-based competitive advantage.

Highly competent IT human resource. A well-developed IT human resource asset is one that "consistently solves business problems and addresses business opportunities through information technology." This asset has three dimensions.

1. IT staff had the technical skills needed to craft and support applications and infrastructures and to understand and appropriately apply new technologies.
2. IT staff had superior working relationships with the end-user community and were effective at furthering their (the IT staff's) understanding of the business, it's directions, cultures, work processes, and politics.
3. IT staff were responsible, and knew that they were responsible, for solving business problems. This orientation goes beyond performing discreet tasks and leads IT staff to believe that they "own," and have the power to carry out that ownership, the challenge of solving business problems.

The technology asset. The technology asset consists of "sharable technical platforms and databases." The technology asset had two distinguishing characteristics.

1. A well-developed technology architecture that defined the rules for the distribution of hardware, software, and support.
2. Standards that limit the technologies that will be supported.

Failure to create a robust architecture can result in applications that are difficult to change, not integrated, expensive to manage, and unable to scale (Weill and Broadbent, 1998). These limitations hinder the ability of the organization to advance. IT resources, efforts and capital can be consumed by the difficulty of managing the current base of infrastructure and applications, and relatively modest advances can be too draining.

The relationship asset. When the relationship asset is strong, IT and the business unit management share the risk and responsibility for effective application of IT in the organization. A sold relationship asset is present when the business unit is the owner, and is accountable for, all IT projects, and top management leads the IT priority setting process.

The study noted the interrelationships between the assets. IT and user relationships are strengthened by the presence of a strong IT staff.

A well-developed, agile infrastructure enables the IT staff to execute project delivery at high levels and be more effective at solving business problems.

McKenney, Copeland, and Goodhue

McKenney, Copeland, and Goodhue (1995) studied those factors that resulted in successful managerial teams creating and implementing innovative information systems. They were particularly interested in those examples where the resulting information systems became the dominant design in a particular industry. They studied American Airlines, Bank of America, United States Automobile Association, Baxter Travenol/American Hospital Association and Frito-Lay.

Their study generated several conclusions.

Management team. All IT innovations were led proactively by a management team driven to change its processes through the means of information technology. The management team had to have three essential roles.

1. The CEO or other senior executive who was both visionary and a good businessmen. This person had sufficient power and prestige to drive technological innovation.
2. The Technology Maestro, often the CIO, who had a remarkable combination of business acumen and technological competence. The CIO must deliver the system and they must recruit, energize, and lead a superb technical team.
3. The Technical Team who understood how to apply the technology in innovative ways and were capable of developing new business processes that leverage the technology.

In addition to exceptional competence in each role, there was a rare chemistry between the players in the roles. A change in a role's incumbent often stalled the innovation. This suggests that a great CIO in one setting may not be a great CIO in another setting.

Evolution of the innovation. The innovative systems evolved over time and generally went through several phases of evolution.

- A business crisis develops (e.g., Bank America being overwhelmed by the volume of paper transactions), and a search begins for an IT solution.

- IT competence is built as necessary research and development is done of potential IT solutions, particularly the application of new technology.
- The IT solution is planned and developed.
- IT is used to restructure the organization and processes and to lead changes in organization strategies.
- The strategy evolves and the systems are refined. Competitors begin to emulate the success.

In these phases, the capabilities of the technology heavily influenced and constrained the operational changes that were envisioned and implemented.

This series of phases occurs over the course of five to seven years, reflecting the magnitude of the organizational change and the time required to experiment with, understand, and implement, at scale, new information technology. This interval suggests that CIO (or CEO) average tenures of three years or less risk hindering the organization's ability to make truly innovative IT-based transformations.

Capitalizing on IT innovation. A particular IT innovation was identified by the organization, early in the life of the technology, as being the breakthrough necessary to resolve the business crisis or challenge. Across the cases studied, the breakthrough was the transistor, time sharing, and cheap mass storage. Today the technology might be the World Wide Web or natural language processing.

Weill and Broadbent (1998)

Weill and Broadbent (1998) studied firms that "consistently achieve more business value for their information technology investment." Their study noted that these organizations were excellent or above average in five characteristics.

More top management commitment to information technology. The leadership of the organization was committed to the strategic and effective application of IT. This commitment was widely known within the organization. The management participated actively in IT strategy discussions, thoughtfully assessed the business contribution of proposed IT investments, and provided seed funding to innovative and experimental IT projects.

Less political turbulence. IT investments often serve to integrate processes and groups across the organization. Political conflict reduces the likelihood and success of interdisciplinary initiatives. IT investments can require that the proposals of one part of the organization be funded at the expense of other parts or other proposed non-IT initiatives. Political turbulence can reduce the likelihood that such "disproportionate" investments will occur.

More satisfied users. If the organization's staff have had good experiences with IT projects, they are more likely to view IT as something that can assist their endeavors rather than a burden or a function that serves as an organizational boat anchor.

Integrated business information technology planning. Organizations that do a very good job at aligning the IT plans and strategies with the overall organizational plans and strategies will be more effective with IT than those that do not align well. This statement is almost rhetorical since the effectiveness of IT will be assessed in terms of how well it supports the organization.

More experience. Organizations that are experienced in their use and application of the technology, and have had success in those experiences, will be more thoughtful and focused in their continued application of IT. They will have a better understanding of the technology's capabilities and limitations. They and their IT colleagues will have a better understanding of their respective needs and roles and the most effective ways of working together on initiatives.

Summary of Studies

The studies discussed in the preceding pages suggest that organizations that aspire to effectiveness and innovation in their application of IT must take steps to ensure that the core capacity of the organization is developed such that high levels of, and sustained progress can be achieved. The development of this capacity is a different challenge than identifying specific opportunities to use IT in the course of improving core processes or ensuring that the IT agenda is aligned with the organizational agenda. As an analogy, the development of core capacity is akin to a runner's training, injury management, and diet, which are designed to ensure the core capacity to run a marathon. This capacity development is different from the discussion of the strategy of running a specific marathon which must consider the nature of the course, the competing runners and the weather.

While having somewhat different conclusions (to a degree resulting from different study questions) the four studies have much in common regarding capacity development:

Individuals and leadership matter. It is critical that the organization possess talented, skilled, and experienced individuals. These individuals will occupy a variety of roles: CEO, CIO, IT staff and user middle management. These individuals must be strong contributors. While such an observation may seem trite, too often organizations, dazzled by the technology or the glorified experiences of others, embark upon technology crusades and substantive investments for which they have insufficient talent or leadership to effect well.

Leadership, in these studies, was essential. This leadership is needed on the part of organizational senior management (or executive sponsors), the CIO, and the project team. This leadership understood the vision, communicated the vision, was able to recruit and motivate a team, and had the staying power to see the innovation through several years of work and disappointments, setbacks, and political problems along the way.

Relationships are critical. In addition to strong individual players, the team must be strong. There are critical senior executive, IT executive, and project team roles that must be filled by highly competent individuals, *and* great chemistry must exist between the individuals in the distinct roles. Substituting team members, while perhaps involving a replacement by an equally strong individual, can diminish the team. This is true in IT innovation just as it is true in sports. Political turbulence diminished the ability to develop a healthy set of relationships between organizational players.

The technology and technical infrastructure enables and hinders. New technologies can provide new opportunities for organizations to embark upon major transformations of their activities. This implies that, while CIOs must have superior business and clinical understanding, they must also have superior understanding of the technology. This should not imply that they can rewrite operating systems as well as the best system programmers, but it does mean that they must have superior understanding of the maturity, capabilities, and possible evolutions of information technology. Several innovations occurred because the IT group was able to identify, and adopt, an emerging technology that could make a significant contribution to addressing a current organizational challenge.

The studies stress the importance of well architected technology. Great architecture matters. Possessing state of the art technology can be far less important than a well architected technology.

The significance of the technology also implies that healthcare organizations will need an IS function that defines and manages the architecture, engages in identifying new promising technologies, experiments with the technologies, and works with the organization to help it understand the potential contribution (or lack thereof) of embryonic technologies to the plans and activities of the organization.

The organization must encourage innovation. The organization's (and the IT organization's) culture and leadership must encourage innovation and experimentation. This encouragement needs to be practical and goal directed; there must be a real business problem, crisis, or opportunity and the project needs budgets, political protection and deliverables.

True innovation takes time. Creating visionary applications or industry dominant designs or an exceptional IT asset takes time and a lot of work. The organizations studied by McKenney often took five to seven years for the technology to fully mature and the organization to recast itself. The applications and designs will proceed through normative phases, which are as normative as the passage from being a child to being an adult. Innovation, like the maturation of a human being, will see some variation in the timing, depth, and success at moving through phases.

Evaluation of IT opportunities must be thoughtful. The visionary and dominant design IT innovations studied were analyzed and studied thoroughly. Nonetheless, the organizations engaged in these innovations understood that a large element of vision, management instinct, and "feel" guided the decision to initiate investment and continue. An organization that has had more experience with IT and more successful experiences will be more effective in the evaluation (and execution) of IT initiatives.

Processes, data, and differentiation formed the basis of the innovation. All of these examples were based on fundamental understanding of current limitations of the organization. Innovations were directed to focus on those core elements, discussed in Chapter 2, as being the basis for achieving an IT-based advantage: significant leveraging of processes, expanding and capitalizing on the ability to gather critical data, and achieving a high level of organizational differentiation. Often an organization pursued all three simultaneously. At times the organization evolved from one basis to another as the competition responded and/or it saw new leverage points.

Alignment was mature and strong. The alignment of the IT activities and the business challenges or opportunities was strong. It was also mature in the sense that this alignment depended on close working relationships rather than methodologies.

The IT asset was critical. Strong IT staff, well-designed IT governance, well-crafted architecture, and a superb CIO were critical attributes.

SUMMARY

Chapter 2 was concerned with strategy formulation. We discussed the process of aligning organizational strategies with IT initiatives and lessons learned from decades of experiences, across a range of industries, in the application of IT to improve the competitive position of the organization. In this chapter we were concerned with the implementation aspect of strategy. The chapter developed these summary observations and conclusions.

- Organizations need to develop robust, efficient, and effective IT assets. These assets have characteristics and strategies and plans are needed to ensure that the asset is healthy and evolves appropriately. Ignoring the asset, or undermanaging and underfunding it, weakens the ability of the organization to effect its strategic IT plans.
- Organizations should be careful of fads, slogans, and surveys that can mislead as often as they provide insight. These sources of information should not unduly influence decisions regarding strategies and changes in assets. Nor should organizations be overly cynical about what can appear to be shallowness in these sources of information.
- Several studies of IT effectiveness have identified a relatively small number of IT-centric organizational attributes that have a significant influence on effectiveness. These attributes bring together much of what has been discussed in Chapters 2 and 3.
- Effective means to develop IT and organizational alignment
- A focus on organizational processes, data, and differentiation
- A strong IT asset
- Thoughtful means to evaluate proposed initiatives

And added factors such as the following.

- IT and organizational relationships
- Senior leadership
- Organizational experience and satisfaction in working with IT

In the next chapter, we discuss several examples, drawn from the experiences and plans of Partners HealthCare System, of the strategic application of information technology in healthcare. These examples will depict the alignment of organizational strategies to IT plans and the development of the related IT asset. Chapter 4 will also discuss the ideas of "foundational concepts" and "strategic views."

REFERENCES

Anderson, H. (1998). 1998 Market Leaders Report *Health Data Management,* June.

Bazzoli, F. (1998). Justifying Where the Dollars Go. *Health Data Management,* February.

Bresnahan, J. (1998). What Good is Technology?" *CIO Enterprise,* July 15.

CHIME. (1998). *The Healthcare CIO: A Decade of Growth.* Ann Arbor, MI: College of Healthcare Information Management Executives.

Computer Sciences Corporation. (1997). *Critical Issues of Information Systems Management, 10th Annual Survey of IS Management Issues.* El Segundo, Calif.

Dempsey, J. et al. (1998). A Hard and Soft Look at IT Investments. *McKinsey Quarterly* (1):126–137.

Drazen, E., Staisor, D. (1995). Information Support in an Integrated Delivery System. *Proceedings of the 1995 Annual HIMSS Conference.* Chicago: Healthcare Information and Management Systems Society, V2:191–199.

Drazen, E., Metzger, J. (1998). *Strategies for Integrated Health Care.* San Francisco: Jossey-Bass.

Earl, M.J. (1993). Experiences in Strategic Information Systems Planning. *MIS Quarterly* 17(1):1–24, March.

Earl, M., Feeney, D. (1995). Is Your CIO Adding Value? *McKinsey Quarterly* (2):144–161.

Feeney, D., Willcocks, L. (1998). Core IS Capabilities for Exploiting Information Technology. *Sloan Management Review* 39(3):9–21, Spring.

Freedman, D. (1993). Where Are We Now? *CIO Magazine,* January.

GartnerGroup. (1998). Defining a Flexible IT Architecture. GartnerGroup Management Strategies and Directions Research Note. SPA-03-3708, April.

GartnerGroup Research notes SPA-TECH-050, KA-04-5517, QA-03-4925, TU-TECH-051, SPA-TECH-052. *CHIME Connection,* September, 1998.

Glaser, J. (1991). Managing the Management of Information Systems. *Healthcare Executive,* Jan/Feb.

Glaser, J. (1996). The Siren Call of the Slogan. *Healthcare Informatics,* July.

Glaser, J. (1997). Beware 'Return on Investment' *Healthcare Informatics,* June.

Glaser, J., Williams-Ashman, A. (1990). Keeping the Database Healthy. *Information Week,* June 25.

Healthcare Information and Management Systems Society. (1995). *Healthcare Information and Management Systems Society and Hewlett-Packard Leadership Survey*, February 12–16.

Healthcare Information and Management Systems Society. (1996). *Healthcare Information and Management Systems Society and Hewlett-Packard Leadership Survey*, March 3–7.

Healthcare Information and Management Systems Society. (1997). *Healthcare Information and Management Systems Society and Hewlett-Packard Leadership Survey*, February 16–20.

Healthcare Information and Management Systems Society. (1998). *Healthcare Information and Management Systems Society and IBM Leadership Survey*, February 22–26.

Keen, P. (1997). *The Process Edge*. Boston, MA: Harvard Business School Press.

Kilbridge, P. et al. (1998). Information Systems for IDNs: Best Practices and Key Success Factors. *Proceedings of the 1998 Annual HIMSS Conference*. Chicago: Healthcare Information and Management Systems Society, V2:229–241.

King, J. (1997). IS Labor Drought Will Last Past 2003. *Computerworld,* June 30.

Lacity, M., Willcocks, L. (1998). An Empirical Investigation of Information Technology Sourcing Practices: Lessons From Experience. *MIS Quarterly* 22(3):363–408, September.

Levitin, A., Redman, T. (1998). Data as a Resource: Properties, Implications, and Prescriptions. *Sloan Management Review* 40(1):89–101, Fall.

Marietti, C. (1998). Bullet-Proof Warehouses. *Healthcare Informatics,* September.

McKenney, J., Copeland, D., Mason, R. (1995). *Waves of Change: Business Evolution Through Information Technology.* Boston, MA: Harvard Business School Press.

Quinn, J.B. et al. (1994). *Information Technology in the Service Society.* Washington, D.C.: National Academy Press.

Ross, J., Beath, C., Goodhue, D. (1996). Develop Long-Term Competitiveness through IT Assets. *Sloan Management Review* 38(1):31–42, Fall.

Sambamurthy, V., Zmud, R. (1996). *Information Technology and Innovation: Strategies for Success.* Morristown, NJ: Financial Executives Research Foundation.

Scheier, R. (1997). 15 Ways to Keep Your People. *Computerworld,* September 8.

Strassman, P. (1990). *The Business Value of Computers.* New Canaan, CT: The Information Economics Press.

Strassman, P. (1997). *The Squandered Computer.* New Canaan, CT: The Information Economics Press.

Weill, P., Broadbent, M. (1995). *Leveraging the New Infrastructure.* Boston: Harvard Business School Press.

Wible, S. (1997). Reeling in the Keepers. *Healthcare Informatics,* October.

CHAPTER 4

Examples of IT Strategy

In this chapter we focus on the development of the concepts, ideas and definitions that govern how we view a particular IT challenge or opportunity. The importance of foundational concepts and "view" can be found in all aspects of our lives and the ramifications of different views are significant.

- One can view the Bible as literal, allegorical, or something that one doesn't think about at all.
- One can view the role of the federal government to be protection of shores and individual freedoms, or to compensate and overcome injustice and deficiencies in the free market
- One can view an individual's destiny as being heavily influenced by the environment and genes, largely determined by the choices made in life, or preordained by larger forces in the universe.
- One can view the goal of a college education to be the preparation for a job, the garnering of knowledge of one's society and civilization, or an opportunity for a prolonged party.

There is no one formula or cookbook for arriving at a strategic view. The strategic planning frameworks discussed in Chapter 2 begin with a strategic view (e.g., the value chain and the competitive forces are different views of the world to be used as the basis for strategy). This chapter will not attempt to present a methodology for view development. Views emerge from complex and not well-understood phenomena involving insight, discussions between members of the organization's leadership, examination of the strategic efforts of others, an organization's successes and failures (and the reasons it assigns for success and failure), and the organizational values and history that form the basis for judging views. Despite the lack of methodology in this chapter, the basis for view formation is a small number of questions. The questions are often easy to state. Developing thoughtful and insightful answers is much more difficult. Nonetheless, forming such views is critical. This chapter, through its discussion, presents some of the basic questions and, for three areas, answers them in an attempt to show what such views "look like."

We will discuss the areas of clinical information systems, integration and the World Wide Web (WWW). In the course of this discussion, we will focus on the definitions of the core concepts and ideas that form the view of these areas developed at Partners HealthCare System. This discussion will also, as appropriate, bring together the concepts and ideas of strategy discussed in the previous chapters.

- The alignment of IT plans with organizational strategies and plans
- The creation and modification of IT-centric capabilities and characteristics and the IT asset

Each of the three areas (clinical systems, integration, and the WWW) starts from a very different premise or basic presentation of the problem or opportunity.

- Clinical information systems are an IT response directed to improving the essential capability of the provider organization: the provision of medical care. As such, clinical information systems are an example of a set of IT activities that are directly derivable from organizational strategies, plans, and competitive activities.
- The integration of very heterogeneous applications and technologies is the fundamental technical challenge confronting the IDS. Integration generally doesn't result from a single aspect of IDS strategy. Rather it is a necessary IT asset characteristic to support, as a foundation, a significant set of strategies of the IDS.

- The WWW, unlike clinical information systems and integration, does not fall naturally from IDS strategies. It is hard to imagine an IDS strategic discussion concluding that "We need a thing like the WWW if this core initiative is to succeed." Nor is the utility of the WWW as a component of the organization's IT asset well understood. An organization can develop a home page and publish policies on an Intranet but those activities, while good ideas, seem to be a pale utilization of the WWW. Rather the WWW is fundamentally a profound social technology. The technology of the WWW is not nearly as remarkable as its likely impact on society. In this case the IDS challenge is to understand the role of this technology: to determine which strategies and organizational activities the technology can leverage, if any. The WWW is an example of a technology looking for a strategic fit.

CLINICAL INFORMATION SYSTEMS

There is a portion of the conversation that links IT initiatives to overall strategic initiatives and plans that is conceptually straightforward. For example, if the organization intends to manage physician practices then there is a need for application systems that support the related administrative operations of billing and scheduling. If the organization intends to improve its abilities to measure the quality of its care, then there is a need for appropriate databases and analytical tools. While the mapping of strategy to IT response may be clear, the implementation of the response may be quite complex and difficult. Moreover, it may not be clear from the linkage statement which capabilities of the application system are the critical capabilities.

There can be a portion of the conversation that can be more profound. The strategy implies (or is explicit about) deep changes in the organization and significant changes in the nature of the application systems. For example, an HMO moving from a staff model, where physicians are salaried, to a model where its physicians are paid for performance will undergo deep change. The application systems needed to support performance measurement are also likely to represent a significant change in the application portfolio and the data of the HMO. The implementation will be difficult because of these factors and the extensive changes in the professional reward system.

Several questions should be asked as the organization examines its strategies and the linkage to IT activities.

Does the strategy imply that there are new and significant concepts that govern how we organize, practice, incent, or structure the work? There are many examples of strategies that would provide an answer of "yes."

- An effort to decentralize decision making at a provider organization with a national presence
- A strategy to aggressively pursue capitated business and assume as much delegation as possible
- An effort to move as many patients as possible to protocol-driven care
- A strategy to develop a continuum of care

What are the underlying concepts behind these strategies?

- An effort to assume a significant amount of delegation, for a majority of patients that a provider organization sees, can represent the concept that the provider organization will engage in the full spectrum of medical management believing that it can do it better and for less money than managed care organizations and improve its leverage over managed care organizations.
- The development of a continuum of care can represent a concept that purchasers of care will want to deal with one organization for all of their care needs and that the provider will be able to rationalize care across the continuum leading to cost reductions and service and care quality improvements.

Does the IT response represent new concepts for applications, architecture, or any other part of the asset? What are the concepts?

- A continuum of care, if it involves linking a wide range of diverse clinical information systems, may require that the concepts and techniques behind the integration of systems become far more robust and diverse.
- The movement to protocol-driven care may require that clinical information systems and clinical support systems like scheduling, have deep and powerful capabilities to add and integrate

algorithms, complex logic checks, and pathway development into existing applications.

Applications that are based on new concepts are inherently risky to implement. What are the risk factors that will accompany the IT response and what strategies and steps are available to overcome the risks? The risks may not involve the information systems group or the technology (e.g., a provider organization assuming capitation may have its greatest risk in the HMO competitive response or the organization getting into a line of business for which it has little experience). The information systems group or the technology may be the focal point of risk (e.g., can today's integration technologies provide adequate integration between heterogeneous platforms and applications?).

In the duration of this section we will focus on clinical information systems. These systems are an example of an application portfolio and agenda that can be derived directly from the organization's strategies. They are also an example of an area where there is often significant change in the underlying concepts of both the business and the applications and hence organizational and IT risk is involved. In this section, the approach to care improvement undertaken by Brigham and Women's Hospital (BWH) and now Partners Healthcare System, Inc. (PHS) is discussed.

The discussion will proceed along the following steps.

- A review of the underlying concepts that guide efforts to improve care
- A presentation of the related core IT concepts
- A discussion of the major sources of complexity that confront the application of IT to care improvement
- An examination of BWH efforts to reduce adverse drug events and unnecessary utilization of medications, procedures, and tests. This examination discusses changes in the IT asset that resulted from these efforts and major implementation challenges
- A discussion of PHS efforts to deliver clinical information systems to support a continuum of care. These efforts include additional asset changes and raise an additional set of challenges

Underlying Core Business Concepts and Views

Healthcare providers face several significant cost, quality and access pressures on their care delivery. To meet these pressures they must, with increasing sophistication and effectiveness, do the following.

- Measure and report the quality of care outcomes and processes
- Identify and manage "optimal" medical care processes
- Streamline or redesign care-related operations
- Reduce the cost per unit of care, per encounter, and per covered life
- Improve customer satisfaction

In their efforts to respond to these pressures, the organization may realize that there are two major concepts that will guide the response to these pressures. These concepts, which must be defined and implemented, follow.

- An increased emphasis on organizational clinical management of care. Care processes and outcomes can be measured, best practices defined and implemented, and conformance to these practices monitored. These practices can be applied, by the organization, to specific care acts (e.g., encouraging providers to use cheaper, therapeutically equivalent medications). The practices can be applied to an encounter, e.g., a clinical pathway for a coronary arterial bypass graft surgery. And the practices can be applied to care that spans encounters (e.g., guidelines for the treatment of hypertension).
- Care should be viewed as a process: a series of interdependent tasks and activities performed by a diverse set of healthcare professionals and the patient. The processes can be analyzed, measured, and reengineered. These processes span providers, departments, organizations, and time. The view of care as a process is different than the view of care in terms of discrete knowledge domains (e.g., oncology), or in terms of departments and roles (e.g., nursing or the clinical laboratories).

IT Application Concepts

The focus of clinical information systems should be the support of organizational efforts to implement its definition of these two approaches.

Clinical information systems are those application systems used by providers to support the immediate provision of care. Example systems include the computerized patient record, provider order entry, and databases that are used to measure care quality.

Drawing from the pressures and the approaches presented above, three major goals for clinical information systems can be stated.

1. Improve the efficiency and effectiveness of care-centric processes. Example processes include accessing data about a patient, ordering something, and referring a patient. Information systems should enable these processes to be less error prone, less expensive, faster, and more convenient.

2. Improve provider and patient decision making. In their efforts to implement best care practices, organizations would like to ensure that, as decisions are made, the most appropriate decision is made. These decisions can range from ordering the most appropriate radiology modality given the clinical question, to defining the right care activities on postoperative day two for a specific procedure, to the best diet for someone with high cholesterol. At times the objective is to prevent an adverse decision (e.g., the ordering of a medication to which the patient is allergic). If the organization has no position on the best decision, it can offer knowledge resources (e.g., medical textbooks, guidelines developed by professional societies, or literature searching capabilities).

3. Evaluate the efficiency and effectiveness of care. Databases and analyses capabilities should be provided to enable the organization to understand its care practices, identify optimal practices, monitor its conformance to those practices, and report its outcomes and measures of care processes to a variety of constituencies.

Drawing from the discussion of concepts and goals, the view of clinical information systems can be stated in the form of philosophies and concepts that guide clinical information systems activities and plans.

The objective is care process improvement. This statement is seemingly self-evident. However, it suggests that one deduces the applications and application capabilities needed from a thorough analysis of care process problems and opportunities for improvement. The organization should not leap to the conclusion that it needs computerized records or any other application until it is sure that it has developed an understanding of the care problems to be solved, and the specific linkages between application capabilities and problem reduction or removal are very clear.

There are a relatively small number of core care processes. Perhaps the use of the word *core* makes the adjective "small" self-fulfilling. Nonetheless, for example, the application of IT should focus on accessing clinical data, ordering something, and referring a patient for an admission or to a specialist. This set of processes will span organizational boundaries. It is with these processes that the IT asset response must be an "A+."

Process leverage points are poorly understood. Our knowledge of how best to apply IT to improve care is crude. There is insufficient industry experience with these systems and insufficient measurement of experiences where they have occurred. We have much to learn. Hence clinical information systems must be designed in an intelligent way such that the systems can continuously and efficiently be changed to respond to new patterns of care and improved knowledge about the care process.

An important IT concept is the information-rich process. Most clinical decisions are made in the context of a process (e.g., the decision to refer initiates the referral process and the decision to order a medication initiates the ordering process). Information systems directed to improving the process have an opportunity to deliver information or check decisions at key points in the process. For example, the application, while capturing clinical data to be transmitted to the consulting physician, can check to see if the referral is being directed to the right specialist or is even necessary. As medications are ordered, the system can check for allergies, contraindications, and opportunities to suggest less expensive and therapeutic equivalents.

The use of IT to improve care is a form of guerrilla war. There is no single application system, no core set of capabilities, no single database that once installed will turn the tide in the battle to improve care. Care is too complex. There is no Battle of Midway here. Rather care improvement is a year in year out, continuous set of initiatives: a form of guerrilla war. Wars can be won this way.

The implementation of clinical information systems is a 1,000 project journey for which there is no end point. Advances in basic science, medical practice, pharmaceuticals, and diagnostic technologies will mean that no matter how advanced our medical practice is, it will always be able to be better. Hence no matter what capabilities our clinical systems have, there will be care improvement opportunities if additional capabilities were present. We will never be done in our efforts to applying IT to improving medical care. Defining and building the ultimate clinical information system is a wasteful exercise since it implies that we know the endpoint and that there is an endpoint.

Organizations should focus. Organizations should not, per se, embark upon efforts to make care paperless or to fully automate the medical record. Instead, for any given year, there should be a set of well-defined initiatives.

- Designed to solve very clear, measurable care problems or opportunities to improve care
- That comprehensively focus on processes
- With systems that are developed and implemented within an overall clinical information systems architecture[1]
- Leveraging an IT ability to support the iterative improvement in care

The computerization of the record is a byproduct of these initiatives. In aggregate, and over time, these focused initiatives will lead to increasing levels of computerization of the paper record. The computerization of the record becomes a secondary outcome of the application of IT to improve care, not the primary objective.

Sources of Complexity

The design and implementation of clinical information systems has always been complex. Three major factors or sources have contributed most of the complexity: the process of care, health and medical data, and care boundaries. These sources create challenges that are in addition to challenges, which occur at times, posed by new technology that doesn't work as advertised, recalcitrant providers, and organizational confusion.

Before the advent of the IDS, these challenges existed. However, the creation of integrated delivery systems, an increasingly stringent reimbursement environment and demands for more accountability for the cost-effectiveness of care have led to pressures that have aggravated the complexities. The industry is adding, for example, to its traditional challenge of integrating departmental systems, the challenge of integrating systems across organizations. The industry's interest in implementing clinical

---

[1] See, for example Figure 3–1, the Partners clinical information system architecture.

systems is moving beyond traditional hospital-centric systems to systems that support a continuum of care. And, while the cost of care will always be a basis of competition, quality, and proving quality, is ascending in importance to the purchaser of care.

These sources of complexity have a significant impact on the difficulty of implementing clinical systems and are unlikely to be resolved quickly.[2]

Complexity of the Process of Care

If one were to view the process of care as a manufacturing process (sick people as inputs, a "bunch of stuff" is done to them and better or well people emerge), it is arguable that medical care is the most complex manufacturing process that exists. This type of complexity has three major sources: defining best care, care process variability, and process volatility.

Our current ability to define the best care process for treating a particular disease or problem can be limited. Process algorithms, guidelines, or pathways are often the following.

- Based on heuristics that makes consensus within and between organizations difficult or impossible. There are often insufficient facts or science that can act as the final arbitrator leading to a consistent, let alone the most effective, approach. We often arrive at competing guide lines or protocols being issued by payors, provider organization committees, and provider associations.
- Condition or context specific. The treatment of a particular acute illness, for example, can depend on the severity of the illness and the age and general health of the patient.
- Reliant upon outcome measurements that can have severe limitations (e.g., be insensitive to specific interventions), serve as proxies for "real" outcomes or reflect the bias of an organization or researcher.

Often a defined approach to care has not been defined or adopted. A defined approach may also permit substantial latitude on the part of the provider. In these cases, one confronts the great variability in treatment that can occur. In an academic medical center, a physician may be able to

---

[2] Reprinted/adapted with permission from, Glaser J. (1998). *Topics in Health Information Management,* The Challenge of Integrating Clinical Information Systems in an Integrated Delivery System 19(1):72–77. ©1997 Aspen Publishers, Inc.

order one of 2,500 medications (each with a set of "allowable" frequencies, dosages, and routes), 1,100 clinical laboratory tests, 300 radiology procedures, and large numbers of other tests and procedures. The sequence and time relationship of the above along with patient condition and comorbidity all determine the relative utility of a particular approach to treatment. The variability within a pathway or guideline is compounded by the diversity of disease and problems. There are 1,000 diseases, each of which, in theory, has a different pathway or guideline.

This variability, or opportunity for variability, is unparalleled by any other manufacturing process. No car maker produces 1,000 different models of cars or provides for each model 2,500 different types of paint, 300 different arrangements of wheels, or 1,100 different locations for the driver's seat.

If we presumed that, through hard work and a very agreeable group of providers, we finally developed a large number of guidelines and algorithms and had significantly reduced the options in test, medication, and procedure ordering we would be confronted with the volatility of the medical process. In an average year, 60,000 articles are added to the base of refereed medical literature, which may lead us to need to continuously revisit our consensus. In addition, medical technology often induces us to change practices before the studies that measure their efficacy can be completed.

The complexity of the medical process places unique and tough demands on the design of clinical information systems, our ability to focus our efforts to support provider and patient decision making, and measure the quality of the care that we deliver. It is a complex undertaking to rationalize or standardize these processes within one provider organization. Clearly we compound the problem as we move across organizations within an IDS and, from there, expand beyond the IDS boundaries. We may be faced with attempting to have systems interoperate, which support different approaches to care.

Complexity of Health and Medical Data

The health status and medical condition of a patient is difficult to describe using comprehensive, coded data. Factors that contribute to this problem include the following.

- Although research is ongoing, well-accepted methods to formally decompose many key components of the patient record (e.g.,

admission history and physical), into coded concepts have not yet been developed.
- Even when such data models have been developed, vocabularies to represent the terms within the model in a standard way are difficult to develop. The condition of a patient is often complex, probabilistic, and describable in nuance. Multi-factorial and temporal relationships can exist between pieces of data. This complexity makes it inherently difficult to develop codes for medical data.
- Even when the model has been developed and coded terms defined, entry of coded data, by the provider, is more cumbersome and constraining than using free text.
- Finally, there are several additional factors that contribute to the complexity of data. There is no single way to organize automated medical data. The relational model does not serve the medical domain particularly well. And one encounters, across sites and often within a site, idiosyncratic ways to code data that have been often developed for good reasons, and because of the significant investments made to define and implement this way, change will not happen unless it is very compelling.

Because coding schemes can be idiosyncratic, nonexistent, or insufficient within and across organizations in an IDS, establishing clinical meaning, measuring care, determining the health status of a patient, and developing clinical information systems that interoperate can be exquisitely difficult.

Complexity of Care Boundaries

An organizational boundary (e.g., the physician groups, hospitals, and sub-acute facilities that make up an IDS), does not adequately bound the patterns of healthcare encounters experienced by people considered to be "members" of the organization. A person may receive care at hospitals or physician offices that are part of the IDS. That person may also receive care in settings outside of the IDS, or data about patients may be generated by organizations outside of the IDS (e.g., a retail pharmacy).

If the IDS desires to create a composite clinical picture of a person, for example through the implementation of a clinical data repository, it needs clinical data from multiple care settings, some of which are part of the IDS, some of which are not. The IDS may decide that it needs applications to span all of these settings (e.g., it may need to have a computerized record in all of these settings or at least have these records interoperate). The complexity created by this leakiness or bluriness in organizational boundaries shows up in several ways.

Thousands or millions of people, who an IDS considers to be its membership, may receive care, in aggregate, in potentially dozens or hundreds of settings that are not part of the IDS. An IDS may decide to connect its systems to these other settings. The connection could be in the form of providing terminal access through a workstation at one of these settings or through the placement of one of the IDS workstations at one of these settings. The resulting pattern of system interconnections, when carried out over a region or a state, is a complex network topology model; almost every provider connected to every other provider.

We complicate this pattern by random dispersion of data. One site, despite having a clinical data repository, may need to access data being kept at other sites. But the requesting site may not know where this data exists or if it exists or whether the data is relevant. One may not know, for a patient who presents at the emergency room, whether the patient has been seen in other hospitals in the city.

Should we be able to effect this interconnectedness and effect it efficiently, we would still have to grapple with the complexity created by the fact that we often want to do more than provide access to applications across these sites. We want to exchange data and have application processes interoperate. However, we see, across settings, significant variations in data, clinical processes, definitions of "optimal" processes and the extant base of information systems. We will also see the nature of the relationships between organizations change.

Data definitions vary across settings. These variations range across problem lists, laboratory tests, procedures, and other types of clinical data.

Care processes vary. Referrals, medication ordering, care documentation, and other processes are not done the same way across settings.

Definitions of "optimal" care vary. Frequency of visits, standard batteries of tests and appropriate medications for a particular problem are not consistent across settings.

One will clearly encounter different technologies, vendors, and levels of IT sophistication across settings. One will also find different levels of computerization (e.g., some settings will have provider order entry while others will not).

The nature of the relationships between organizations, both within the IDS and across its boundaries, will change over time. Hospitals in the IDS may decide to consolidate to one microbiology laboratory but leave other parts of the clinical laboratory unintegrated. A provider and a payor may decide that both organizations need not do utilization review and decide to integrate that function between them.

An integrated delivery system, if it desires to have a comprehensive database about the health status and care received by one of its members or have clinical applications interoperate, is faced with a daunting challenge created by the fact that care is often boundary-less. The complexity of boundaries compounds the complexities of the medical process and health and medical data.

Brigham and Women's Hospital Care Improvement Efforts

The next set of sections discusses some of the specific efforts of Brigham and Women's Hospital (BWH) to apply IT to improve the process of care. The sections will focus on BWH efforts to reduce adverse drug events. These efforts, discussed in depth elsewhere (Teich, 1996), are illustrative of several of the concepts discussed in this chapter.

- Medical care was examined as a process with the studies identifying deficiencies in the process.
- Information system capabilities were derived as a result of understanding process failure points.
- The studies highlighted the need to have information systems support of an information-rich process.
- The information systems had to possess a high degree of agility, and generality (e.g., a set of tools to allow efficient construction of order sets), so that the system could respond efficiently to the progressive understanding of the care process and its deficiencies and opportunities for improvement.
- The efforts to reduce the incidence and severity of adverse drug events involved change and growth of all aspects of the IT asset.

This section begins with BWH efforts to reduce adverse drug events.

Adverse drug event reduction at BWH

Leape, et al. (1995) and Bates et al. (1994) examined the incidence and nature of adverse drug events at Brigham and Women's Hospital and Massachusetts General Hospital. The study found the following.

- 6.5 adverse drug events (ADEs) occurred per 100 non-OB admissions, an estimated 2,340 annually at BWH.

- 28% of ADEs or 655 ADEs are preventable.
- 5.5 potential ADEs occur per 100 non-OB admissions, an estimated 1,980 annually for BWH. These errors, such as the order for a medication that was contraindicated, did not result in an event because they were caught, for example, by a nurse or pharmacist before execution of the order was complete.
- The average cost of each ADE is $6,000 for an annual estimated cost, at BWH, of $3.9 million.

The ADE problem was clearly significant. Further analysis examined the nature of the IT solution (Bates et al., 1994).

- 56% of the ADEs occur at time of ordering: the physician is unaware of, or forgets about, an allergy, a contraindication, or a problematic laboratory result
- 34% of the ADEs occur at time of medication administration with some of these being due to order legibility problems
- For BWH, a provider order entry system could prevent an estimated 480 ADEs per year for an annual savings of $2.9 million. This system would need to have the following capabilities.
- Drug-drug checking
- Drug-lab checking
- Drug-allergy checking
- Drug dosing based on age and renal status
- Informational displays of current results

The ADE study pointed to the need for a provider order entry system. For maximum reduction of ADEs, the system would have to be used by the ordering physician for the entry of all medication orders.

An internal BWH study examined the ordering of six common laboratory tests in the Surgical Intensive Care Unit. The study concluded that 35% to 50% of the tests were clinically unnecessary, the result of "pre-programmed" ordering. A provider order entry system could also reduce problems of inappropriate test ordering if entry were expanded to include the entry of all orders by the physician.

Impact on the IT Asset

An organizational decision to pursue the implementation of a provider order entry system clearly requires an investment in the application component of the IT asset: an order entry application. The previous sentence should not disguise the complexity of designing and developing a provider order entry system. However, the asset impact was more extensive than an application system.

Application utilities software are software tools that are part of the application. Example utilities include tools to allow schedule creation and editing in an outpatient scheduling system or editing of payor dictionaries in an accounts receivable system.

The provider order entry system required utilities software; in particular, software to process medical logic or rules, tools to enable users to construct order sets, and tools to link order screens to knowledge resources.

The *technical infrastructure* required upgrading primarily to ensure very high degrees of reliability and significantly enhance potency. Downtime for an order entry system is highly problematic particularly if these is no corresponding paper copy of the orders. If a results reporting system fails, the provider can call the laboratory. There are fewer options when order entry downtime occurs.

Upon entering an order, the system would engage in a series of checks to ensure that the order was safe or did not represent a potential inappropriate consumption of resources. Several dozen rules might be invoked for each order and these rules had to potentially check dozens of pieces of data. Since most orders will be acceptable, this checking process has to be exceptionally fast since few providers want to wait more than a second only to be told that their order was "correct." Hence, order entry had to be assisted by very fast processing power and data access. These needs, and others, led to the BWH implementing a very large client server platform (Roberts, 1995).

Organizational data and databases required progress in two major areas. First, order checking logic meant that coded allergies and reasons for an order had to be established and implemented. Vocabularies for medications, procedures and laboratory tests, and associated results had to be reviewed and augmented.

Second, a database of orders and related clinical information was to be created from the order transactions. This database would allow BWH to assess its ordering patterns and outcomes on an ongoing basis.

Two major categories of *IS staff* had to be defined, organized, and hired to support this system and others that were similar in nature. Medical Informatics talent was hired to provide the knowledge base and effort to develop medical logic processors, define vocabularies for data to be coded, work with the medical staff to analyze and design care interventions, and lead the design of the order entry system such that it fit well with clinical work flow and thought processes.

Care management analysis talent, who had health services research training, were recruited to support ongoing analyses of care processes and to measure the impact of the order entry system and other clinical information systems to determine if the desired improvements in care occurred following system implementation

IT governance was altered in two major ways. First, the guidance for clinical information systems, beginning with the provider order entry system, was placed under the jurisdiction of existing BWH care quality improvement forums. The BWH Care Improvement Steering Committee (CISC), composed of senior clinical and administrative leadership (including the BWH CIO) had been formed to provide overall direction, policy setting, and resource allocation for efforts designed to improve care operations and practices. In addition to order entry, for example, this committee initiated the development of clinical pathways. A Clinical Initiatives Committee (CIC), reporting to the CISC, had been formed to identify and prioritize those care processes and areas that would be assessed for opportunities for improvement, develop improvement plans, and monitor progress. Members of the IS Medical Informatics and care management analysis staff were on the CIC.

Second, knowledge domain committees were established or existing committees had their role expanded. The Pharmacy and Therapeutics Committee was tapped, and laboratory and radiology utilization committees formed to do the following.

- Provide ongoing review and definition of new logic to be applied in an effort to reduce adverse events and improve utilization
- Ensure that the logic was defensible either based upon the literature or the consensus of the committee's medical expertise
- Ensure that the medical staff was informed of the rationale for the logic
- Monitor the impact of the logic on care practice
- Update the logic as advances in medical practice occurred
- Respond to questions about the logic and its clinical rationale

Figure 4–1 provides a diagram that illustrates the broad IT asset impact of clinical information systems at BWH.

FIGURE 4-1

Clinical Information Systems IT Asset

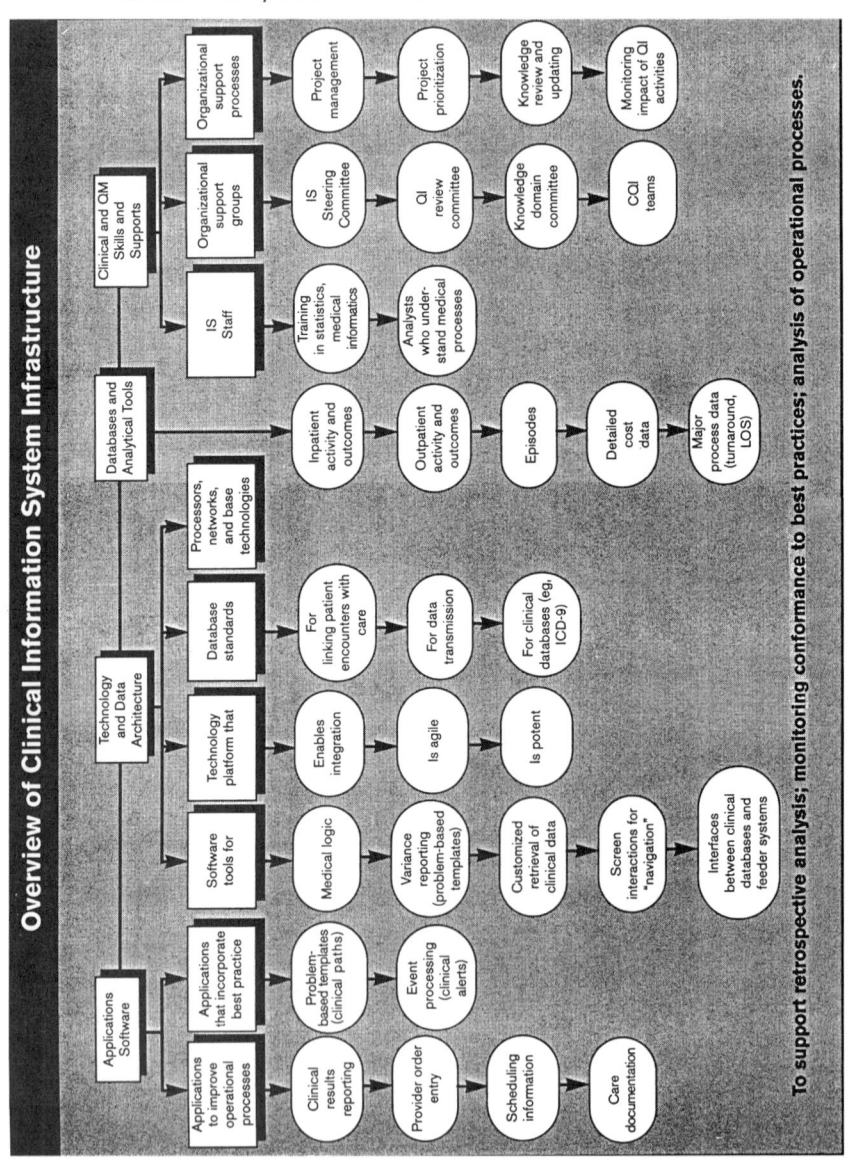

A clinical information system must encompass four key components: application software, technology and data architecture, databases and analytical tools, and clinical and quality management (QM) skills and supports. LOS, Length of stay; IS, information services; CGI, continuous quality improvement; QI, quality improvement.

Source: Glaser, J. (1994). *Developing a Clinical Information System: The Role of the Chief Information Officer.*

Strategies Surrounding Implementation

This book hasn't discussed strategies that might surround the implementation of a specific system. Implementation strategies have largely been in the context of the organization being structured, resourced, and organized such that multiple implementations can occur and occur in a way, if possible, that provides some form of sustainable advantage. An example of a broad structural implementation strategy is the creation of a group of Medical Informatics staff to be applied across multiple clinical systems implementations or the establishment of a highly reliable technical infrastructure to support multiple clinical systems.

Strategies surrounding the implementation of a specific application generally are designed to overcome major sources of implementation risk or address an implementation critical success factor.

The BWH provider order entry system had two major critical success factors.

1. Direct physician use of a complicated application
2. Physician acceptance of their clinical judgment being challenged by a computer

Strategies designed to address one factor also addressed the other.

Physician Use Strategies There is no substitute for a well-designed, easy to use application that "thinks" like the user. The design approaches and guidelines of the BWH provider order entry system is described by Teich (1995) and will not be repeated here. Some of the other use strategies are described below.

- *The system was developed internally.* The complexity of the application meant that it was inevitable that the initial specifications were, at best, 80% right. The system also had a suggestion button where users could forward ideas. While some of these ideas had to do with the removal of parts of the anatomy of the IS staff, most of the ideas were helpful. The IS staff was able to respond rapidly to these suggestions and enhance the system or correct bugs. The mantra was "If there are ten suggestions on Monday, six will be implemented by Friday. There will be ten on the following Monday and four will be left on the following Friday." The system evolved rapidly based on real experience with its use. This also meant that medical staff

saw sustained improvement in the system and a willingness to listen to their ideas.
- *Once implementation was started in a service, the implementation would move at "warp speed" through the service.* A lull would ensue to enable everyone to catch their breath and then implementation would resume again. For example, the Medicine service was implemented in four weeks. A two-month lull occurred before a six-week push through surgery. This pace of burst-lull-burst minimized the amount of time that physicians spent straddling manual and computer-based orders as they made their rounds.
- *All care units were staffed with personnel around the clock for the first two weeks of the system's introduction* to ensure that help was available in the form a person within eye shot. Training classes are sparsely attended and retention of training is poor. People will not read the manual nor are they likely to call the number posted on the workstation. They will respond to a pleasant person coming up to them and asking if they can help. Delivery of this help early in the implementation is essential to ensuring use.

Challenging Clinical Judgment The implementation of a system which has, as its core premise, the intent to challenge real-time the decision making of the physician can appear to be threatening. Hence while this implementation, like all implementations, had to address issues of software capabilities, training, and infrastructure readiness, the implementation of provider order entry had the additional burden of developing strategies to handle the potential problems of real-time decision support.

To address this critical success factor, the following strategies were developed and implemented.

- *The analyses of the incidence of adverse drug events and the utilization of laboratory tests in the SICU provided the basis for significant political support on the part of the clinical leadership.* The support was almost in the form of a moral imperative. The analyses of care deficiencies were of very high quality, conducted by physicians who were respected as health services researchers. It was difficult to attack the quality of the study or the credentials

of the researchers. The data indicated a serious problem that was not only a financial problem but also, in case of the adverse events, were counter to the core medical ethos of the medical staff leadership. To a large degree the motive to solve this problem was based on core values and not dollars or notions of efficiency.
- *The first interventions or medical logic focused on interventions that were "no brainers."* It is hard to argue with the utility of a piece of logic that points out allergies or medication contraindications.
- *The system was packaged as an experiment.* It would be piloted and evaluated. It would be implemented and evaluated. If the evaluation showed that the system created more problems than it solved or failed to live up to its expectations, it would be removed. This packaging eased the sense that the system was a "given" with administration doggedly committed to implementation regardless of the consequences. This packaging also fit with the culture of the BWH, an academic medical center, which was quite comfortable with the notion of conducting well-designed experiments with the intent of seeing whether the intervention improved care or did not.
- In addition to the label of "experiment" *other aspects of system implementation were designed to ensure that the rules were "safe."*
  - Resources were committed to ongoing evaluation of the impact of the system.
  - Knowledge domain committees were established to ensure that the appropriate expertise was brought to the task of constructing logic
  - Rules were often introduced as part of a trial (e.g., the rules were activated for half the patients and not the other half, to ensure a trial period before full implementation)
  - Computer generated advice could be overridden by the physician (although as the system made the transition from an experiment to an accepted aspect of the clinical management of care, medical leadership became increasingly comfortable in not permitting immediate over-riding.)

Impact

The provider order entry system, utilizing a core concept of an information-rich process, has had a significant impact on the care at BWH (Teich, 1996). Examples of the improvements are highlighted below.

- On an average day, 13,000 orders are entered by a clinician.
  - 386 of these are changed as a result of a computer suggestion.
  - A 55% decrease in serious medication errors was observed (Bates et al., 1998).
- The event detection system generated 1,730 alerts in a 6-month period.
  - Treatment was changed as a result of the alert 72% of the time.
  - A 35% decrease in time to correct the problem resulted.
- In a 6-month period, 898 warnings were generated for excessive chemotherapy order doses, 167 (19%) of the warnings resulted in order cancellation or change in the dose.
- Ondansetron and Ceftriaxone guidance saved $500,000 and $250,000, respectively, in annual charges.
- System guidance on H_2 blocker use shifted Nizatidine from 4% to 97% of orders.
- Reminders about redundant tests resulted in cancellation 69% of the time.
- KUB assistant (1,200 displays yr.) led to 14% of examination orders being canceled; 33% changed.
- IV/PO shift led to 20% to 40% shift (20,000 orders) saving $1 million in charges.
- Vacomycin guidelines decreased its use 37%.

Appendix B contains the set of impacts of a range of BWH clinical information systems including order entry.

Clinical Information Systems Across a Continuum of Care

When we examine the challenge of clinical information systems across an IDS, we find that the concepts and views developed for inpatient care support can be extended, although they undergo some transformation.

The two core views of clinical management of care and the perspective of care as a process remain the same. However, they are not completely the same. The focus of clinical management can change, For example, the clinical management over a continuum (in contrast to an encounter) rises in importance if the organization is under a payment mechanism that is based on per capita or per disease. The relative importance of a process can change. For example, the presence of capitation may place more emphasis on streamlining the process of referrals than on inpatient procedure ordering.

Core views, if they are well conceived, tend to remain intact over long periods of time. This does not mean that they remain unaltered. However, organizational competence in the clinical management of care, for example, will serve as a strength even as the view evolves.

The three IT goals of care process improvement, enhanced decision making and measuring the quality and cost of care remain. Nonetheless, they too undergo change. The continuum introduces new processes or changes the relative importance of processes. The referral becomes more important both as a means to channel patients to within the system, minimizing "leakage," and to support medical management. The accessibility of data, always an important process, moves from a hospital-centric issue to an IDS-centric issue leading to the creation of a clinical data repository. If an organization places great emphasis on wellness, the focus of decision making improvements changes.

The clinical information systems complexity factors loom larger in an IDS than an acute care hospital. The IDS inherently spans multiple organizations, and hence the complexity of boundary spanning is exacerbated and the need for integration is heightened. The IDS involves collecting data on care patterns from disparate organizations that compounds the complexities of differences in data definitions and care processes.

The observations on the care process remain intact. Care improvement is still iterative. Organizations should still begin with process examination from which the capabilities of applications can be derived.

Problems/Opportunities in Outpatient Care and the Care Continuum

As in the adverse medication error example, the formation of clinical systems for a continuum begins with an analysis of care processes to identify their deficiencies. Internal studies at Partners of such processes generated the following data (Sittig, 1998).

- In a study of clinic patients, 18% reported problems or unexpected symptoms after taking their medications. 48% of

those with problems sought medical attention. Those with problems had lower satisfaction with their care. In essence, it appears that 9% of the outpatient visits may be associated with problems with medications prescribed at a previous visit.
- In a study of primary care provider (PCP) and specialist (SSP) satisfaction with the referral process (Gandhi, 1998)
  - 63% of the PCPs and 35% of the SSPs were dissatisfied with the referral process.
  - PCPs reported that only 36% of the time did they receive an SSP follow-up within 7 days.
  - For 23% of the referrals, SSPs did not have enough information to adequately address the patient's problem.

The analysis suggested that care improvement opportunities might be extensive. Table 4–1 presents hypothesized improvements.

TABLE 4–1

Potential Care Improvement with Outpatient Clinical Information Systems

Impact	Clinical Information System
25% overall decrease in PMPM outpatient medication drug costs	AmbOE
50% decrease in inappropriateness rate for targeted tests, e.g., Digoxin, PSA, and thyroid function tests	AmbOE
15% net decrease in radiology utilization	AmbOE
80% decrease in outpatient medication errors	AmbOE
50% improvement in speed of processing of referrals	Ref
99% complete data for key referral fields, e.g., diagnosis, number of visits, and who the patient is to see	Ref
30% decrease in out-of-network referrals	Ref
100% documentation of follow-up for abnormal Paps	LMR
70% vaccination rate for all eligible patients	LMR

AmbOE, Ambulatory order entry; LMR, computerized medical record; pmpm, per member per month; Ref, referral application.
Source: Bates, D. (1998). Internal document, Partners HealthCare System.

Continuum IT Asset

Analyses of the above data and discussions with other delivery systems and Partners' providers led to the identification of a set of applications and related features necessary to support an effective and efficient continuum of care. Moreover, changes to all aspects of the IT asset were identified as being necessary. The impact on the asset is discussed below.

Applications. Several application needs were identified (Teich, 1998).

- A computerized medical record to support the documentation of care (structured according to flowsheets where appropriate), the accessibility of clinical data between providers, and the incorporation of health maintenance reminders
- A referral application to support the comprehensive communication of data between the referring and consulting physician, provide logic to check for any referral preconditions and determine referral necessity, establish linkages to scheduling systems to ensure that the referral was scheduled and completed, and create linkages to the resulting consulting physician findings
- Provider order entry for outpatient visits focused on medication ordering and prescription generation, but also supporting radiology and laboratory orders; logic, similar to that utilized for inpatient order entry to check the orders to help avoid errors and guide utilization
- A clinical data repository, with a viewer and analytical tools, to support cross-continuum access for care, research and care quality, and outcome measurement
- Algorithms, guidelines, and other knowledge resources to support the care decisions of all physicians in the system and patients and consumers seeking health information

In addition to improving the continuum-based processes of care, Partners strategies also called for the extension of the clinical reach of its specialists. As the clinical management of care across a continuum and managed care cost pressures increased, the volume of patients seen by the specialists would be expected to decrease. A Telemedicine program was initiated to extend the reach of the specialist throughout the region and the globe. The program also intends to improve the ability of Partners to support the remote management of the chronically ill at their home. A program to support the development of Radiology Picture Archival and Communications (PACS) applications was initiated.

The Clinical information systems infrastructure evolved to incorporate new demands placed by the view of care as a continuum and the heightened emphasis on clinical information systems in the ambulatory care settings. These infrastructure elements included flowsheet templates for the gathering of structured outpatient data, guideline and algorithm development templates, and additional confidentiality and access restriction algorithms to protect the confidentiality of patients. Confidentiality looms as a significantly larger concern as clinical information systems grow to encompass relatively large numbers of care settings and patients.

Technical infrastructure strategies were augmented, largely in the arena of application integration, which will be discussed later in this chapter. In addition, the technology architecture was moved to "lowest common denominator technologies" (e.g., TCP/IP, SMTP, and browser-based front ends). This term is by no means pejorative. Rather, the movement recognizes that the IDS systems must be extended to and loosely integrated with systems in care settings in which the IDS has little or no control (e.g., an affiliated health center for which there is a referral arrangement). The IDS is unlikely to have much interest in expending the capital required to place a workstation on the desk of this health center or being responsible for the support of invasive applications that interfere with the client configuration adopted by the health center. And yet, the IDS desires to quickly extend its reach. Lowest common denominator technologies enable its infrastructure to be supportable and agile.

Most of the *clinical data* in a continuum have to be mapable to a common vocabulary. Laboratory tests can be mapped to the LOINC standard. Problems can be mapped to the ICD-9 codes. Medications can be mapped to one of several national standard dictionaries. It may be quite difficult to force extant application systems to adopt these standards, but new systems can be implemented using the standard and the clinical data repository can have all incoming data mapped to these standards before being stored.

The construction of a database of IDS-wide quality measures will bring forth a range of inconsistencies and data quality issues. A simple quality measure such as unplanned returns to the operating room may encounter different definitions of "unplanned" and, in the various organizations, different individuals (e.g., operating room nurses versus billing clerks), who decide if the second procedure was unplanned or planned.

IS staff may have to undergo some change. In the case of Partners, a small number of new IS groups were created.

- The Telemedicine Center conducts trials of the use of Telemedicine to monitor patients remotely and the ability of Telemedicine to support the extension of the specialist over a wide geography. The group also supports videoconferencing activity used by the integrated residency programs and to extend access to medical education and rounds throughout the region.
- The Data Analysis unit supports the databases and analysis of Partners-wide care quality measurement and care pattern assessment.
- The Radiology Information Systems group is developing Picture Archival and Communication Systems to support improvements in radiology care and the extension of radiology services to community-based practices.

In addition, existing groups (the Medical Informatics group and those staff who developed clinical applications and implemented them) had to develop an appreciation for care practice and organizational cultures that were not academic medical center-based. The world of a two person physician practice in rural New Hampshire and the world of the suburban community hospital are not the same world as that of a Harvard teaching affiliate. These differences are not instantly appreciated nor understood by staff who grew up in an academic medical center.

IT governance The guidance of clinical information system activities at Partners evolved to the following current form.

- The Partners Executive Committee, composed of the member organization CEOs and the physician leadership, provides overall direction on strategies and priorities and approves the final budgets.
- An Information Systems Physician Advisory Group, composed of physicians from across Partners, works with IS to develop strategies, monitor implementations, resolve issues such as implementation tactics and vocabulary development, and review the results of analyses of the impact of these systems on medical practice.

- Each hospital has a physician advisory group that works on issues and needs for its local physician community.
- The practice medical directors contribute guidance on systems issues related to primary care and medical management.

Observations and Issues

The implementation of information systems to support a continuum of care is a new experience for Partners and the industry. It appears that the industry is still in the early stages of thought and experience gathering in both the formulation and implementation aspects of strategy development. Very fundamental questions and concepts remain to be resolved or clarified.

Understanding the Care Leverage Points Knowledge of the high leverage points in continuum-based care processes remains limited. Preliminary data, presented earlier in this section, suggest that there are many leverage points and much leverage is needed. However, IDS leadership should be careful to ensure that their IT investments solve real problems or provide real improvements. For example, consider the following.

- A clinical data repository may add little value unless patients are receiving care across the delivery system with some regularity. If the percentage of time is small (less than 5% of the physician to physician referrals) that physicians associated with one hospital refer patients to physicians associated with another hospital in the delivery system, it is not clear how the clinical data repository will help significantly improve the direct provision of care.
- If a computerized medical record is implemented in a small practice that has few problems with the paper records, it is not clear how provider productivity will be enhanced.
- If there is little risk-based pressure on medication ordering in the outpatient arena, it is hard to imagine most providers being excited about an ambulatory medication order entry system regardless of its potential quality improvement gains.

Well Conceived Stating of the Application It is insufficient to state that the organization needs a "computerized medical record." Such a statement may fail to sufficiently understand what actually happens during an outpatient visit. Analysis of such visits indicates, for example, that a flurry of activity happens at the end of the visit: the core recording of findings, generation of orders, and, potentially, initiation of referrals all can occur within a relatively small amount of time. While this flurry doesn't mean that the computerized record is a bad idea, if the statement of the application is too superficial, the critical support needed for end of visit processing may be overlooked. This deeper view and statement helps to understand the small time window within which system interaction must occur and the interdependence between the care activities of documentation, order, and referrals.

Developing a Crisp Definition of Integrated Care While this industry is full of "integrated delivery systems" developing "integrated care," it is not clear that we have a well-developed understanding of what that means. We have semi-fantastic descriptions of how it all might work with lots of words like "seamless" and "transparent." But we lack a large number of real, pragmatic examples of continuum-based care really working at scale. Drazen and Metzger (1998) present one of the first comprehensive and thoughtful descriptions of what integration can mean.

The value of integration is not well understood and, at times, is directly challenged (Herzlinger, 1997). An organization needs to create a technical and application infrastructure that enables it to adapt to integration as it develops its understanding of it. Strategies that presuppose an understanding of integration, such as all participants using the same system, may be quite wrong. Understanding the meaning and value of integration will be an area of experimentation, require application and infrastructure agility, and organizational focus on measuring and evaluating its experiences.

Summary of Clinical Information System Concepts and Views

In the preceding series of sections, we reviewed the concepts or view underpinnings of clinical information systems at BWH and PHS. These ideas were formed over the course of years and were guided by the mistakes and successes of experience.

- Two major organizational concepts were defined that form the core view of care: care as a process and the clinical management of care.

- These views led to three IT goals: improve care-centric processes, enhance patient and provider decision making, and measure the process of care.
- Discussion of the implementation of the above, and learning from the experience of others, suggested that applications focus on improving care processes that had been thoroughly studied, leading to a clear linkage between care improvement opportunity and IT capabilities.
- Care improvement is fated to be an ongoing, iterative set of analyses and interventions because of the following.
  - Our knowledge of what works and doesn't work in care can be limited.
  - Our understanding of the impact of clinical systems on care improvement is often deficient.
  - The design and implementation challenge confronted several sources of significant complexity that defy quick solutions.

These statements, referring back to Chapter 1, represent the formulation component of strategy. Discussion, in the preceding sections, on changes in the IT asset driven by a focus on care improvement, represents the implementation component of strategy.

INTEGRATION OF INFORMATION SYSTEMS

As discussed in Chapter 3, the IT asset has characteristics. The governance structure can be decentralized or centralized. Data can be accurate or not. Organizations will always find that there are aspects of the asset that need to be improved, and hence will embark upon activities designed to strengthen the asset

Often the needed activities are straightforward to state even if they are hard work to implement. The IDS may decide to improve the consistency of its measures of care quality by tightening up the definitions of data. The organization may decide to improve the supportability of its infrastructure by investing in new, powerful network management tools.

There are other times when the asset characteristic is quite complex and difficult to define with precision, and yet the characteristic is seen as critical. In these cases the organization would be well served if it spent time forming a thoughtful view of the definition and nature of the characteristic before it embarked upon the commitment of resources directed to its "improvement." For example, agility would seem, at face value, to be a very important characteristic of applications and infrastructure (and the organization as a whole), but what does it really mean? What does agility look like? How much does agility cost? How would we assign a value to agility?

As organizations think strategically about and develop plans for their IT assets, there are several questions that should be posed.

What asset characteristics are important to us? Organizations often find all of the asset characteristics to be important to at least some degree. However, some characteristics are more important than others. This ranking of importance can be a reflection of today's issues and priorities. The integration of the infrastructure may be a more immediate concern than the agility of the infrastructure early in the life of an IDS. The ranking can also reflect a "normative" sequence of importance. If the data is of very poor accuracy, then characteristics of accessibility and understandability may diminish to close to irrelevance until the accuracy is at least barely acceptable. The importance of asset characteristics can reflect the nature of the industry and its basis of competition. When the basis of competition varies by metropolitan area, a national healthcare provider may choose a governance structure that emphasizes local responsiveness.

Can we define the characteristic crisply or does the definition seem to be complex, multifaceted, and elusive? What does potency mean to us? What does data understandability mean? Assigning a definition (and measure) to potency can be very difficult. Object technology would appear to be potent because it supports reusability of standard programs. But how would one know if one object offering was more potent than another? A common definition (understandability) of a data element (e.g., primary care provider), would seem to be easy to define. It is. But effecting it can be elusive because there are strong reasons that various constituencies have for their specific, crisp, and individually correct but collectively inconsistent definitions.

If the definition is elusive or complex, what principles, views, and strategies should guide our pursuit of improving the characteristic? We may find it hard to define potency or to measure it. But, nonetheless, we can decide to replace our technical infrastructure every four years because we believe that will enable us to keep up with the most potent technology. We may not be sure how to define or measure an "innovative" IS organization, but we will undertake some of the steps outlined in Chapter 3.

What is our plan for ensuring that the asset has the characteristics desired? What plans, tactics, and resources do we need to have in order to advance the asset? Is the plan straightforward or something less than that?

In the remainder of this section, we pursue the aspect of the technical infrastructure asset called "integration." Integration is an example of an asset characteristic for which the definition is complex, multifaceted, and elusive. And yet, arriving at an integration strategy is critical.

Integrated delivery systems are investing enormous energy attempting to operationalize the word "integrated."[3] This effort is generally and correctly believed to require IDS efforts to integrate clinical, administrative, and financial information systems and system utilities such as electronic mail. A critical undertaking for the Information Systems group of any IDS is to develop strategies for facilitating integration. These strategies and tactics ideally are effective, efficient, and capable of a high degree of leverage (e.g., an interface engine can be applied across a wide range of integration tasks).

What Does Integration Mean?

Defining (and effecting) integration of applications and technologies is an exceptionally difficult challenge. This challenge results from several factors.

Integration can mean many things.

- A single password and look and feel for all systems
- The ability to access all IDS applications from any workstation in the IDS
- The ability to interface existing applications
- Common data definitions and a common database
- Common clinical and operational application processes (e.g., a single way to perform a referral, order supplies, or schedule an appointment across all entities in the IDS)
- A single application system to support consolidated administrative functions (e.g., human resources and materials management), but not clinical services (e.g., Dermatology)

---

[3] Reprinted/adapted with permission from, Glaser, J. (1998). *Topics in Health Information Management, The Challenge of Integrating Clinical Information Systems in an Integrated Delivery System* 19(1):72–77, ©1997 Aspen Publishers, Inc.

- Different implementations of the same system to support the consolidation of administrative functions, which allows for different modes of operations (e.g., different benefits packages for the academic medical center and the primary care network)
- A single application to support the consolidation of a subset of ancillary departments (e.g., two out of four Radiology departments)
- A common application to support the integration of some clinical services (e.g., Oncology), but not others (e.g., Cardiology)
- Some combination of the above and other examples not listed

Integration means all of these things. At any given time the IDS will decide the following.

- It should have the ability to effect all of the types of integration cited above.
- Different IDS situations will require different degrees of integration (and different willingness to bear the costs of loose versus tight integration).
- A situation might move between degrees of integration or change its needs for integration.

There is no single IT integration answer. A "single system" for all systems in an IDS, may be politically, economically, and time prohibitive. It is not clear that a single system can accommodate the variation listed above nor that a single system improves the above situation. A single system may require a degree of control over an affiliate's IT decisions, which isn't in the cards. Similarly an interface engine will be useful in some situations but not others. Common vocabularies for data will be useful in some situations (e.g., the definition of a primary care provider), but unnecessary work in others (e.g., reasons for no-shows).

There will be no one way to integrate these systems. The nature of the needed integration will vary from being able to access a system to a very tight coupling of applications. The "openness" of the installed base of systems will vary; at times one can leverage a standard interface and at other times one is confronted with the ugliness known as screen scraping. The maturity and potency of the integration tools will vary. Hence, like a good carpenter, the IS organization will need to develop a set of integration tools and know which one to apply in which situation.

At times one defines a phenomenon based on the tools that one has to address it. The presence of a diverse set of tools that are useful in certain contexts but not others means that the phenomenon is diverse and difficult to pin down.

No matter what the set of IT integration answers are, integration will be very hard and in some cases not achievable. Partners, for example, has a total of approximately 600 applications, 44 platforms, and 60 programming languages. The IT strategies of its member organizations vary from best of breed to heavy internal development to single vendor solution (although the single vendor is different from organization to organization). Few of these applications and platforms were designed with integration with other applications and platforms in mind. The definition of integration, and any other asset category, is often defined within the boundaries of what is achievable.

The IDS processes to be integrated are complex. Per the discussion in the previous section, the integration of care data, processes and patient care systems must confront the complexity of care. Administrative and fiscal processes and data are also complex.

Views That Guide the Improvement of Integration

Given the complexity of the definition of integration, the diversity of IT ramifications and the need to integrate the IDS, the organization will have to develop a view that will guide its integration strategy. Potential conclusions of that view development are discussed below.

Decompose the problem. Not all applications need to be integrated with every other application, no more so than all departments in all IDS organizations need to be integrated with every other department. There are pockets of integration need and the strength of that need will vary; ranging from an enterprise-wide need to send e-mail to anyone in the IDS to acceptance of diverse, nonintegrated technology in the research community. One needs to identify where integration matters and where it doesn't.

Recognize the evolution that will occur. Integration will evolve as organizations understand where integration makes sense and where it doesn't. Organizations will integrate functions that will need to be unintegrated later. Organizations will initially establish some level of integration between functions and then change that level as they become smarter about what works and what doesn't.

One integrates processes and data. Before one leaps to the conclusion that a common system is needed for integration to occur, one should try to understand what processes and data form the basis of integration and whether there are degrees of integration. The need for IDS-wide financial reporting may require common definitions of certain pieces of data, but may not require common closing schedules or a common general ledger. IDS desire to standardize its care of asthmatics may require common protocols and measures of outcomes but these can be implemented in the systems offered by different vendors. The desire to have a composite clinical view of the care delivered across the system may require one IDS-wide clinical data repository and standards for clinical content in that repository but not require the replacement of existing patient care systems or that the data in those systems be transformed to the standard.

Adopt standards including industry technology standards across a wide gamut of technology, data, and process interoperability. For example, infrastructure standards (e.g., Windows NT and Ethernet), transaction standards (e.g., HL-7), identifier standards (e.g., the HCFA National Provider Identifier), and data content standards (e.g., LOINC for clinical laboratory data). It is more important to adopt a standard, preferably a viable and robust standard, than it is to pick the standards that will eventually "win." Those banks that launched ATMs, using internal standards prior to the adoption of banking industry standards, "won" in a very big way, despite the fact that they implemented before standards were national in scope.

Promote the adoption of standards through appropriate contributions to and presence in standard setting processes at the national level (e.g., the Andover Working Group or Active-X for Healthcare), or at the local level (e.g., the Affiliated Health Information Networks of New England).

Wait for clarity. Often members of an IDS voice slogans such as "Integration is good," and "We want integrated systems," without knowing what an integrated application should really do or how much money and effort is reasonable to expend in order to get one. One should be hesitant to integrate until it is clear what integration really means to the proponent and why it will be worth the trouble.

While waiting, don't compound the problem. The clarity may take time to emerge but organizations can take the opportunity, when selecting a new application, to choose one from a vendor already installed at an IDS site. Organizations can demand that new applications conform to certain standards that ease integration. Application, technology, and data decisions should seize opportunities to ease future (although potential) integration needs.

Move opportunistically. The IDS can adopt a strategy of progressive or opportunistic homogeneity and integration. This strategy looks for, and capitalizes upon opportunities to standardize processes, data, and technology or reduce organizational IT asset heterogeneity. Several examples exist.

- IDS concern with losing money on its medication sub-capitation provides an opportunity to standardize the formularies
- An organization in the IDS that wants to replace its radiology system provides an opportunity to choose a replacement system used by other organizations in the IDS
- HCFA announcement of a National Provider Identifier provides an opportunity to standardize that data element across the IDS
- IDS concern with its management of hypertensive males provides an opportunity to rationalize that care process

Progressive or opportunistic homogeneity does mean that integration may be somewhat idiosyncratic. However, it also means that the organizational interest in achieving at least partial integration will be high.

Recognize the length of the journey. Integration will take a long time to accomplish. Organizations, and the industry, will go through several iterations, experiments, successes, and failures until it settles on a mature understanding of integration. This may take decades to accomplish.

The specific implementation component of the strategic integration response can take the form of several types of IT strategies.

Integration IT Strategies

IT integration strategies can focus on four levels of integration.

1. The ability for a person to access, from anywhere within the IDS, "their" set of applications and services subject to user authorization. This set may not be integrated with each other.
2. The ability to have a set of consistently defined data across the IDS. These data can be used for reporting purposes or as the basis of data exchange between two applications.

Examples of IT Strategy

3. The ability to establish common processes across the IDS. A common process can be a referral, the identification of a patient, or the sending of an e-mail message with attachments.
4. The ability of applications to behave the same way across an IDS (e.g., a common look and feel and command set or the implementation of the same application across all IDS organizations).

One can make several general comments about these strategies.

- As one goes from the first to the fourth type of integration, the degree of integration generally increases.
- Addressing one type invariably requires that one address at least some elements of the remaining types.
- Work performed to address one type eases the work required to effect subsequent types.
- The IDS can also adopt one type of integration for a class of systems or a portion of the IDS and another type of integration for another class of systems or different portion of the IDS. For example, two IDS members may have the same radiology system but across all four radiology departments the vocabulary of procedures may be standardized.
- Strategies carried out to support integration often support the improvement of other infrastructure characteristics (e.g., standardizing the workstation and its operating system also enhances supportability).

Example strategies within these four types will be discussed below.

Access Strategies

Access strategies generally require the development or identification of the following.

- A common presentation technology (e.g., a browser or an IDS-wide Visual Basic front end)
- Consistent names and definitions for the applications and services presented
- A common security service that maintains information on authentication (e.g., a person's password), and authorization (i.e., what services and applications they can access)

Data Commonality Strategies

There are several data commonality strategies.

Define common syntax and semantics. Data commonality strategies center on arriving at a common syntax for the exchange of information between applications (e.g., HL7 and ANSI X.12), and a common semantic that defines data meaning and coding conventions (e.g., ICD9 for patient problems and LOINC for laboratory test results).

Adopt exchange technology standards that provide the technical environment for the exchange of messages, transactions, or specific elements of data. Example technology standards can include XML, CORBAMed, and Active X for Healthcare.

Develop competency in a range of interfacing technologies. Interfacing technologies are diverse and varied in elegance. An IDS should be able to implement an interface engine, screen scrape, file transfer, and perhaps scan documents and printouts into machine readable form.

Move toward component-based and message-based architectures and encourage vendors to move to these architectures. The use of well-defined application components that expose their capabilities or services to other applications, through well-defined messages, will, over time, enable a marked improvement in application process interoperability. An IDS may evolve to the point where applications that need the identity of a patient or member are able to utilize a standard message exchange mechanism regardless of which vendor supplies the code that does the identification.

Common Process Strategies

Common process strategies are diverse and complex. This should not imply that arriving at a common semantic for clinical data across the IDS is not a complex task.

Define and implement the core IDS implementation applications. The need for and degree of integration for an IDS may be unclear but it may be clear that the IDS strategy will involve the integration of care at some nontrivial level, and hence a clinical data repository will be needed. The IDS may be working to assume delegation under capitation, and hence will need a common managed care application to support its eventual operations. Basic needs for communication may point to a common telephone directory on an Intranet, a common paging system, and a common e-mail directory if not a common e-mail system. While eventual

IDS integration may be forming, there will be some core integration capabilities that will be clear because it is "obvious" that some classes of processes (and data) will need to be integrated.

Utilize browser-based or browser front-end applications where possible. These technologies allow the IDS to be less worried about the workstation environments upon which these applications have to run. Not all applications need to be browser-based and some applications, or parts of applications, are constrained by current browser technology. Nonetheless a large number of very valuable capabilities (e.g., retrieve results), determine eligibility or examine care algorithms, can be delivered through browser-based technology. Browser-based technology helps integration in two ways.

1. By reducing the need to replace infrastructure before one can extend an "integrating" application or process out to IDS member organizations. The expense of replacing infrastructure (and the time required) can thwart efforts to integrate.
2. A browser-based application can enable the IDS to "layer" a common process on top of individual member organization's applications. This process may not be integrated at all with extant applications. For example, the IDS may provide a common way to determine eligibility or order a medication. In neither example would integration with, or the presence of, existing applications, although valuable, be required.

Develop applications in a manner that enables the delivery of "components" or "parts" of the application to a setting and not require that the full application be implemented. For example, some physician offices would benefit from an application component that enables the recording of problems, editing of a transcribed note, or the flowsheet capture of data. That office may not need or be interested in the full computerized record. Similarly, a site may be interested in medication order entry but not procedure order entry. By allowing components to be implemented, an IDS may speed up delivery of information systems value, find a more receptive customer, and reduce the integration demand. If the basis of process integration is 20% of an application, one can slow integration down by requiring the implementation of 100% of the application.

Limit the list of acceptable applications to some small number which, in addition to reducing the cost of these applications and improving supportability, can enhance integration if the integration supplier is told that winning the business requires the presence of integration technologies in their application, and if the implementation of a common systems is used as a catalyst for standardizing data and processes.

Develop a vendor anchor/tenant approach.[4] In this approach the IDS defines one vendor as the core supplier of its applications (the anchor). All other application vendors must coexist or integrate (as tenants) with the applications provided by the anchor vendor.

Develop a process architecture. Common processes form the basis of a high degree of integration in an IDS. These processes can be common across the enterprise or between some groups of IDS members. Such groups, or constellations, are discussed below.

While it may not be clear how an IDS will achieve these common processes, it will have a better chance of arriving at "commonness" if it has a fairly clear definition or architecture of the processes and related sub-processes (Drazen and Metzger 1998). This architecture requires that the processes be defined (e.g., engage and retain members, assess health, and develop care and wellness plan). Moreover, the related sub-processes must be defined. Example sub-processes of the develop care and wellness plan process include the following.

- Set standards and monitor performance
- Develop wellness plan
- Develop care plan
- Engage and manage referrals

Reasonably detailed sub-process flow narratives and mock computer screens can be developed (Drazen and Meztger, 1998). This process architecture serves to guide specific implementation decisions. Such decisions can either move an IDS toward its process vision or hinder the ability to achieve the vision.

Develop integration concepts which bound the need for integration. The IDS should develop an approach to four major integration concepts: constellations, clusters, transcendent processes, and levels. These concepts are diagrammatically presented in Figure 4–2.

Not all parts of an IDS need to have an equal level of integration with every other part. The physician practices surrounding a hospital may need to be well integrated with that hospital but have less of a need to be

---

[4] Larry Grandia, CIO of Intermountain Health Care, personal communication, October 22, 1998.

Examples of IT Strategy

FIGURE 4-2

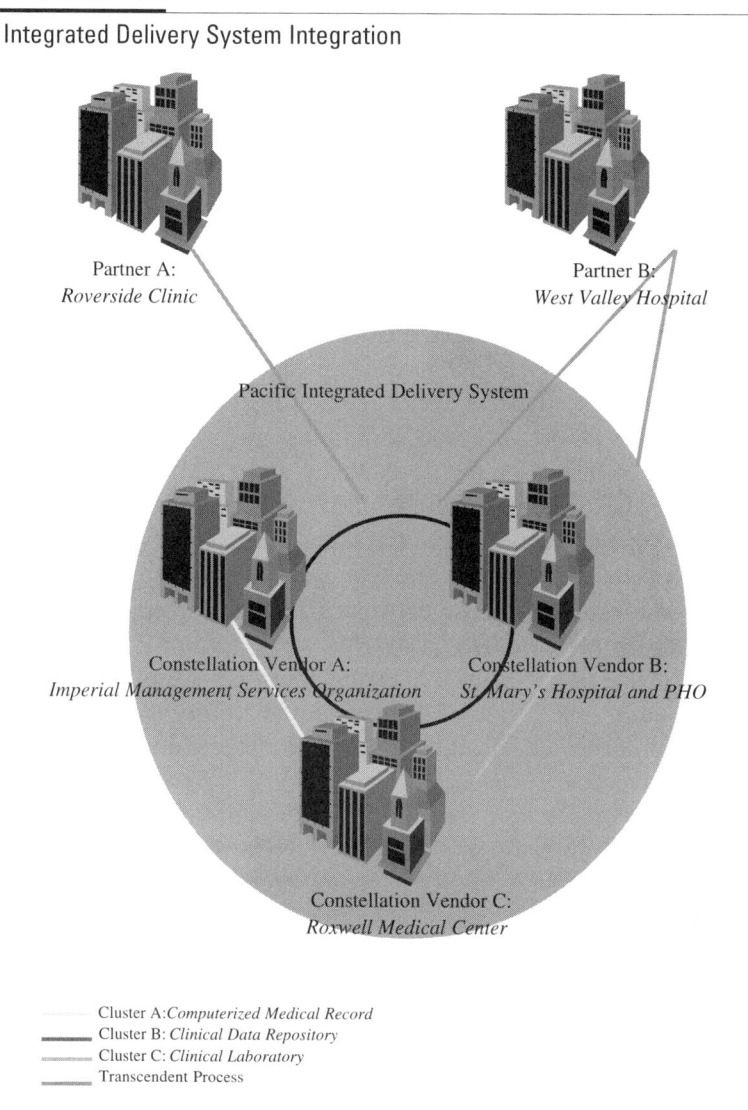

Integrated Delivery System Integration

Partner A: *Roverside Clinic*

Partner B: *West Valley Hospital*

Pacific Integrated Delivery System

Constellation Vendor A: *Imperial Management Services Organization*

Constellation Vendor B: *St. Mary's Hospital and PHO*

Constellation Vendor C: *Roxwell Medical Center*

Cluster A: *Computerized Medical Record*
Cluster B: *Clinical Data Repository*
Cluster C: *Clinical Laboratory*
Transcendent Process

integrated with another IDS hospital twenty miles away. There are constellations of care activity (or some administrative processes) within which a high degree of integration is valuable. An IDS may have half a dozen constellations, each perhaps centered around an IDS hospital. There may be less of a need to integrate between constellations than within a constellation. For example, if 99% of the physician to physician referrals occur within a constellation, that process should be tightly integrated within the constellation. If 1% of the referrals cross constellation boundaries, cross-constellation integration of that process may not need to be tightly integrated with the systems of the respective constellations. In this scenario, the referral can be faxed.

An IDS should focus on ensuring a high degree of integration within a constellation even if that means a different vendor supplier, for example, than the one chosen by another constellation.

A cluster recognizes that there may be compelling reasons to have the same application implemented across the IDS (e.g., a managed care application). However, the IDS may decide that having a common laboratory system is not needed since the degree of integration between the laboratories will be modest. An IDS should thoughtfully define those clusters. Defining a cluster is a big deal; it may mean that one is committing to an expensive, time-consuming, and potentially politically-charged whole-scale replacement of a set of systems that probably work just fine.

A transcendent process is one that spans organizational boundaries. These boundaries can be those between IDS member organizations and the boundary between the IDS and its "partners." Example processes may include retrieving of results by a referring physician regardless of whether that physician is "one of ours," determining eligibility, ordering medical supplies, or ordering a medication or radiology procedure. The number of transcendent processes is generally small, probably fewer than ten critical processes. Support for transcendent process requires that the IT integration response be minimally invasive (i.e., the IDS is unlikely to be able to require that all process participants change their applications and infrastructure). For example, the transcendent process may need to be extended to affiliates.

The process has to be able to tolerate no integration. For example, a referral application may prompt for allergies if it is unable to integrate with a computerized medical record or if no such record exists. Standard interfaces (or messages) and browser-based applications form the essence of the transcendent process integration response.

The concept of levels brings together ideas of clusters, constellations, and transcendent processes and extends these ideas by listing specific types of capabilities and degrees of integration. For example, an IDS may have relationships with affiliated provider organizations. These relationships may involve a modest degree of integration that can be met by offering a standard level of integration (e.g., SMTP-based integration of e-mail, insurance EDI capabilities to the IDS managed care application but not to the payor applications, and browser-based ability to generate a referral). On the other hand, a member organization of the IDS may be offered a different level of integration (e.g., the IDS common e-mail system, insurance EDI capabilities to the IDS managed care application and all payors, full order entry, a browser-based referral application and a common financial system). Within the IDS, other levels can be created (e.g., levels that might be defined due to full or partial consolidation).

The Partners levels of integration are presented in Appendix A. This document, while synthesizing most of the discussion in this section, is focused on levels of integration.

These concepts of constellations, clusters, transcendent processes, and levels can help the IDS focus on those areas where commonality is needed; boundaries can be defined, processes rationalized, and data content standardized.

Consistent Application Behavior Strategy

If the IDS desires that any of its staff can go to any of its sites and use the applications the same way that they would at any other site, then a common system commonly implemented application would be needed. The delivery of "chunks" would also help ensure that that process has consistent behavior across the enterprise.

The value of a consistent applications behavior, where consistency is absolute, is not clear. We all confront inconsistencies in our use of the ATMs from different banks or the location of the headlight switch in different rental cars. This variation can be annoying (e.g., groping for the volume knob in a rental car where the rental car employee left the radio on full volume on a station that appears to focus on playing trash compactor sounds). But it is not clear that this level of inconsistency is debilitating.

Summary

Organizations will seek to improve their IT asset and develop strategies and plans to effect the desired improvements. At times, they confront asset characteristics that are critical but very complex. The complexity generally results from difficulty in arriving at a crisp definition of the characteristic and the fact that the characteristic is multifaceted and intricate.

In these cases of complexity, organizations need to develop views and concepts that frame their understanding of the characteristic and the nature of the efforts to improve or effect it. These views may not lead to a crisp definition or necessarily reduce the complexity. But they provide very important guidance to improvement efforts.

Failure to be thoughtful can be highly problematic. Treatment of the integration problem as one that can be solved by the implementation of a single system for all systems, for some IDS (not all), can result in exceptional expenditures and time frames that are quite disproportionate to the gains in integration that might be achieved, assuming there is any budget left. A single system also does not adequately address the problem of affiliates where replacing their applications is not a meritorious conversation.

In the case of Partners, integration is viewed as an evolving, opportunistic, and idiosyncratic phenomenon involving clusters, constellations, levels, and processes. The IT response is one of view and the ability to develop proficiency with a range of infrastructure and application tactics.

THE WORLD WIDE WEB

From time to time, information technologies emerge that have the ability to significantly influence the strategies and plans of an organization and/or the manner in which it architects its infrastructure and applications. Examples of these technologies include transistors, time-sharing, networks, bar codes, global position satellites, and the personal computer. There is also the steady emergence of information technologies which, while important, have not had a widespread and deep impact on organizations and their information systems (e.g., CASE technologies and artificial intelligence).

A critical component of strategy development for IT is to understand, for a given new technology, whether it belongs in the first cohort or the latter and why. An organization that miscategorizes runs the risk that it either invests heavily in a technology that is unable to provide a commensurate leverage of the organization or the organization misses an opportunity to take advantage of a technology that can help effect significant organizational change or improvements.

In analyzing new technologies, the organization needs to answer four major questions.

What are the core characteristics of the new technology? A simple question to state. But the answer must demonstrate insight and be based on essential capabilities of the technology. For example, the core characteristics of an airplane are that it does the following.

- Allows one to go from point A to point B in less time than other modes of transportation
- Does not require a track or a road or some other element of infrastructure to be in place and hence it costs less to achieve scope (go to lots of places) and can achieve greater range (go to places where it is impractical to create infrastructure [e.g., the jungle])

The core characteristic of refrigerators is that they enable perishable goods to last longer before they spoil.

Client server technology has three core characteristics.

1. The processing of an application is meaningfully distributed between at least two computers, the client that controls the application processing and a server that provides application services requested by the client (e.g., database services).
2. Servers can communicate with each other specifically to fulfill client requests for services a particular server cannot satisfy.
3. All clients can access all services on the network.

These capabilities enable the application to accomplish more work over a defined period of time by splitting up across several machines all of the processing tasks that make up an application.

The definition of core characteristics is critical if an organization is to begin to understand how the technology might contribute and if the contribution will be significant.

What has the use of this new technology, by others, taught us? If the organization is not the first adopter or an early adopter, it should ask about the experiences of others. Are there some types of uses that are more successful than others? What troubles or disappointments have been encountered? To what degree are the disappointments the result of inexperience, inferior implementations of the technology, or technology immaturity rather than the technology concepts being fundamentally flawed? For example, early efforts to fly were plagued with crashes and pilots who got lost. Early client server implementations were difficult to manage, expensive, and unreliable. These problems were a reflection of the immaturity of the field with the technology rather than the technological concepts being shown to be of little merit.

What roles or general categories of use does the technology appear to fill? In other words, given the core characteristics and perhaps the experience of others, how might the technology be applied. For example, bar codes can fill roles such as those listed below.

- Track an object as it moves from place to place
- Identify an object so that it can be linked to other data (e.g., the bar code of a can of soup can be linked to current price information)
- Serve as a "permanent," nonmagnetic storage device that can be applied to irregularly shaped objects

Similarly, the characteristics of client server technology enable it to fill roles such as the following.

- Supporting the addition of a Graphical User Interface, which has high processing demands, on top of legacy, production systems
- Allowing multiple applications and systems to "seamlessly" utilize scarce or expensive "services" such as fax, slide making, database management and high volume printer services
- Permitting an application to utilize extensive logic checks, which run on another computer (the server), of a transaction without slowing down the entry of the transaction on the client

Given the strategies and plans that we have, the lessons learned from others, and the roles that the technology might play, how does the technology significantly leverage our plans and strategies? Why do we care about the technology? And do we care in a very big way or is the technology a minor contributor to our efforts?

The answers to these questions can vary from industry to industry and organization to organization. Bar codes are strategically important to retailers and less important to a law office.

Client server technology was critical to the BWH (Roberts, 1995) in the example of order entry discussed earlier in this chapter. Running expert system-based rules past an order transaction required that an enormous amount of processing be completed within sub-seconds. Any response time longer than a second might slow the transaction to the point of unacceptability to the medical staff. In this case the checking of the order ran on another computer minimizing the interference of that processing with the processing needed to support the entry of the order. On the other hand, client server technology may be far less important to a very high volume credit card processing operation.

TABLE 4-2

Growth in the WWW Worldwide

	1996	2002
Number of devices accessing the WWW	32M	300M
Number of Web users	28M	175M
Percentage of users buying goods and services on the Web	25%	39%
Web-based commerce	$2.6B	$220B

Source: International Data Corp, "Internet Commerce Market Model."

The World Wide Web (WWW) is an example of a new information technology that might have significant strategic implications to a healthcare provider organization. While the WWW is being subjected to all of the hype and accretion of mystical properties that often accompany new technologies, there is some evidence (see Table 4–2), before one even answers the questions posed above, that something powerful is occurring here.

To date, in calendar year 1998, more than 17 million people in the United States have looked up medical data through the Web, an increase of 35% from 1997 and 30.8 million people, 46% of online users, looked up information about a personal or medical problem (Green, 1998).

In the sections that follow, we pursue the "answers," generated by Partners, to the questions cited above for the WWW. These answers served to define a view of the potential contribution of this technology to the strategies and initiatives of healthcare organizations in general, and hence to Partners. The sections conclude with a discussion of the impact of the WWW on one aspect of the IT asset, governance.

Core Characteristics of the WWW[5]

The WWW has four characteristics that mark it as a truly revolutionary technology.[6]

---

[5] This section first appeared in Glaser, J. "Business Opportunities in the Delivery of Health Care Information Over the Internet" *Spectrum* Monograph. (Waltham, MA: Decision Resources, Inc., 1998).

[6] The Internet and the WWW are less remarkable for their sophistication as technology than they are for the impact of that technology on society. The ability to create a spark (and hence a fire), using flint, on demand and the moveable type set are examples of technologies that have had remarkable societal ramifications that dwarfed the sophistication of the technology.

- *The WWW utilizes an extant, nearly ubiquitous, and open network.* WWW access leverages, and goes beyond, the phone system network. Moreover, little incremental capital is required for an individual consumer or a service provider to become part of that network.
- *WWW-based systems are minimally invasive of the client or workstation.* Hence, the provider of WWW-based services and information is not concerned with the cost of supporting remote hardware or network connections. Nor do suppliers of WWW services confront the need to homogenize the workstation base in order to effect widespread use of their services.
- *The WWW uses a very standard (e.g., HTML and HTTP) environment.* Hence WWW developers are reasonably sure that their software will work on the WWW and have a sufficient level of interoperability with other WWW offerings.
- *Adding a new service to the WWW is trivial.* A URL created today can be found by millions of browsers tomorrow. This is both a strength (we can be on the WWW tomorrow), and a weakness (hundreds of our competitors can be on the WWW tomorrow).

Fundamentally, the WWW is an exceptionally inexpensive and extraordinarily ubiquitous mechanism for the distribution of information, software, and shared processing by millions of suppliers to hundreds of millions of consumers and businesses. Keen (1991) refers to this attribute as "reach" (i.e., the organization is able to significantly extend the reach of its applications). The advent of the printing press dropped significantly the cost of information distribution. The television expanded significantly the dimensions of media that could used to convey information. The WWW has a comparable impact on dropping the incremental cost of information distribution to almost zero (i.e., there is a small but real cost to print and distribute the incremental book but the cost, to the publisher, for the next user to access their WWW-based content is almost nothing). The WWW also extends the media that can be distributed by adding the power of computation to text, sound, pictures, and video.

Examples of Use by Healthcare Organizations

The HIMSS/HP survey in 1997 found extensive interest in the Internet and the WWW. Of the respondents:

- 87% of organizations used the Internet
- 59% were "most likely" to adopt Web-enabled applications.
- 53% were currently or considering using tele-healthcare.

WWW use by healthcare organizations is very diverse. Uses include the following.

- Clinical results transmission and retrieval (including images) (e.g., primary care providers accessing test results on a patient they sent to the hospital)
- Organizational home pages
- Directories of providers and their areas of expertise
- Descriptions of clinical trials, criteria for enrollment and enrollment request forms
- Medical school, residency, and fellowship applications
- Subscriber determination of health insurance benefits, referral status, and claims status
- Access to medical text, algorithms, FAQs, and chat sessions
- Insurance, supply, and clinical data EDI among healthcare business partners
- Patient and physician request for a consultation by a specialist
- Application of WWW front-ends to current healthcare application software to enable remote access to the application

While, in healthcare, interest is high and impressive examples of WWW use exist, in general WWW use has been limited, crude, and non-strategic. Several factors hinder use.

- Concerns with the security of the WWW and the ability of WWW-based applications and access to preserve patient confidentiality
- Perceived and real limitations in the ability to develop robust/complex applications using WWW technologies
- Perceived and real concerns over the reliability and performance of WWW-based applications
- A tradition of information technology conservatism in the healthcare industry
- Limited understanding of "enabling" that the WWW provides (i.e., what exactly does the technology allow us to do that we couldn't do before?)

- Limited understanding of viable business models and the technology's ability to leverage existing businesses
- Limited understanding of how a "customer" will use and value WWW-based services and information and the ways in which the WWW will supplement other service delivery modes (e.g., when will a patient want to see a provider versus communicate with them through e-mail?)

Roles of the WWW in Healthcare

There are three major roles that the WWW is likely to play (and is playing) in a healthcare organization.

1. The WWW can serve as an integration technology by providing an inexpensive network linking the organization to itself and its business partners and patients and WWW tools provide inexpensive, although crude, technologies to integrate applications at the display level (e.g., a WWW-based "physician's workstation," which enables a physician to access the results reporting systems at two different hospitals). The advent and maturation of WWW technologies (e.g., XML), will significantly enhance the ability of the WWW to support integration.
2. The organization can use the WWW to provide broad access to information or content (e.g., directions to the clinic, care algorithms, or disease-specific chat sessions for the chronically ill).
3. The organization can extend and enhance existing services or create new services that link customer and supplier or patient and provider (e.g., a patient scheduling an appointment, a subscriber changing health insurance coverage, or a primary care provider holding a consultation with a specialist on the appropriate treatment course for a patient).

Information System Integration

The healthcare industry is in a period of aggressive merging and forming of alliances. Industry participants are also pursuing the introduction of information technology to reduce the cost and improve the effectiveness of transaction processing that occurs between them (e.g., supply ordering and claims submission).

This consolidation and search for efficiency has led several healthcare organizations to examine the WWW in two roles: as a network and as an application integration tool.

The WWW may provide an inexpensive network between the components of a merged organization and between that organization and its business partners. Most integrated delivery systems, for example, are acquiring or affiliating with primary care providers in the community. A large number of the primary care providers in the United States are in one- or two-person groups. The WWW appears to be a much more cost-effective means of providing a network connection to these groups than dedicated T1 lines.

Organizations are examining the WWW as a substitute for Value Added Networks (VANs), which currently support insurance and supply related transaction movement between organizations. The VAN business is very price sensitive and the WWW may permit further reduction in per-transaction costs or replace a large segment of VAN business.

As healthcare organizations merge, they come under immediate pressure from the merged entities to provide some level of application integration across a very heterogeneous base of technologies and IT vendors. These applications include common electronic mail, a single view of patient data regardless of the locations of patient interactions with the delivery system, or a common view of the claims experiences of a company's employees. While the merged organization may have long-term plans to arrive at a single application platform for those applications that require integration, execution of that plan is multi-year in nature. Organizations are examining and implementing WWW-based solutions as a means to provide some level of integration as a short-term measure. These short-term measures may become long-term solutions if the short-term measures continue to benefit from enhanced functionality and superior performance.

Content

Healthcare organizations will develop, and at times purchase, and publish content. They will do so for two major reasons.

1. To establish brand name recognition in the eyes of the public and the general medical community
2. To support their efforts to improve the management of patients with a chronic disease, direct patients to the right healthcare resources, or improve customer interactions with administrative and clinical services

Advances in WWW-related technologies should enable significant advances in the industry's ability to deliver sophisticated content. Content based on passive text and static images will evolve to encompass the following.

- *More extensive use of healthcare simulations.* An example of a simulation might include, for the patient faced with heart surgery, the beating of the heart with significant occlusion of an artery. Another example, for the patient recently diagnosed with cancer, might show, through animation, how chemotherapy fights tumors.
- *Personalization of information delivery.* An example might include subscriptions to services that "push" to a patient or well person all of the articles that appeared in the last week on a particular healthcare topic. The user should also be able to establish the reading level of the content they are to receive.
- *On-demand "long videos"* (e.g., videos showing someone how to change a wound dressing for the postoperative patient now at home, or breast feed the colicky baby, or watch families talk about the stress and coping strategies, of having a member with Alzheimer's).
- *Support for the unclear question* (e.g., natural language support to help steer the patient who has typed in "My stomach really hurts what should I do?" or "Is a red bumpy rash a sign of AIDS?" to the appropriate information source. This source could be WWW-based text or a suggestion to call a 24-hour support number).

Despite these advances, content delivery is quickly, if it isn't already, becoming a commodity business. There are 15,000 health and medical WWW sites today (Green, 1998). Developing content, albeit crude, and "publishing it" on the WWW is almost trivial. Differentiating content can be very difficult.

Content is increasingly being given away. CD ROM-based medical text often comes with PC purchases. Several well-developed, Web-based content offerings, from respected sources, have appeared (e.g., Mayo Clinic Health Oasis, BetterHealth, and DrKoop.com). Health and medical knowledge sources are part of the bundle of services offered by Internet Service Providers (ISPs). A content provider may arrange a relationship with the ISP to be the mass market health and medical content provider, but that relationship will be under constant price and feature pressure that results from the fact that adding new services to the WWW can be trivial. It will be difficult for the vast majority of providers to compete with national offerings of content.

There are several strategies that can be applied to improving one's odds at being successful in the development and distribution of content.

- *Being seen as authoritative, trusted, and unbiased in the eyes of the consumer.* The consumer of health and medical information wants to know that the content represents the best thinking and knowledge available today.[7] The consumer will make very important personal decisions based on this information. Content that carries a logo from an authoritative academic medical center is likely to be more well received than the content offered by a pharmaceutical company (which may be perceived as biased) or an unknown medical source.
- *Creatively leveraging WWW technology.* Too often medical content is simply a book on the WWW. The content does not take advantage of the graphics, video, audio, or computer processing capabilities of the technology. The publishers of WWW-based material often don't realize that WWW navigation strategies by the user are different from the navigation strategies used when people read books (i.e., people look up information differently). Use of the technology can make the information more accessible, understandable, and entertaining. A dry academic discourse on breast cancer will suffer when compared to the same discourse that is not only written for the lay person but includes videos of women talking about their disease, provides animation simulations of the mechanisms of chemotherapy, and enables the patient to plot survivor likelihood curves.
- *Providing access to a human provider.* Often, in the course of seeking information about their health, a person simply wants to talk to someone who is a provider. The person may be confused by the information, want emotional support, or feel the need to double check before they take action. Content providers can supplement their WWW-based offerings with access to providers who can perform some level of consultation.

---

[7] Health and Human Services will launch a site (http://www.scipich.org) that intends to help consumers evaluate the quality of health sites.

While these strategies may enhance the likelihood of success, the challenge of differentiating on the basis of content will remain a difficult one.

Despite the commodity nature of content, some players will win at the national, mass market level of content provision just as Encyclopedia Britannica won its market for encyclopedia books. The book *Our Body, Our Selves* was fabulously successful as a health and medical book for women. Some players will win in the focused medical market just as Gray's Textbook of Anatomy is on the shelf of virtually every physician in the country. However, skills in publishing, pricing, and distributing books may have modest value on the WWW. Skills and experience in developing documentaries or computer games may be more important.

There will likely be niche roles for those who deliver highly focused and specialized content. Example content areas might include nutritional advice or information about a chronic illness that afflicts a large segment of the population (e.g., congestive heart failure). In these cases, because of patient personal interest in getting the right answer or finding any answer to a highly focused or arcane question, there will be a market willing to pay some noncommodity rate for information.

Increasingly one will find consulting or "information brokering" services that supplement the pure delivery of content. For example, access to a financial planner to help interpret and implement the suggestions of financial planning software obtained from the planner's Web site.

Similarly, an information brokering service could be established that enables a patient to find the "best" specialist or treatment site for a disease. Or to talk about the WWW-based material they have read.

Process Improvement

There are, and will continue to be, significant and multifaceted efforts on the part of current participants in the healthcare industry to use the WWW to improve the delivery of service, both medical and administrative. Services are carried out and supported by core organizational processes. These processes are critical in that customers judge the organization as a whole based on their interaction with these processes. Examples of service processes include patient scheduling of an appointment, patient seeking answers to healthcare questions, pharmaceutical benefits manager informing a physician of the appropriate use of a medication, and determination of patient eligibility for insurance coverage of an encounter.

The greatest leverage point of the WWW will be in its ability to support service improvement through the leverage of organizational processes. The WWW can achieve this by doing the following.

- *Enabling the customer to directly initiate the service or determine the status of a service.* The customer can schedule the appointment or find answers to questions. This enabling makes the process more efficient, eliminates "middle men" and the related inefficiencies and sources of error, and tailors the service to the customer
- *Enabling closer ties between patient and provider.* For example, a system could be created that provides rapid feedback on the management of the chronically ill (e.g., entry of data by the diabetic or patient with congestive heart failure, transmission to the provider, calculations run at the provider site to see if management is "on course," feedback sent to the patient in the form of graphs to show how well the patient is doing, etc.). This may improve care and create a stronger bond between the patient and their provider. Patients can also communicate to their providers through electronic mail.
- *Providing an information-rich service.* As questions are answered, appointments scheduled, or medications ordered, the WWW can deliver "just-in-time" information and information tailored to the customer in the context of the service or task in which they are engaged. This information may suggest, based on the responses the patient gives when pursuing a health-related question, that a provider call the patient to discuss this issue or question. This information may remind the patient, for example, to not eat for 24 hours before the appointment or have a particular lab test done before arriving for day surgery. This information may inform the physician ordering the medication that there is a less expensive alternative.
Another example might include a remote consultation with a physician who specializes in weight management. The patient (perhaps anonymously) enters a personal history of lifestyle, blood levels and food intake into a guided WWW-based form. This information is reviewed by a physician who returns a personalized weight reduction program.

- Providing an integration technical infrastructure to assist in the integration of services that span organizational boundaries or heterogeneous technologies within an organization. For example, the scheduling of an appointment may require information from the managed care organization's information systems as well as the systems of the physician's office. The ordering of a medication by a primary care provider may involve interaction with that provider's computerized record system, the systems of the pharmaceuticals benefits manager, and the systems of the retail pharmacy.

There is no cookbook approach to the leveraging of service through the WWW. Effective leverage requires the following.

- Understanding which processes customers use to judge the performance of the organization and its products and services
- The attributes of the process deemed critical by the customer and the current deficiencies in those processes
- Thoughtful application of WWW technologies in an effort to improve these processes

Despite the potential for WWW use to improve processes, it is often not clear how current organizational processes will work or be transformed when placed on the WWW. Subtle but powerful aspects of the technology and the business process are discovered when placed on the WWW.

WWW-based ordering of products works well for rare items (e.g. obscure Jazz recordings), and when the potential inventory exceeds the inventory capacity of any single distribution site (e.g., the number of book titles dwarfs the number of books that any book store can carry). WWW ordering has limitations when there is a social element to purchasing (e.g., a teenager shopping for clothes), when the purchasing involves multiple senses such as taste, touch, and smell (e.g., grocery shopping), or when it is difficult to specify what you want (e.g., "pants that make me look thinner"). We learn this because people try applications and some number fail.

Organizations are discovering that branding works differently on the WWW than it does through other media (Neuborne and Hof, 1998). TV and magazine ads can effectively create an emotional response on the part of the viewer who associates that emotion with a company or its products (e.g., whiter teeth make one more attractive and successful and toothpaste X provides such teeth). However, when using the WWW, customers are seeking specific information or are performing some other "task." As such, emotion-based messages, which take several seconds to send down the wire, are viewed as annoying and task impediments. People resent them. Healthcare organizations should learn from such experiences.

In healthcare we would expect that WWW use may alter the physician–patient relationship.

- The patient may know more "facts" than the provider about an aspect of care or care alternatives.
- The patient may know more "myths and bad information."
- The role of the specialist and the interpretation function may be strengthened as patients believe that they've garnered the fact base that their primary care provider could have conveyed.
- Visits may be fewer but communication with providers and management of care may be more frequent and focused.
- Medical decisions will become more "shared."
- The patient will expect the provider to be a more active participant in the patient's care.

It is also not clear how much of the above will occur, how satisfying it will be to the participants, and whether care is improved.

It is not clear how much leverage of existing services, the WWW will provide to today's participants in the healthcare delivery system. One can imagine WWW-based systems that answer patient's questions and steer them to the care facilities that developed the systems. However, how important will this referral channel be? Will it account for 2% or 20% of all referrals? Currently the vast majority of referrals to a hospital are made by the patient's doctor not the patient. Will the WWW reduce that relationship or strengthen it?

WWW Support of the Healthcare Organization's Strategies

Given the definition of characteristics, examples of use and factors that hinder use, healthcare organizations are in a position to begin to develop more specific understandings of the potential role of the WWW to support organizational strategies. The WWW may be able to support strategies in the following areas.

- Management of the chronically ill
- Management of the well (worried or not)
- Provision of high quality administrative services

These challenges, and potential roles for WWW-based applications and information, are briefly discussed below.

Management of the Chronically Ill

Managed care organizations and providers are under pressure to manage the chronically ill patient in a way that reduces the cost of that care and improves the quality of life and longevity of the patient. Over 50% of the population in this country has a chronic illness, and that percentage will increase as people live longer and as medical advances, while not always preventing or eradicating a disease, reduce the likelihood that the disease will unduly shorten a life-span. The chronically ill consume a disproportionate amount of the healthcare.

Management of the chronically ill patient is difficult. Patient compliance with their treatment may be problematic. Hypertensive men, for example, often don't take their medication because they are asymptomatic and the medication has side effects. Small changes in the patient (e.g., weight gain of the patient with congestive heart failure or blood oxygen saturation for the patient with chronic obstructive pulmonary disease), can indicate a deterioration that needs to be corrected quickly. However, the patient does not detect these change until too late and the result can be an expensive visit to the emergency room.

The WWW could be used to do the following.

- Have the chronically ill patient record information daily or weekly, transmit that information to the provider who analyzes it for deterioration and/or compliance, provide feedback to the patient commending him or her if the disease appears to be well managed, or suggest remedial steps if further management is required
- Provide content that supports that patient's periodic need for information and emotional and behavior change reinforcement (e.g., changes in diet and beginner exercise program information for the hypertensive)
- Provide guidelines, protocols, and text to ensure that the provider has the benefit of the latest medical thinking on the topic of managing a patient with this disease
- Provide chat sessions for patients and their families to help them through some of the difficult emotional and life style change issues that often accompany a chronic illness

Keen (1998) observes that successful WWW-based offerings are successful because they thoughtfully address three aspects of the service provider-customer relationship.

1. They provide access to information content.
2. They support relevant transactions.
3. They create for the customer a sense of community.

For example, Amazon.com provides information about books, enables the customer to order books, and creates a sense of community by enabling customer to contribute reviews, ask questions of authors, and have Amazon.com provide information about new books that are based on prior ordering patterns.

These three dimensions, perhaps important in any successful WWW-based service extension by a provider, would seem to be most important in supporting the chronically ill.

Management of the Worried Well

Providers and managed care organizations would like to ensure that patients stay healthy. They would also like to ensure that patients receive care when they need it but don't seek care when it is not needed.

Information can be provided over the WWW on healthy behaviors and behavior change. Summaries of new health research findings (e.g., the benefits of estrogen replacement therapy for postmenopausal women), may be offered and updated. Viewers of the information could leave questions on the material for a response by a provider.

Health risk appraisals could be offered with a provider calling the patient to discuss the results, if appropriate.

Patient access to guidelines (e.g., for persistent coughs or abdominal pain), as they determine whether they should seek care, may reduce the number of outpatient visits. A large number of patient self-referrals to a specialist should not have occurred because the problem corrected itself, a primary care provider could have provided treatment, or the patient chose the wrong type of specialist. Reducing unnecessary encounters could have substantial impacts on the quality and cost of care.

In an effort to guide the seeking of care and determine if a patient needs a visit or a referral, the WWW could be used to do the following.

- Offer triage guidelines based on problems or symptoms (e.g., back ache or rashes)

- Suggest an appointment, person to call, or visit to the emergency room if the interaction with the guidelines indicated that an encounter with a provider was warranted
- Enable the patient to book the appointment, instruct a provider to call, or dispatch an ambulance to the home
- Transmit the session to the provider who will follow up on the care

High Quality Administrative Services

Patients and subscribers often base their judgment of a hospital or health plan more on the quality of administrative services than on the quality of medical care they receive. Patients feel comfortable judging convenience and courtesy. They are not always comfortable judging the medication regime they have been given.

As providers and payors compete, they may find that the WWW offers a means to improve the quality of administrative services. To support this objective, the WWW could be used to do the following.

- Provide access to the specifics of coverage that a subscriber has and enable the subscriber to leave a question for a benefits counselor, avoiding a lengthy wait on the telephone
- Enable a patient to schedule an appointment to see a physician, renew a medication or leave a non-urgent care question for follow-up in the next day or two
- Enable the subscriber to check the status of a disputed claim, referral authorization, and/or the remaining number of allowable visits to a specialist

Impact of the WWW on IT Governance

The advent of the WWW as a potent information technology has multiple ramifications to the IT asset of an organization like Partners. Technical and application infrastructures must incorporate a new class of technologies. WWW developers must be hired. Discussions with organization staff regarding their plans and initiatives must ensure that the WWW is introduced, as appropriate, as a potential technological "solution."

However, one of the most complex set of changes occurs in IT governance. Departments and individuals can and do develop WWW sites and applications. Partners has an estimated two hundred such locally authored sites. This development can go undetected for long periods of time. Unlike WWW applications sponsored and managed by the IS organization, these local developments may have highly variable quality of content and introduce risks (e.g., misrepresenting the organization or engaging in inappropriate clinical practice), which escape organizational notice.[8]

However, when an organization is confronted with a phenomenon like the WWW that holds great promise but for which great uncertainty exists surrounding the most appropriate uses, the organization may decide that it needs to develop policies that encourage innovation while it protects the organization from risks that the technology creates. Prior to the WWW, personal computers in the early 1980s were such a technology. Organizations, at the time, established polices to govern PC use and often had committees that reviewed PC requests. Such PC policies and committees are largely extinct at this time since organizations now "understand" how best to utilize the technology (or, the cynic might note, have given up any hope of managing personal computers).

WWW Policy Strategy

Essentially there are three philosophies by which an organization can govern initiatives and expenditures on local WWW development. The choice of philosophies is central to the formation of the policy. An organization can fund and manage projects on the basis of strategic alignment, return on information (or some other rigorous evaluation method), or an incubation strategy.

Generally strategic alignment is not a central concern for a specific locally developed WWW applications (although alignment can be of concern for the portfolio of applications). If the linkage between the organizational plan and the IT activities pointed to the need for a departmentally-based WWW application, the control over that development and operation would likely be given to the IS organization. The vast majority of local WWW development is likely to have no particular strategic interest.

WWW applications that have strong ROIs are not abundant. Justification of WWW activity on cost-benefit analysis alone could lead

---

[8] Reprinted/adapted with permission from, Hamff, C., Glaser, J. (1997). Internet Policy and Procedures for Healthcare Organizations: The Approach of Partners HealthCare System. *Topics in Health Information Management* 17(4):40–61. ©1997 Aspen Publishers, Inc.

the organization to ignore many projects that could later become beneficial to the organization. Cost-benefit analysis is often done to ensure the appropriate consumption of scarce, significant resources. However, the costs of publishing a WWW page can be trivial. ROI, as a resource protector, may be a less than relevant role for a large number of WWW activities.

The incubation strategy recognizes that WWW technology is so new that many of the strategic ramifications of this technology are not readily known to anyone. An organization may want to encourage learning so that it improves its ability to assess effective and ineffective uses of the technology. This strategy is akin to a decentralized PC strategy of the early 1980s that encouraged PC use in an effort to facilitate organizational learning. A contrasting PC policy might have required an ROI for each computer purchase; this, although emphasizing prudent organizational consumption of capital, would have had the effect of hindering innovation. An incubation strategy aims to foster innovation while maintaining corporate interests and was deemed most appropriate for Partners' local WWW development. This strategy also frankly recognized the potential futility of trying to regulate most decentralized WWW development.

Clearly, the three methods are not mutually exclusive, an incubation strategy does not preclude efforts to identify uses of the WWW to further major strategic initiatives. And large scale WWW investments, locally developed or not, can potentially be subjected to a rigorous quantitative analyses.

WWW Policy Objectives

The WWW policies and procedures at Partners are designed to achieve several objectives.

- Manage risk (e.g., identify acceptable approaches to the conveyance of clinical information that balance improvements in care delivery and customer service with confidentiality and malpractice risks)
- Foster innovation so that the organization learns about effective and ineffective uses of the technology
- Ensure that organizational resources are used appropriately (e.g., by offering centralized WWW support)
- Ensure that WWW initiatives are consistent with the overall organizational and associated information systems directions

(e.g., by standardizing on a browser and declaring certain applications "off limits")

There are several types of risks that the policy needed to address.

- Publishing of information that is libelous, offensive, or misrepresents the organization
- Publishing of medical care information (e.g., guidelines), that is incorrect or does not represent best practice as defined by appropriate members of the medical staff
- Engaging in transactions that fiscally expose the organization (e.g., ordering supplies using Partner's contracts or inventory)
- Engaging in clinical dialogue that results in inappropriate medical advice
- Establishing an inappropriate or inadvertent provider-patient relationship
- Protecting the copyrights of the organization or others
- "Warranting" the information of others by connecting a department's pages to the pages of other organizations or sites
- Protecting data confidentiality
- Protecting the organization's WWW activities from the activities of hackers

The organization's policies developed an inventory of risks, established policies and procedures for guiding WWW development so that risk is reduced, and monitored WWW development, as well as it can, across the organization to ensure that risk reduction or avoidance policies and procedures are being followed.

Supporting WWW Development

Because of a limited ability of the central Information System's function to stop WWW development or tightly control it, and the ease with which WWW development can be performed by semi-skilled staff, the policy must recognize that local development is a fact and provide policies and procedures that help ensure that this development is well performed and well maintained.

This policy philosophy is analogous to that for control of PC development. Once a user has a PC, one has limited ability to manage the use of that PC. Hence policies, procedures, and management mechanisms should be developed that encourage effective use and provide support mechanisms (e.g., help desk and training classes). Centralized support of decentralized development must be a component of the WWW policy.

Composition of the Partners WWW Steering Committees

Most of the member organizations of Partners have a WWW Steering Committee. These committees are charged with developing, monitoring, and amending the organization's WWW policies and procedures. The steering committees recognize that the organization is learning about the technology and that it may be necessary to continue to evolve the WWW policies and procedures.

Because no single profession fully understands all the aspects of healthcare WWW publishing and service extension, WWW policy at Partners was developed by a multidisciplinary group. The group consisted of information system professionals, attorneys, auditors, physicians, managers, medical informatics professionals, and other clinicians. The rank of the individuals present varied, but there was significant upper management participation, which is crucial to effective policy development.

The role of the committees is to do the following.

- Refine and understand the nature of risks and, where possible, develop risk reduction strategies
- Ensure WWW support is responsive and effective
- Develop an organizational understanding of the most appropriate and high leverage uses of the WWW

WWW Summary

Organizations are periodically confronted with new technology that they (and no one else) understand well. Moreover, the organization suspects that the technology has great potential and hence a lack of understanding is a problem.

When this occurs, the organization needs to develop a view or an understanding by defining the core characteristics of the technology, learning from the experiences of others, and determining potential roles for the technology. This should lead to the definition of ways that the technology can further organizational strategies or create new strategies.

Experimentation with the technology will be required and, if the experiments show promising results, investment in the technology and associated IT staff should occur. An important finding of the studies, conducted by McKenney, et al. (1995) on organizational excellence in IT and reviewed in Chapter 3, was the importance of identifying new and promising technologies, developing understandings of their possible roles, and experimenting with their use.

The adoption of new and potent technologies will clearly affect the IT asset and not just the technical architecture and IT staff components.

SUMMARY

In this chapter we discussed three major current IT issues, clinical information systems, integration and the World Wide Web. During the discussion, several points were made.

- Whether they intend this to be the case or not, organizations develop views or governing concepts that frame their definition of these three topics and others like it.
- These views are very powerful since they guide subsequent, significant decisions about the role of these technologies and applications, the organization's approach to their implementation and management, and the manner in which an organization evaluates the success of the technology.
- While view formation is a complex, frankly mysterious process, asking a small number of questions and thoughtfully developing answers can assist in ensuring that the view is well conceived.
- In the development and implementation of each of these topics, as presented from the experiences at Partners, the role of and the impact on the IT asset was pervasive and significant.
- In addition to the formulation aspect of strategy which largely leads to the creation of a view, in the discussion of the three examples we saw the implementation aspect of strategy.
- We also saw, recalling the discussion in Chapter 2, that the concept of leveraging organizational processes was prominent in all three discussions.

REFERENCES

Bates, D., et al. (1998). Potential Identifiability and Preventability of Adverse Events Using Information Systems. *Journal of the American Medical Informatics Association* 1:404–411.

Bates, (1998). Internal Partners Analysis.

Bates, D., et al. (1998). Effect of Computerized Physician Order Entry and a Team Intervention on Prevention of Serious Medication Errors. *JAMA* 280(15):1311–1316.

Brodwin, D., Kline, D. (1998). Information Publishing enters a Post-Web World. *Upside,* February.

Drazen, E., Metzger, J. (1998). *Strategies for Integrated Health Care.* San Francisco: Jossey-Bass.

Green, H. (1998). A Cyber Revolt in Health Care. *Business Week,* October 19.

Ernst and Young. (1996). *The Role of the Internet in Health Care.* Atlanta: Ernst and Young.

Gandhi, T., et al. (1998). Satisfaction with the Referral Process from the Primary Care and Specialist Perspectives. *Journal of General Internal Medicine* 13(suppl):47.

Glaser, J. (1995). Lessons Learned from a Client Server Pioneer. *Healthcare Informatics,* October.

Glaser, J. (1994). The Role of the Chief Information Officer in Forming Clinical Information System Strategies. *The Joint Commission Journal of Quality Improvement* 20(11):614–621.

Glaser, J. (1998). *Business Opportunities in Delivering Health Care Information Over the Internet,* Spectrum Monograph Waltham, MA: Decision Resources.

Hamff, C., Glaser, J. (1997). Internet Policy and Procedures for Healthcare Organizations: The Approach of Partners HealthCare System. *Topics in Health Information Management* 17(4):40–61.

HIMSS. (1997). *Eighth Annual HIMSS/Hewlett-Packard Leadership Survey.* Chicago: Healthcare Information Management and Systems Society.

Herzlinger, R. (1997). *Market-Driven Health Care.* Reading, MA: Addison-Wesley.

Keen, P. (1991). *Shaping the Future: Business Redesign through Information Technology.* Boston: Harvard Business School Press.

Keen, P. (1998) All Change: The IS Organization as Competitive Advantage. Lecture given at Boston University, November 4.

Leape, L., et al. (1995). Systems Analysis of Adverse Drug Events. *Journal of the American Medical Association* 274(1):35–43.

McKenney, J., Copeland, D., Mason, R. (1995). *Waves of Change: Business Evolution Through Information Technology.* Boston: Harvard Business School Press.

Neuborne, E., Hof, R. (1998). Branding on the Net. *Business Week,* November 9.

Roberts, P. (1995). Client Server at Brigham and Women's Hospital: An Enterprise of PCs. *Integrating Personal Computers In a Distributed Client-Server Environment.* Khanna, R. (Ed.). Englewood Cliffs, NJ: Prentice Hall.

Sittig, D. (1998). Partners Internal Analysis.

Teich, J., et al. (1995). Enhancement of Clinician Workflow Using Computer Order Entry. *Journal of the American Medical Informatics Association* 2(Suppl):459–463.

Teich, J, et al. (1996). Towards Cost-Effective, Quality Care: The Brigham Integrated Computing Systems. *Proceedings of the Nicholas E. Davies CPR Recognition Symposium* 2:3–34. Chicago: Computerized Patient Record Institute.

Teich, J., et al. (1998). Components of the Optimal Ambulatory Care Computing Environment. *Proceedings of the Ninth World Congress on Medical Informatics,* 1273–1277. Edmunton, Alberta: International Medical Informatics.

CHAPTER 5

Conclusion

In this chapter we will attempt to summarize the discussion and material presented in the previous four chapters.

Healthcare organizations are making, and will continue to make, significant investments in information technology (IT). They will do so in an effort to further organizational goals of improving care quality, reducing costs, enhancing service, growing market share, and, at times, transforming themselves into a tightly integrated delivery system.

The efforts and investments can be thwarted or hindered by a myriad of problems and issues. However, the two core IT risks are the failure to conceptualize or develop a sound IT strategy and the failure to implement that strategy well. Strategy conceptualization failures may be the more significant of the two. A brilliant implementation of an incorrect strategy is not exceptionally helpful.

Strategy development permeates several aspects of IT: the linkage between organizational strategies and IT plans and activities, the development and advancement of internal IT capabilities and characteristics, and the creation of concepts or views that frame an organization's understanding of a major IT initiative, challenge or technology (e.g., establishing the role of the Internet).

The linkage of organizational strategies to IT strategies and plans is a complex exercise. Frameworks and methodologies exist that can assist the development of the linkage between the two. These frameworks can help derive the IT strategy directly from organizational strategies or via core formulations and views of organizations (e.g., the world can be defined in terms of value chains or competitive forces). While these frameworks and methodologies can be very helpful, linkage may always be difficult and fraught with problems.

Organizations can also draw from the lessons learned by others in their linkage efforts directed toward applying IT to enhance the competitiveness of the organization. These lessons on IT-based competitiveness highlight the leverage that IT can provide to improving or reengineering core, critical organization processes, capturing and reporting critical data, and delivering new or differentiated products and services. An IT-based competitive advantage is very difficult to sustain, although the sustainability is enhanced if IT leverages some other significant organizational strength such as having a large market share. In all cases, IT cannot overcome inadequate assessments of the environment, poor organizational strategies, weak management, or limited abilities to execute. The aggressive application of IT to improve a competitive position can also carry baggage such as a "permanent" increase in operating costs without a comparable increase in margins.

The IT asset is composed of applications, architecture, data, IS staff, and IT governance. These assets have characteristics and different ways of contributing to organizational performance. Asset strategies must be developed. These strategies should be directed to ensuring that the ability of the organization to implement its IT plans is strong, robust, and improving. Strategies will form views of the asset (e.g., a view of the nature of the integration needed by the organization), and lead to plans to advance the asset (e.g., standardize technology).

In addition to the asset, IT effectiveness is also governed by intangible but real factors such as the relationship between IS and the rest of the organization, and the chemistry between the CIO and other members of organizational senior leadership. Organizations must establish and nurture these intangible factors. These factors, and the IT asset, may be the greatest contributor to an organization's ability to significantly affect IT-based contributions and to sustain those contributions over time.

As IT-asset plans and strategies are developed, organizations should be careful of surveys, fads, and evaluation techniques that can mislead as well as inform.

Conclusion 201

In Chapter 4, clinical information systems, integration, and the World Wide Web were discussed. These three topics, while quite different in many ways, have several common elements of strategy.

- The formulation of a view or governing concept of the topic was essential. For clinical information systems, this view resulted in the definition of the core of the IT response being the support of information-rich processes. Integration was defined in terms of concepts such as clusters, constellations, and transcendent processes. The World Wide Web was defined in terms of four core characteristics.
- The formulation of this view can be guided by the answers to a small number of questions. The questions are easy to state. Thoughtful answers are difficult to develop.
- Early in the development of the strategy for the area, there was a focus on organizational processes and from that focus, and other analyses, application and other asset needs were determined. Organizations should be careful about premature conclusions that certain applications are needed.
- Implementing the view required significant alteration and extension of the IT asset. Strategies were necessary to define changes in applications, staff, data, architecture, and governance. In each of these areas, the component of the asset that represented the most challenging change varied.

The authors hope that this book has been informative and perhaps enlightening. It is clear from our experience that IT can help effect very significant improvements in care and the ability of healthcare provider organizations to thrive.

Too often, however, healthcare IT leadership immerses itself in conversations of which vendor is the best at delivering a certain type of application, whether a component of technology (e.g., hand held devices), has promise, or whether phenomena such as outsourcing are real or otherwise. These conversations are not inappropriate; these areas require discussion and thought. But these conversations are not complete. The effective and strategic application of IT in healthcare is a vastly broader and deeper challenge than these conversations would imply. Too narrow of a focus does not serve well the organization's effort to craft IT-based effectiveness.

We hope to advance that effectiveness. The stakes are too high to do otherwise.

APPENDIX A
Levels of Integration of Information Systems at Partners (1997)

There are six levels or groups of application integration. These levels summarize different classes of relationships between organizations within and outside of Partners. The groups also reflect degrees of operational integration. The groups are presented below and the degree of integration increases in the order presented.

LEVELS OF INTEGRATION

PCHI [1]*Affiliates* include Melrose-Wakefield Hospital and Emerson Hospital. An affiliate receives, at a minimum, managed care contracting support from PCHI and may purchase other Partners services and joint ventures.

Partners-Wide includes all organizations that are wholly owned subsidiaries of Partners (e.g., BWH, MGH, PCHI, Faulkner, NSMC, and potentially NWH).

Urban Core integration results because of the clinical integration between the BWH, MGH, and DFCI and the consolidation of administrative and financial operations between MGH and BWH.

Constellations refers to the integration within a subsidiary of Partners (e.g., the integration between the ancillary systems at the MGH and the integration between MGH and MGPO).

Clinical Joint Ventures are a very diverse set of arrangements (e.g., Radiation Oncology Joint Venture between MGH and Emerson; DFPCC; BWH, and Faulkner operating room integration; Partners Mental Health; and the Radiology Joint Venture between Partners Radiology and

---

[1] Partners Community Healthcare Inc. (PCHI) manages the primary care network and the administrative activities associated with delegated risk contracts. If PCHI provides services to an organization that is not owned by Partners, then that organization is an affiliate.

Brigham and Women's Hospital (BWH), Massachusetts General Hospital (MGH), and North Shore Medical Center (NSMC) are hospital-based delivery systems in Partners. Partners has a joint venture with the Dana Farber Cancer Institute (DFCI) to provide adult oncology services throughout the region; Dana Farber/Partners Cancer Care (DFPCC). The MGH Physicians Organization is referred to as MGPO. Faulkner Hospital (Faulkner) is also a member of Partners. Newton-Wellesley Hospital's (NWH) membership is under negotiation.

Hawthorn group practice). Each arrangement is idiosyncratic and will have a different need for application integration.

External Linkages are relationships that exist between Partners and its "trading" or "business" partners. Example relationships include electronic transmission of a supply order to Owens and Minor, electronic transmission of insurance transactions to a payor such as BCBS, and the potential linkage of medication order entry to a retail pharmacy.

The following sections present the application capabilities and degree of integration to be developed between now and the end of Fiscal Year 2000.[2]

PCHI AFFILIATES

The following capabilities will be delivered to PCHI affiliates.

- Electronic linkage to the PCHI managed care application for insurance transactions (e.g., eligibility determination)
- Access to medical management information
- Access to the Partners e-mail and telephone directory
- Access to clinical knowledge resources (e.g., algorithms and text)

PARTNERS WIDE

For FY98–00, it is anticipated the integration that is truly Partners wide (i.e., involves all Partners entities) will be modest. The following capabilities will be delivered.

- Communication
- Look up an e-mail address and send a message with attachments
- Look up a telephone number and mail address
- Conduct a video-conference session
- Look up administrative policies/procedures
- Managed care
- Support core insurance transactions and data flows, for PCHI contracted patients, between PCHI and the RSOs[3]

---

[2] This document doesn't discuss the distribution of payment responsibilities for these systems.

- Support insurance transaction flows to payors for other insurance products
- Clinical information systems
- Linkage to the Partners Clinical Data Repository
- Linkage to the Partners Enterprise Master Person Index
- Access to clinical knowledge resources (e.g., care algorithms and medical textbooks)
- Technical infrastructure
- Provide the ability to install a Partners workstation at the site enabling access to applications discussed under the urban core category
- Connection of the site data communication network to the Partners core network
- Common data definitions and reporting
- Care quality and outcomes
- Goals Monitoring System
- Financial performance measures

CONSTELLATIONS

Within Partners there are ten current/potential constellations; groups of organizations with a current or potential high degree of internal integration of operations and care provision.

These constellations are defined as (1) having movement of patients within them that is much "higher" or more "extensive" than between them, (2) distinct markets, (3) common senior management team, and/or (4) some significant level of local support operations (e.g., clinical laboratory), provided to members of the constellation but rarely to non-members.

Strategies, specific to each constellation, have been developed to strengthen integration within that constellation (and meet application needs).

- Faulkner—pursuing a Meditech strategy.
- North Shore Medical Center—pursuing an SMS strategy.

---

[3] Regional Service Organizations (RSOs) are geographically defined groups of PCHI practices.

- Spaulding—pursuing an SMS strategy.
- McLean—pursuing an IDX strategy.
- Newton-Wellesley Hospital—pursuing a Meditech strategy.
- PCHI-owned and managed practices—pursuing an IDX strategy.
- Urban core (BWH, BWH, MGH, DF/PCC)—Discussed below.

The strategies adopted by any constellation are reasonably independent of the strategies adopted by any other constellation. Central Partners Information Systems will alter the strategy of a constellation only to the degree that it jeopardizes the ability to deliver the Partners-wide capabilities outlined above.

The capabilities described as Partners-wide will be provided to each constellation.

URBAN CORE

In the urban core:

- The Partners centralized support departments (Finance, HR, etc.) provide support to all elements of the core.
- There will be an increase in clinical integration.
- There will be a sufficient number, many yet to be defined, of ancillary and administrative consolidations to require a common technical infrastructure.

For the urban core, the following components are common and go beyond the Partners-wide areas outlined above.

- Technical infrastructure (e.g., Microsoft Outlook)
- Clinical information systems (e.g., the computerized medical record)
- Systems to support consolidated operations

The above components, and those listed below, will be applied across those Partners sites, outside of the urban core that don't have these systems (e.g., clinical systems for PCHI-owned and managed practices), need technical infrastructure help (e.g., McLean) or are in the process of replacing these systems (e.g., Spaulding payroll). Hence we should expect that our definition and scope of "urban core" will expand over the next three years.

Partners-wide capabilities will also be provided to the urban core.

Levels of Integration of Information Systems at Partners (1997)

Technical Infrastructure

- Server platform (NT) provides a "home" for the following.
- Partners-wide and urban core applications (e.g., PeopleSoft and provider order entry)
- Partners-wide and urban core resources (e.g., e-mail and shared file areas)
- Win95 workstation provides the following.
- Access control (passwords) to all Partners and urban core applications
- Ability to run Partners and urban core applications
- Common utilities include the following.
- Exchange (e-mail)
- Remote access
- Virus protection
- Interactive television
- Telephony including voice mail and paging

Clinical Information Systems

- Provider Order Entry (inpatient and outpatient)
- Computerized Medical Record
- Referral Application
- Radiology PACS
- Results View
- Telemedicine

Consolidated Operations

- General ledger
- Accounts payable
- Materials management
- Accounts receivable
- Philanthropy information system
- Facilities management
- Research support

If not listed above, individual urban core organizations can choose systems that are different from those implemented by other urban core organizations subject to infrastructure and integration constraints.

An urban core organization seeking to replace or acquire a new system should select a system currently used by another organization (e.g., the MGH implementation of a system derived from the BWH operating room system).

Where pragmatic, if more than one organization is seeking to acquire the same kind of system they should engage in a joint selection (e.g., the current joint BWH and MGH examination of anatomic pathology systems).

We ought to anticipate that infrastructure will "lead" integration (i.e., the Partners infrastructure will become common and pervasive well before application integration or commonality is extensive outside of the urban core).

Following are examples of systems that are and will continue to be different across the urban core (unless some consolidation or integration initiative directs otherwise).

- Ancillary department systems (clinical lab, pharmacy, etc.)
- Outpatient registration and scheduling
- Admitting

CLINICAL JOINT VENTURES

A series of diverse clinical joint ventures has been formed or is forming. Example ventures include the following.

- Radiation Oncology between Emerson and MGH
- DFPCC
- Mental Health
- Radiology services for Hawthorn
- East Boston and MGH for OB
- Several initiatives in which physicians from the urban core assume clinical and administrative responsibilities at non-urban core sites

There is no uniform means to address the information systems needs of these ventures and others that will emerge. However, based on examination of these to date, the majority of them will adopt the technology infrastructure and clinical information systems being developed for the urban core in addition to be provided with the capabilities outlined in the Partners-wide category.

EXTERNAL LINKAGES

Two external linkage discussions are active.

Partners Materials Management systems will link to Owens and Minor.

Partners, CareGroup, Lifespan, Harvard Pilgrim, and TAHP [4] are working with Computer Sciences Corporation to develop a common insurance electronic data interchange mechanism.

Both of these cases, and others to follow, will integrate based on standards transaction formats and content.

---

[4] CareGroup and Lifespan are integrated provider systems. Harvard Pilgrim Health Care (HPHC) and Tufts Health Plan (THP) are HMOs. These organizations have formed the New England Healthcare EDI Network (NEHEN) to facilitate the development of a common insurance EDI infrastructure.

APPENDIX B
The Impact of Clinical Information Systems in Brigham Women's Hospital

Order Entry

Intervention	Description	Means of Benefit	Potential # events/yr	Effect	$/year
Allergy warning	Warns if the patient is allergic to the ordered drug	Prevents ordering of dangerous drug	1,500 warnings; 40 adverse events/yr	70% of orders canceled after warning	$250,000 in costs[1]
Enhanced allergies	Warns of definite or possible allergies to the ordered drug; checks all members of cross-allergenic drug families	Wider scope of prevention of drug errors	80 adverse events/yr	60% of orders canceled after warning	$500,000 in costs[1]
Drug-drug interactions (DDI)	Checks for hazardous interactions between ordered drug and other drugs patient is taking	Prevents adverse events due to interactions	27 adverse events/yr	Nearly 100% change in serious DDIs	$160,000 in costs[1]
Conflict warning	Warns if the patient is already on the ordered drug	Prevents overdose of drug due to multiple orders	100,000 warnings/yr	30% changed, 30% canceled	not measured
Relevant results display	Shows relevant lab results when ordering medications	Prevents errors that may stem from overlooking lab results	200,000 displays/yr	display only	not measurable

[1] Estimated hospital cost savings based on prior analysis which shows that each adverse event costs $6,000 to the hospital. These costs are primarily due to extended length of stay and to additional testing and therapeutic measures needed because of the adverse event. This figure excludes cost and detrimental effect to the patient, and also excludes any liability the hospital may bear.

Order Entry

Intervention	Description	Means of Benefit	Potential # events/yr	Effect	$/year
Lab charge display	Shows charges for lab tests being ordered	Once aware of relative costs, doctor may choose less expensive orders	700,000 orders/yr	5% reduction in ordering	1,000,000 in charges
Radiology charge display	Shows charges for radiology procedures being ordered	Once aware of relative costs, doctor may choose less expensive orders	250,000 orders/yr	2% reduction in ordering	$100,000 in charges
Redundant labs	Warns if order for lab test inappropriately soon after previous test	Doctor is made aware that result is unlikely to have changed from last test; doctor may rescind order for new test	4,500 warnings/yr	50% canceled	$75,000 in charges
Human growth hormone (HGH) guidance	Warns and requires documentation of reason for HGH use	Reduce excess use of HGH	reduced to 3–8 orders/wk	85% reduction in ordering	$177,000 in charges
Ondansetron guidance	Changed default frequency for IV ondansetron	Doctors guided toward an effective but less-expensive dose of ondansetron	3,000 displays/yr	92% switch to new dose	$500,000 in charges
Ceftriaxone guidance	Changed default frequency for IV ceftriaxone	Doctors guided toward an effective but less-expensive dose of ceftriaxone	3,000 orders/yr	85% switch to new dose	$200,000 in charges

Order Entry

Intervention	Description	Means of Benefit	Potential # events/yr	Effect	$/year
Cephalosporin assistant	Asks for indication for 3rd generation ceph use; guides user to more appropriate drug use based on indication	Reduce use of expensive 3rd generation cephalosporins; promote use of effective antibiotics without increasing resistance patterns	8,000 orders/yr	currently under study	under study
Vancomycin guidance	Prompt to guide initial use of vancomycin and to consider stopping after 3 days	Reduce overutilization of vancomycin; decrease spread of vancomycin-resistant enterococcus	5,000 orders/yr	currently under study	under study
Chemotherapy dose ceiling	Warns/restricts when daily, weekly, or overall dose of chemotherapy exceeds limits	Prevent overdosage of chemotherapy agents	2,000 orders/yr	100% of high doses generate display	under study
Chemotherapy per-protocol ceilings	Sets limits for chemotherapy dosing based on particular diagnosis or protocol	More specific limitation of chemotherapy overdosage, allows limits to vary for different protocols	2,000 orders/yr	100% of high doses generate display	under study
Chemotherapy approval	Requires attending approval of chemotherapy regimen	Prevent giving chemotherapy agents to wrong patient	2,000 orders/yr	Nearly 100% prevention	under study

Order Entry

Intervention	Description	Means of Benefit	Potential # events/yr	Effect	$/year
Chemotherapy parameter checking	Requires reentry of height, weight at regular intervals; checks for height/weight outside of limits	Prevent wrong dosage of chemotherapy due to incorrect body-surface area calculation	2,000 orders/yr	Rechecking on each entry	under study
Chemotherapy rescue prompt	Prompts for 'rescue' drugs such as leucovorin when certain chemotherapy agents are ordered	Prevent adverse events due to giving toxic chemotherapy agent without rescue drug	300 orders/yr	Nearly 100% prevention	under study
H_2 blocker shift	Guides orders toward PO nizatidine and IV ranitidine as H2 blockers of choice	Doctors guided toward ordering effective but less expensive medications	22,000 orders/yr	99% switch to new drug	$250,000 in charges (PO)
Nephors/Gerios	Changes recommended dosing of drugs based on patient's renal function and age	Prevent adverse events due to failure to reduce drug dosing in these populations	106 adverse events/yr	not measured yet	$640,000 in costs[1]
Dose checking	Checks for single, daily, cumulative overdosing	Prevent over- or underdosing of all drugs	53 adverse events/yr	not measured yet	$320,000 in costs[1]

[1] Estimated hospital cost savings based on prior analysis which shows that each adverse event costs $6,000 to the hospital. These costs are primarily due to extended length of stay and to additional testing and therapeutic measures needed because of the adverse event. This figure excludes cost and detrimental effect to the patient, and also excludes any liability the hospital may bear.

The Impact of Clinical Information Systems in Bringham Women's Hospital

Order Entry

Intervention	Description	Means of Benefit	Potential # events/yr	Effect	$/year
Guided dose algorithms	Provide advanced calculation of dose for drugs which require it	Prevents overdose and underdose of drugs that required special calculation, such as heparin, digoxin	53 adverse events/yr	not measured yet	$320,000 in costs[1]
Cosign reminder and documentation improvement	Notifies doctor, upon logging in, if there are orders to be cosigned on his/her patient	Reduce un-cosigned verbal orders. Before OE, 80% of charts had un-cosigned orders, 25% of orders had unidentifiable MD	See box at left	All orders have MD; >95% of charts fully cosigned	improved reimbursement potential
Therapeutic bed guidance	Guides proper use of therapeutic beds	Promotes proper use while preventing overutilization	pending	not measured yet	not measured yet
Sputum induction	Order form guides ordering toward 3-day sputum induction protocol	Reduces risk of unsafe sputum induction outside of isolation rooms; manages utilization of insulation rooms	1,000 inductions; 20 adverse events/yr	under study	$120,000 in costs[1]
Order sets	Standardized orders for various situations	Reduces ordering errors and omissions	1,200,000 orders/yr from sets	35% of all orders	variable

[1] Estimated hospital cost savings based on prior analysis which shows that each adverse event costs $6,000 to the hospital. These costs are primarily due to extended length of stay and to additional testing and therapeutic measures needed because of the adverse event. This figure excludes cost and detrimental effect to the patient, and also excludes any liability the hospital may bear.

Order Entry

Intervention	Description	Means of Benefit	Potential # events/yr	Effect	$/year
KUB assistant	Asks for indication for KUB; offers suggested alternatives based on indication	Reduce overutilization of KUBs	1,200 displays/yr	14% of exams canceled; 33% changed	$40,000 in charges
Reasons for transfusion	Requires doctor to specify reasons for transfusion; shows relevant lab results	Promotes more appropriate ordering of blood products. Next step: restrict to appropriate reason	30,000 orders/yr	80% now have reason	In next step
Restrict advance lab ordering	Reduced advance ordering from 7 to 3 days	Reduces unnecessary tests	400,000 orders/yr	10% decrease in labs ordered	>500,000 in charges
Anti-epileptic drug level guidance	Suggests appropriate use of drug levels when ordering	Reduces overutilization of these lab tests	10,000 orders/yr	20% decrease in levels done	$80,000 in charges
C. difficile guidance	Removes default ordering of C. difficile where not needed	Prevents excess test ordering unless true positive results likely	2,300 orders/yr	7% canceled	$12,000 in charges

The Impact of Clinical Information Systems in Bringham Women's Hospital

Event Engine and Surveillance programs

Intervention	Description	Means of Benefit	Potential # events/yr	Effect	$/year
Panic lab results	Alerts on positive medical logic modules centered on lab-result abnormalities +/- other patient data	Rapidly provides needed information to doctor so abnormality can be managed	10,000 alerts/yr	Reduced median time to respond from 2.1–0.7 hours	under study
Drug-lab interactions	Alerts on drug orders and lab results that are in conflict	Prevents adverse events due to interactions such as heparin-induced thrombocytopenia	30 adverse event/yr	under study	$180,000 in costs[1]
Drugs in renal failure	Alerts on orders for drugs inappropriate for renal-failure patients	Prevents adverse events due to altered metabolism of these drugs	400 alerts/yr	under study	under study, combined with Nephros
Missed TPN alert (pending)	Alerts when patient on TPN has no new order as daily ordering deadline	Prevents delays and adverse events due to missed day of parenteral nutrition	2,000 missed doses/yr	Permit timely dose in nearly 100%	not measured
Adverse drug events monitor	Records indications that adverse event has occurred	Counts adverse events before and after interventions; finds areas for new interventions	1,600 events/yr screened	20–30% reflect actual adverse events	not an intervention in itself

[1] Estimated hospital cost savings based on prior analysis which shows that each adverse event costs $6,000 to the hospital. These costs are primarily due to extended length of stay and to additional testing and therapeutic measures needed because of the adverse event. This figure excludes cost and detrimental effect to the patient, and also excludes any liability the hospital may bear.

Event Engine and Surveillance programs

Intervention	Description	Means of Benefit	Potential # events/yr	Effect	$/year
Allergy entry prompt (pending)	Prompts for allergy entry when orders suggest new reaction (e.g., Benadryl order)	Prevents second allergic reaction due to failure to enter new allergy which occurred during inpatient stay	300 events/yr	prompt recapture of almost 100%	not yet measured
IV-to-PO shift	Nightly report finds patients on IV meds who are taking other PO's (meds or diet)	Reduces use of expensive IV medications where equivalent or better PO medications may be used	20,000 orders/yr displayed	25% result in change in PO	$500,000–$1,000,000 in charges
Drug–drug interaction pharmacist report	Nightly report shows potential interactions, for pharmacist review	Prevents adverse events that occur through such interactions; more detailed than physician review.	10,000 orders/yr displayed	5.7% result in charge	under study
Sign-out	Daily exchange of information for covering physician	Prevents adverse events due to poor information exchange to covering physician	120 adverse events/yr	Relative risk of cross-coverage reduced 6-fold	$700,000 in costs[1]

Copyright © 1996 by Computer-based Patient Record Institute.

Source: CPR Recognition Symposium Proceedings, May 1–2, 1996

[1] Estimated hospital cost savings based on prior analysis which shows that each adverse event costs $6,000 to the hospital. These costs are primarily due to extended length of stay and to additional testing and therapeutic measures needed because of the adverse event. This figure excludes cost and detrimental effect to the patient, and also excludes any liability the hospital may bear.

ABOUT THE AUTHORS

John Glaser is Vice President and Chief Information Officer of Partners HealthCare System, Inc., an integrated delivery system founded by the Brigham and Women's Hospital and Massachusetts General Hospital. Previously, he was Vice President, Information Systems at Brigham and Women's Hospital.

Dr. Glaser was Founding Chairman of the College of Healthcare Information Management Executives (CHIME) and Past President of Healthcare Information and Management Systems Society (HIMSS). He is the 1994 recipient of the John Gall award for Healthcare CIO of the Year.

Dr. Glaser is on the editorial boards of *CIO, Healthcare Informatics, Report on Healthcare Information Management, Healthcare Intranet Report,* and *Topics in Health Information Management.* He is a fellow of the Healthcare Information and Management Systems Society and the College of Healthcare Information Management Executives. He has been elected to the American College of Medical Informatics. He has lectured at the Wharton School, MIT, Duke University, University of Michigan, and Harvard's Kennedy School, School of Public Health, Business School and Medical School. He has authored more than 50 publications.

Prior to Brigham and Women's Hospital, Dr. Glaser managed the Healthcare Information Systems consulting practice at Arthur D. Little. He holds a Ph.D. in Healthcare Information Systems from the University of Minnesota.

With a background in graphic design, Web design, health promotion, and information technology management, **Leslie D. Hsu** is a recent graduate of Harvard University Graduate School of Public Health, specializing in Health Communications. Her studies in the strategic use of information systems in healthcare settings and personal tragedy drive her toward a dedication to empowering consumers to be better managers of their own health through technology.

An Albert Schweitzer Fellow, she co-founded and was Executive Director of the Hepatitis B Education and Prevention Boston Initiative, a collaborative public health and medical student–initiated mass-media campaign that provides culture and age specific outreach efforts and free hepatitis B screenings and vaccinations. At the same time, she consulted for the Navajo Reservation in partnering traditional Indian medicine with biomedical healthcare systems.

She is the recipient of the first *Julius B. Richmond Young Leader in Public Health Award* for outstanding dedication to the health and well being of the community and demonstration of initiative and advocacy in public health, the first *National Award for Excellence in Public Health Leadership*, the *Sun Memorial Award* for exemplifying a commitment to improving the health and well being of people in underserved populations, and the *Schweitzer Award* for reverence for life.

She holds a Biology and concentration in English and Communications degree from UCLA, where she graduated as a *Distinguished Scholar* with Summa Cum Laude and co-founded UCLA's first cancer support organization.

Leslie Hsu was recently an Applications Analyst in Clinical Information Systems Research and Development, Partners HealthCare System, Inc., an integrated delivery system founded by Brigham and Women's Hospital and Massachusetts General Hospital.

She is now the Project Manager of Consumer Health Informatics and Telehealth Team for the Office of Disease Prevention and Health Promotion (ODPHP), within the U.S. Department of Health and Human Services. She manages and designs/develops consumer online services especially that of Healthfinder (www.healthfinder.gov) and the soon to be released Surgeon General's site (www.surgeongeneral.gov). Ms. Hsu also monitors legislation and funding related to Telehealth and assists in forging the future of information technology and health, through the development of interactive health communication for the next decade and the National Health Information Infrastructure. In her free time, she enjoys mountain climbing, hiking, snowboarding, and painting.

INDEX

Acquisition
   applications, 67–69
   strategies, 68–69
Advantage
   core sources of, 40–48
   sustainability of, 48–54
Affiliates, 204
AHSC. *See* American Hospital Supply Corporation
Alignment
   limitations of, 31
   persistence of, 30–31
American Airlines, 34–36
American Hospital Supply Corporation (AHSC), 36–38
Analytic Systems Automatic Purchasing (ASAP), 36–38
Applications, 155, 158–159
   acquisition, 67–69
   asset characteristics, 64–65
   asset value, 65–67
   portfolio assessment, 67
   systems, 64–69
Architecture
   capabilities, 71–72
   changes, 74
   characteristics, 71–72, 74
   for clinical information systems, 75
   representation, 74–77
   strategies, 72–74
   technical, 70–77
   typical, 77
ASAP. *See* Analytic Systems Automatic Purchasing
Assessment, 104–106
Asset(s)
   applications, 65–67
   composition of, 62–63, 200
   continuum IT, 155–158
   decisions, 98–118
   investment in, 96–98
   plans for, 95–96

Attributes, organizational, 118–125
Brigham Women's Hospital (BWH), 144–152
   impact of IS in, 211–218
BWH. *See* Brigham and Women's Hospital

CAM. *See* Component Alignment Model
Capabilities
   internal 10–11, 61–62
   organizational, 9–10
Care
   complexity of, 140–141
   continuum of, 152–159
   integrated, 159
   leverage points, 158
   outpatient, 153–154
Characteristics of the organization
   change in, 47–48
   internal, 10–11, 61–62
Chief information officer (CIO), 93–95
CIO. *See* Chief information officer
Committees
   IT information, 147
   WWW steering, 194
Competitive forces, 25–27
Complexity
   of care boundaries, 142–144
   sources of, 139–144
Component Alignment Model (CAM), 22
Computer-based referral system, 5
Concepts
   core business, 136
   IT application of, 136–139
Constellations, 205–206
Coordination, 44
Cost reduction, 102
Critical thinking, 108
CRLC. *See* Customer resource life cycle
Curves, 109–111
Customer resource life cycle (CRLC), 27–29
Customization, 47
Data, 77–81, 156

accurate, 45
characteristics, 79–80
complexity of, 141–142
critical, 44–46
integrated delivery system, 78
role of, 46
rapid, 45
strategies, 80–81
Departments, 85–86
Dis-intermediation, 43
Drug events, 144–145

Evaluation, 98–100, 104
Excellence rating, 97

Fads, 106–111
Federal Express, 39–40
FedEx. *See* Federal Express
Financial Executives Research Foundation, 118–119
Form, change in, 47–48
Formulation, 2–3
Frameworks
  observations on, 29–33
  strategic IT planning, 18–33

Goals, linkage to, 8–10
Governance, 91–93, 157
Grand slams, 54–55

Home page, 5

IDS. *See* Integrated delivery system
Immaturity, 115–116
Impact, 152
Implementation, 3–4
  strategies, 149
Information systems (IS)
  clinical, 133–160, 207
  clinical goals, 137
  concepts and views, 159–160
  philosophical concepts, 137–139
Information technology (IT), 1, 57
  advantages, 27
  asset impact, 145–148

as competitive weapon, 33–57
concepts that frame, 11–12
governance, 147
Infrastructure, 70, 101, 156
  technical, 207
Initiatives, linkage to, 8–10
Integrated delivery system (IDS), 5
Integration, 2–3, 160–174
  defining, 162–164
  delivery system, 5, 171
  improvement of, 164–166
  IS, 180–181
  IT strategies, 166–173
  levels of, 203–204
Intermediation, 43–44
Internet technologies, 12
Investments
  categories of, 101–104
  evaluation of, 98–106
  mandated, 102
Issues
  emergent, 116–117
  transient, 116–117
IT. *See* Information technology

Java, 13–14
Joint ventures, 208–209
Judgment, 150–151

Leverage
  of IT asset, 51–52
  organizational, 40–44
  of strengths, 49–50
Linkage, 200, 209
  derived IT, 19–23
  IT to organizational, 17
  views on, 23–29

Management
  of chronically ill, 188–189
  of worried well, 189–190
Maturity, alignment at, 31–33
McKenney, Copeland, and Goodhue, 121–122
Methodologies
  generic, 19
  IT strategic, 20
  limitations of, 114–115

Index

Minard, 19–22
strategic IT planning, 18–33
types of, 18–19
Models
component alignment, 22–23
Minard, 21

Operations, consolidated, 207
Organization
agile, 89–90
attributes of, 88–90
form of, 86–87
innovative, 90
smart, 89
structure, 87

Partners, 204–205
level of integration, 203–204
Planning
frameworks, 29–33
IT, 32–33
steps in, 20
Processes, organizational, 40–44
Products
differentiation, 46–47
new, 102–103

Quality improvement, 103

Re-intermediation, 43–44
Rigidity, 56
Risks, 53
Ross, Beath, and Goodhue, 119–121

SABRE, 34–36
Services
differentiation, 46–47
new, 102–103
Singles, 54–55
Slogans, 106–111
curve of, 109
Staff, 157
attributes of, 82–83
capabilities, 83–84
competencies, 83–84

components of, 81
organization, 84–85
Strategies
access, 167
acquisition, 68–69
application behavior, 173
common elements of, 201
common process, 168–173
competitive, 6–7
concepts, 134–135
data commonality, 168
definition of, 1–6
development of, 199
formulation examples, 5
implementation failures, 5–6
IT, 7–10, 17, 131–133
linkage, 17
major initiative, 103–104
need for, 7–12
organizational, 8–9, 17
physician use, 149–150
WWW and, 187–189
Studies, summary of, 123–125
Surveys
CSC, 111
HIMSS, 111–113
leadership, 113, 114
lessons about, 113–117
summary, 117–118
top issues, 112
Sustainability, 48–54
Systems, common, 69

Technology. *See also* Information technology
browser-based, 169
as tool, 52–54
Thinking strategic, 12–14, 14–15

Urban core, 206–208

Value Added Networks (VANs), 181
Value chain, 24–25
VANs. *See* Value Added Networks
Views, core business, 136
Weill and Broadbent, 122–123
World Wide Web (WWW), 132–133
administrative services, 190

content, 181–184
core characteristics, 174–175, 177–178
development support, 193–194
governance impact, 190–194
growth, 177
policy objectives, 192–193
policy strategy, 191–192
process improvement, 184–187
roles of, 180–187
steering committees, 194
strategies and, 187–189
use, 178–180
WWW. *See* World Wide Web